Pelle Lindbergh:
Behind The White Mask

Bill Meltzer and Thomas Tynander

Cover Design: Desire Rappa

Interior Design: Joe Federici

Cover Photograph Courtesy: Thomas Tynander

For Information Write:

Middle Atlantic Press
PO Box 345
Moorestown, NJ 08057

To my son, Benjamin

                        - Bill Meltzer

To my wonderful Rasmus and Mathilda!!

                      -Thomas Tynander

Pelle Lindbergh

ACKNOWLEDGEMENTS

This book would not have been possible without the help and seemingly endless patience of the people near and dear to Pelle Lindbergh and the authors.

The authors would like to thank Pelle's family, fiancee, closest friends and former teammates for their assistance, especially Anna-Lisa Lindbergh, Kerstin Somnell, Göran and Ann-Louise Hörnestam, Björn Neckman, Reino Sundberg, Anders Lånström, Thomas Eriksson, Dave Poulin, Kevin Cady, Jack Prettyman, Mikael Nordh and Rolf Alex. Extra thanks go out to Rolf for his work on Pelle's official memorial Web site (www.pellelindbergh.se) and for securing the private, previously unpublished photos that appear in this book.

We are also extremely grateful for the contributions and time of Bernie Parent, Kurt Mundt, Dave "Sudsy" Settlemyre, Ed Parvin, Jr., Keith Allen, Bob Clarke, Jay Snider, Bob McCammon, Brad Marsh, Brian Propp, Ted Sator, Ilkka Sinisalo, Murray Craven, Al Morganti, Hasse Persson, Gunnar Nordström, Bert Willborg, Gerhard Jörén, Curt Lindström, Bengt Ohlson and Bruce "Scoop" Cooper.

Additional special thanks go out to Artur Ringart, Bengt Jägerskog, Stefan Persson, Annika Nilsson, Anders Ankan Parmström, Micke Bernefjell, Thomas Steen, Arne Hegerfors, Ronnie Hellström, Stephan Lundh, Rolf Edberg, Roffe Ridderwall, Tommy Boustedt, Thomas Dennerby, Bengt-Åke Gustafsson, Tommy Sandlin, Håkan Södergren, Anders Hedberg, Ulf Lill-Pröjsarn Nilsson, Peter Lindmark, Henrik Lundqvist, Tommy Salo, Stefan Liv, Bob Froese, Tommy Söderström, Pat Croce, Jim Evers, Wayne Fish, Tim Panaccio, Zack Hill, Kevin Kurz, Claes Elefalk, Mikael Thelvén, Kjell Ahndén, Lars Nubben Andersson, Mats Ulander, Peter Forsberg, Uffe Jernspets, Janne Wallgren, Pär Mårts, Anders Kallur, Tomas Jonsson, Mats Näslund,

Willy Lindström, Hans Lindberg, Bert-Ola Nordlander, Christer Abrahamsson, Tommy Samuelsson, Leif Boork, Lasse Norrman, Sivert Svärling , Tomas Sandström, Janne Halldoff, Roger Andersson, Lasse Ström, Rolf Tellsten and Lars-Erik Ridderström.

Thank you to Jay Greenberg for the time he spent talking to Thomas but also for writing *Full Spectrum*, which is one of the most thorough year-by-year accounts ever published of the history of a professional sports team.

The authors are indebted to Deborah Sullivan for her yeoman work in proofreading and making style-point suggestions on the first draft of the English text. Big thanks are also owed to Linda Hanna for her painstakingly thorough read and thoughtful edit of the manuscript to a manageable length. In addition, thank you to Middle Atlantic Press for believing in this project.

Thomas would like to thank his former managers and colleagues at Sweden's Aftonbladet newspaper, especially Martin Strömberg, Christer Höglund, Lars-Ove Haraldsson and Fredrik Rubensson. He's also thankful to the publishers and editors of the Swedish version of this book, Sportförlaget and Ruter Media Group. Thank you to Magnus Söderberg, Lina and Bengt.

Most of all, we'd like to thank our families for their encouragement, understanding and patience. And, of course, thank you to Pelle Lindbergh.

Bill Meltzer and Thomas Tynander

TABLE OF CONTENTS

Pelle Lindbergh

FOREWORD

If ever a person were born to play hockey, it was Pelle Lindbergh. Not only did he have a rare talent for the sport, he also had the perfect temperament to become a star on two continents.

While growing up in Sweden, Pelle set his sights on playing in the NHL -- specifically for the Philadelphia Flyers -- in an era when few Swedish players paid much attention to the goings on in North America. Even when he became an NHL star, Lindbergh always kept Sweden (especially his friends and family) close at hand. In a very real way, he lived in both the USA and Sweden simultaneously.

In Swedish, there's a word called "lagom" that has no direct English translation. It refers to what feels just right and comfortable, without being too much or too little. In his lifetime, Lindbergh struck a lagom balance of becoming Americanized while remaining very much Swedish. Perhaps it is appropriate, then, that *Pelle Lindbergh: Behind the White Mask* is an equal team effort between Swedish sportswriter Thomas Tynander and American hockey writer Bill Meltzer.

The American version of this book has its roots in Tynander's 2006 biography of Lindbergh, published in Sweden. Meltzer translated and Americanized the Swedish text, and the authors then put the finishing touches on the book together. The book is illustrated with private photos generously donated by the Lindbergh family and friends of the late goaltender.

For all of his likeable traits, Lindbergh was human and flawed. Like many young athletes, he thought he was invincible. He died a horrible death because he didn't respect his own limits, and drove both recklessly and drunk on the night of his fatal accident. It's our goal to present a balanced portrait of Lindbergh the athlete and the person.

In creating the original Swedish book, Tynander painstakingly researched every aspect of Lindbergh's life and death. He conducted dozens of hours of interviews with Pelle's family members, friends, coaches, teammates, opponents, bosses, journalists who covered the player's career and others who crossed paths with Pelle at some point. He also referred to a host of vintage television and print interviews, contemporary newspaper accounts and books. Meltzer supplemented the research, translated the Swedish manuscript and then edited and Americanized the text. Finally, the English manuscript was edited from roughly 400 pages to the finished product.

A quick note about the book's arrangement: In many ways, *Pelle* is two books in one. There's the story of his life, told in the book's even-numbered chapters. The story of his last days, death and funeral are told in the odd-numbered chapters. In Chapter 26, the two stories come together and then move forward chronologically to look at the aftermath of Pelle's death and the lives of Pelle's loved ones and closest friends in the years since his passing.

We hope that you'll join us in stepping back into Pelle's unique world. Ultimately, we hope you'll discover the human being behind the white goaltender's mask.

Bill Meltzer and Thomas Tynander

CHAPTER 1

THURSDAY, NOVEMBER 7, 1985

The water glistens on the Delaware River. After a week of bad weather, the sun is shining at last. It's the first week of November, and when the late afternoon sun begins to set over Philadelphia, the temperature falls quickly. There's heavy traffic on the Walt Whitman – the huge steel bridge that connects the suburbs of South Jersey to Philadelphia. In the midst of the traffic snare, one car stands out- a bright red Porsche 930 Turbo. Behind the wheel, in the bowl-shaped driver's seat, Pelle Lindbergh sits clad in a suit, necktie, and cowboy boots. He impatiently grips the steering wheel, and is pained that he can't call upon the 380-horsepower motor that awaits the press of his right foot. Traffic jam notwithstanding, Lindbergh is in good spirits. He's living out his boyhood dream, and he knows it.

He's got the car of his dreams. His love of speed is surpassed only by his passion for hockey, music, family, and friends. For as long as anyone can remember, Pelle has been obsessed with sports cars. Now he owns the custom-built Porsche that inches along the bridge. The car cost him $117,380, including $41,000 worth of modifications at the manufacturing plant in Germany.

He grew up in the working-class southern part of Stockholm, and fantasized about playing hockey for the Philadelphia Flyers – the team of his idol, Bernie Parent. Now, at 26 years old, he's in his fourth National Hockey League season for the Flyers. Parent is his goaltending coach and has become a surrogate father of sorts. What's more, he's about to become wealthier than he ever thought possible when he was a boy. As the defending Vezina Trophy winner – representative of the best goaltender in the NHL – he has been rewarded by the Flyers with a long-term contract that will make him the highest-paid Swede in the NHL, and one of the league's best-paid goaltenders, as well. All the terms have been worked out; now all that remain are the signatures.

He's engaged to Kerstin Pietzsch, a beautiful Swedish girl, with whom he's hopelessly in love. The couple shares a lovely home in the peaceful King's Grant section of Marlton, NJ.

To make up time, Pelle accelerates and navigates the car in between the traffic, by switching lanes frequently. Pelle knows that if he's late to the arena, he'll catch hell from Mike Keenan, the Flyers' tyrannical head coach. Two minutes later, he pulls the Porsche into the players' entrance at Pattison Avenue, and parks in the same spot he always uses. He locks the car and walks down to the underground entrance. The rink-level entrance way is poorly lit and untidy. A humming sound from distant fans serenades Pelle as he continues up the broad path against the arena floor. He passes an aging Zamboni that's parked too close to the wide gate that opens to the 17,000-plus-seat arena. He walks past the visiting team locker room to his right, where Chicago Blackhawks players stand outside the door in shorts and t-shirts; some taping up their sticks. Pelle wordlessly greets a former Flyers teammate, Behn Wilson, with a quick nod and continues on his way.

Pelle strides into a smaller room with rows of personal cabinets where the players can hang up their suits and store belongings. This is also where the team post office is kept. As one of the most popular players on the team and the NHL's reigning Vezina Trophy winner, Pelle's stack of mail is usually piled high. The vast majority of the mail is postmarked Sweden and the Delaware Valley. Despite his best efforts to keep up with the fan mail, autograph requests, and postcards he receives, the task has become increasingly difficult.

Stereotypically, goaltenders are supposed to be a moody lot who are unapproachable on game days. But the Flyers players can count on the fingers of one hand the number of times they'd ever seen Pelle in a foul mood – and never when he arrived at the rink. Over the course of the previous season, Lindbergh proved his worth by not only winning the Vezina for his regular-season performance but also backstopping the team to the 1985 Stanley Cup Finals. Such deeds carry a lot of weight in the locker room.

Hockey players in general and goaltenders in particular tend to be creatures of habit and superstition. Pelle is no exception. He's developed a rather elaborate pre-game dressing ritual, and never willingly deviates from it. From a wardrobe at his locker, he takes out his socks and undergarments, including a special long-sleeved athletic t-shirt he purchased many years earlier at Ingvar Eriksson's sport shop in Stockholm. He considers the orange and black shirt to be an old war buddy. Now, many years later, Lindbergh's Flyers teammates often tease him about the shirt's weathered appearance. But to Pelle, the shirt's every tatter and mend adds to its character and comfort.

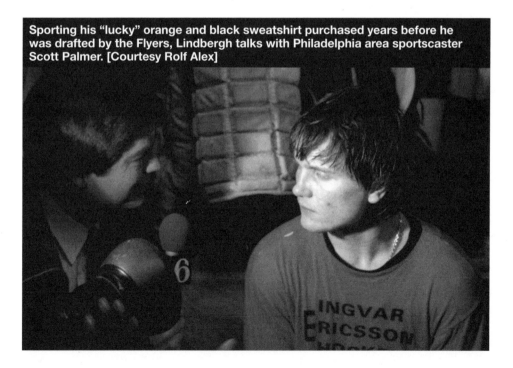

Sporting his "lucky" orange and black sweatshirt purchased years before he was drafted by the Flyers, Lindbergh talks with Philadelphia area sportscaster Scott Palmer. [Courtesy Rolf Alex]

The team's equipment managers have already prepared each player's stall. On a shelf above each position-player station, there's a white helmet and hockey gloves. Players' pads, skates, black pants, and white leggings are also arranged in easy-to-find fashion. The Flyers white game sweater with number 31 hangs neatly, with its orange and black sleeves and player names and numbers visible for anyone to see. As the goaltender, Pelle gets a larger locker space in a corner of the room, lying at a ninety-degree angle to the shower room. He is particular about the placement of his pads, mask, and other equipment, and the staff is very accommodating. Pelle wears a plain white facemask, a replica of the style that Bernie Parent wore and the style that Pelle has preferred for himself ever since he saw films and photos of Parent playing for the Flyers. Bob Froese, the Flyers' backup goaltender, sits in the corner opposite Lindbergh. Their relationship, while cordial on the surface, is tinged by a degree of unspoken tension. On many NHL teams, the two goalies sit closer to one another, but not these two. While Froese and Lindbergh have no personal animosity toward one other, there's little in the way of a quasi-fraternal bond. Froese has made it clear that he believes in his heart that he could have done just as good of a job as Lindbergh if given the opportunity to play more regularly.

The neatly arranged, uniforms, equipment, and sticks quickly become untidy as the players grab their gear. The Spectrum locker room no longer looks quite so spacious. In truth, it's far too small but the room is steeped in the traditions and identity, which the Philadelphia Flyers have forged since their foundation in 1967. The walls are white with two broad orange and black horizontal lines winding around the entire room. There is gray wall-to-wall carpeting with a huge hockey rink in the center. Previously, there was a Flyers logo, but when Mike Keenan took over as coach the previous season he insisted on the rink instead.

Many of the players on the team have come to fear and hate Keenan over the past year. Behind his back, players commiserate and pin unflattering nicknames on him, including "Hitler" for his mustachioed visage, despotic tendencies, and withering stares. Keeping morale up has become a full-time job for the club's leadership group. The players most sought out for advice are Dave Poulin, star veteran defenseman Mark Howe, former Calgary Flames captain Brad Marsh, and emerging young leaders such as Ron Sutter and Murray Craven. Through their prompting and cajoling, the team has become united, and would-be mutinies against the coach are stifled for the sake of winning.

Unable to sit still, Pelle gets up and exits the room to go into the adjacent training room. He's been unhappy with a shipment of goaltending sticks which he recently received and he searches for a particular one he wants, already expertly taped and prepared to his liking by head trainer Dave "Sudsy" Settlemyre. Pelle has known Settlemyre since their time together with the Maine Mariners. Sudsy is a real character, a wisecracking hockey lifer, who has done anything he can think of to stay close to the game and made a successful career of being a "jack of all hockey trades."

Pelle finds the stick he wants in the corridor outside the locker room. When he returns to the locker room, he slips in quietly so that no one will hear or see him. The other players on the team know he wants to be left alone in the room. He's getting himself mentally ready to play. From a preparation standpoint, it's been a typical game day for Pelle and his teammates: a morning skate, lunch and a nap at home, and a drive to the arena in the late afternoon. This Thursday, however, has been a little different than normal for Lindbergh. He has company at home for his mother, Anna-Lisa, and brother-in-law Göran Hörnestam are visiting and have stayed with Pelle and Kerstin for nearly the past two weeks.

Earlier today, after the morning skate, Pelle met up with Gunnar Nordström, a New York-based reporter for the Swedish newspaper *Expressen* ("The Express") and Hasse Persson. Nordström and Persson had arranged with Pelle to come take pictures of him with his custom-built Porsche, which he'd just gotten back from the factory in Stuttgart after some modifications had been made at the star athlete's request. The plan was to use the photos in conjunction with a feature in an upcoming sports supplement in the newspaper.

The three men discussed potential sites for taking photos. At Pelle's suggestion, they agreed on a park near the entrance to the villa development where Pelle and Kerstin live. There's a well-manicured lawn, still green despite the autumn temperatures, next to a man-made lake.

"Come with me," Pelle said to Nordström. "Hasse can follow in the rental car. But you've both gotta stay for lunch. Mama's making meatballs!" Pelle pulled carefully out of the parking lot, and made sure that Persson was still behind him as he headed across the highway and over the bridge into South Jersey. Nordström took out some notes he'd written for the interview and asked Pelle a couple of questions as the car reached a relatively open stretch of road. Suddenly, Lindbergh shifted gears and unleashes the Porsche's staggering acceleration ability. In the passenger seat, Gunnar Nordström was pressed up against the back support. He felt the sensation in his stomach that one gets when riding a steel roller coaster.

"Slow down! Dammit, Pelle, slow the hell down!" he shouted. Pelle smiled without taking his eyes off the road. He applied the brakes and brought the car down to a normal speed. A few minutes later, he parked the car at his house. Nordström couldn't get out quickly enough. He hastily opened the passenger door and tried to stand up, only to hit his head. Still smarting, Nordström complained to Pelle, "You need to calm down. That's no way to drive." "That was calm," Lindbergh replies, stepping out of the driver's side. "I just wanted to show you a little bit of what the car can do."

Anna-Lisa Lindbergh prepared enough Swedish meatballs to feed a small batallion. Over the years, she'd come to expect Pelle to bring company home. A born hostess by nature, she never complained. As Nordström and Persson sat down for lunch, it became immediately clear to them where Pelle got his inquisitive chattiness as well as his expressive facial features.

After lunch, Anna-Lisa cleaned up as her son and his guests excused themselves to go do the photo shoot for the article. They headed to the park on the other side of the man-made lake. Persson's expert eye behind the camera captured the clear blue sky, the green grass, and the red Porsche glistening in the sunshine. Persson took several photos of Pelle posed in front of the vehicle. "Take a picture without me, just of the car," Pelle requested. "I wanna get one to frame and hang on the wall." Persson complied by snapping photos from a variety of vantage points.

When Pelle was finished with Persson, it was Nordström's turn. The reporter wasted no time getting to the big question that he wanted to get answered: How were the negotiations going on the new long-term contract? "I'm optimistic," Pelle said.

In truth, the contract was ready to be signed, but Pelle was reluctant to reveal the details publicly until the ink was dry on the contract. The negotiations between Pelle's agent Frank Milne and Flyers' general manager Bob Clarke had been difficult. Milne was an agent that Clarke didn't particularly like, and Milne held firm on his demands that the Vezina Trophy winner should receive the highest salary in team history to date. For a while, the two sides remained far apart as hopes of getting the deal done before the start of the 1985-86 season faded. Clarke insisted that Lindbergh needed to prove himself over a longer period time to earn the kind of money Milne wanted for his client. Although Clarke never liked to give in on a contract negotiation, he finally made an offer that was close to what the Lindbergh camp wanted by asking for only minor concessions. The two sides had a deal that was a six-year contract, worth $350,000 per season, making Lindbergh both the highest paid Flyer and the highest paid Swedish player in the NHL. "If I stay healthy this year, I won't need to work another job the rest of my life," Pelle finally admitted to the *Expressen* reporter.

When the interview was done, Pelle took Nordström and Persson back to the house. Still a bit shaken up by the harrowing ride to King's Grant, Nordström looks Pelle in the eyes as he steps into the rental car. "Drive carefully and take care of yourself," Nordström said. Pelle nodded as the car pulled away and he headed inside to take his game day nap before it was time to drive to the Spectrum.

As the Flyers prepare to step onto the ice for the pre-game warm-up skate, Lindbergh charges onto the ice first, as is his custom. Right now, 40 minutes before the game, the stands are less than half full and the players' entrance is greeted with a murmur and muted applause. When the Flyers' players return to the ice for the start of the game, they will get a loud ovation from the rabidly partisan sellout crowd of 17,380. Winners of eight consecutive games and 10 of their first 12, the team looks poised to run away with another Patrick Division championship.

When times are good in Philadelphia, the players on the local hockey team can do little wrong in the eyes of Flyers' fans. The athletes and coaches on the other local pro sports clubs, especially the NFL's Philadelphia Eagles and MLB's Philadelphia Phillies have more of a love-hate relationship with their fans – even during winning seasons. The 76ers basketball team has often struggled for attendance through the years, even during periods of prosperity on the court. With the Flyers, the bond between athlete and fan is stronger. That's not to say Flyers players never get booed by the home crowd, but there's a stronger sense of faith in the hockey club. It's been that way ever since Bernie Parent, Bobby Clarke, and Bill Barber led the club to consecutive Stanley Cup Championships in 1974 and 1975. Three appearances in the Stanley Cup Finals have followed in the 10-plus years since the second championship.

During the pre-game warmups, it's customary for the starting goaltender to stand in net first as the skaters on his team shoot pucks from all angles. Having already put on his catching glove, blocker, and mask, Pelle runs his skates hard over the clean sheet of ice in the crease area in front of his net, to scratch up the surface. It's a ritual virtually all goalies perform each time they take to the ice immediately after it has been resurfaced. Some goalies believe that if the ice is too slick, they might slide too far, and insist that scratching the ice evens out any problems. Pelle awaits the first shot. He plucks it cleanly and casually tosses the puck aside. When he's seen enough shots for his muscles to relax and get a comfortable feel for the puck, Lindbergh gives way to Froese. At the end of the warmup, the players return to the dressing room, where coach Keenan will address the team before the start of the game.

Ten days earlier, Pelle's mother Anna-Lisa and brother-in-law Göran left Stockholm's Arlanda Airport on a chilly Saturday morning. Pelle and Kerstin warmly greeted Anna-Lisa upon her arrival and embraced Göran, a bearded fellow whose tattooed arms reveal souvenirs from his years as a sailor. Despite his gruff-looking appearance at first glance, Göran is actually a jovial, avuncular sort who is married to Lindbergh's older sister, Ann-Louise. Göran originally had planned his first visit to the USA to be during the summer. Initially, the intended purpose of the visit was for Göran to help Pelle replace rotting wood on the deck on the back of his house. It seemed as good an excuse as any to arrange a visit. Like Pelle's dad, Sigge, Göran made up for whatever formal schooling he lacked by being handy and resourceful in building and fixing things. "Göran, I need your help," Pelle had said on the phone. "Can you build me a new deck? I'll pay for the plane ticket."

Originally Pelle's father, Sigge, was to accompany Anna Lisa and Göran on this trip. Pelle was thrilled when he heard the news, but disappointed that Sigge chose not to come along this time. Pelle asked his dad to change his mind, but Sigge had once again begged off. "We'll do it next time, Pelle. I don't want to go running to the games dressed in a suit and tie like I had to the last time," Sigge said. "Come on, Dad. You don't have to wear your suit and tie to the games if you don't want to," Pelle protested but Sigge held firm. He was too embarrassed to admit the real reason why he didn't want to go. On past trips to the US, he had received a lot of attention from people once they found out Pelle was his son. Sigge, a quiet and reserved man, felt uncomfortable with all the attention from strangers. More importantly, Sigge couldn't speak or understand English. While younger Swedes speak the language fluently, many people from his generation – especially working folks like himself with little schooling or exposure to the language – cannot. As a result, Sigge inevitably found the trips to the US to be more frustrating than pleasant.

Even for Anna-Lisa, who is much more outgoing than her husband, the trips are difficult because of the language barrier. Her natural inclination is to enjoy meeting and talking to people, which she couldn't do without help. The current trip has been fun for both Anna-Lisa and Göran, as Pelle and Kerstin have made sure his relatives have plenty to do both by day and by night. Tonight, Kerstin drives them to the Flyers-Blackhawks game in her gray Mercedes.

The trio arrives right before the opening faceoff. Pelle has gotten Göran a seat close to the ice behind the goal that he will defend in the first and third periods of the game. Anna-Lisa sits up high in the stands with the other guests in the Flyers' family section.

Mike Keenan stands in the Flyers' locker room, going over final preparations for the game. He's dressed in a beige suite and dark necktie, his hair and mustache well groomed. Ever the perfectionist, the coach is still perturbed by the club's sloppy first period from last night despite the end result. With the club returning to the Spectrum on a winning streak, Keenan wants to guard against a letdown. Hands at his sides, "Iron" Mike's words are sharp and direct,

> Chicago is a better team on the road than at home, but this
> is a club we need to beat, boys. We can't have a start like last
> night. That first period was a disgrace. Tonight, we have to dictate
> the pace from the outset. Keep your feet moving, and keep the
> shifts short.

Keenan glares around the room. Coaching by intimidation is the 35-year-old's stock in trade. A highly intelligent and well-spoken man, Keenan is a workaholic and a stickler for preparation. The coach has claimed in interviews to have a more human, compassionate side away from the ice – but few of his players have ever seen it, much less the sense of humor Keenan professes to have.

With Keenan, the only thing that matters is winning hockey games. The players want to win, too, and realize the coach deserves credit for the team's impressive record in his season-plus behind the bench. But that doesn't mean they have to like his methods. In good times, Keenan nitpicks and micromanages. In bad times, he makes the players' lives a living hell. He screams. He belittles players in front of their teammates. But he also has the young team well prepared for every game, and gives the players he trusts all the ice time they can handle.

Pelle has played the best hockcy of his life under Keenan. Lindbergh privately attributes little of his NHL success to Keenan's presence. Pelle points to Bernie Parent's tutelage, to say nothing of his own desire to work on his game as the secrets of his success. "Bernie focuses on the positive things and how to get better," Pelle tells friends. "Keenan talks only about the things that go wrong."

Keenan's fear of a sluggish start has come true. At 1:09 of the first period, Chicago grabs a quick 1-0 lead as the Blackhawks' Keith Brown gets open and beats Pelle with a shot low to the glove side. From the bench, Keenan screams at Lindbergh and the other players to get their heads in the game. Pelle isn't pleased with himself, either. Despite the coverage miscue in front of him, Lindbergh knows he should have made the save. He had seen the puck all the way.

Less than a minute after the goal, the Flyers draw the first powerplay of the game, but the club fails to score, despite several good chances. A few minutes later, Pelle Eklund gets sent off for a holding penalty (the first penalty of his NHL career) that Keenan considers a lazy infraction with no opposition scoring chance involved. The coach is getting angrier by the minute. An effective penalty kill staged by Lindbergh and company mollifies Keenan slightly. The team begins to settle down and slowly begins to assume control. Pelle sees only five more shots the remainder of the period, and handles each one flawlessly.

At the 15:15 mark, Eklund atones for the earlier penalty by tallying a powerplay goal to even the score at 1-1. Barely two minutes later, oak tree-like power forward Tim Kerr scores his 12th goal of the season to give the Flyers their first lead of the game.

During the first intermission, Pelle returns to his locker to find two plastic mugs that have been prepared for him by the training staff. The first contains a sports drink and the second one is water. Lindbergh, who has suffered from dehydration problems in the past, gulps down the liquid. Soaked in sweat, Pelle holds a towel in one hand and runs his fingers through his dripping dark hair. He doesn't say very much, putting the towel over his head. The Brown goal is still bothering him, although he's trying to put it out of his mind.

Up in the stands, Göran has made some new friends during the intermission. He tries to use his badly broken English to ask some of the people around him about their backgrounds. It's obvious immediately that Göran isn't an American, so the people nearby ask him what brought him to Philadelphia. "I'm visiting Pelle Lindbergh's home," he said with no small amount of pride. A man claps Göran on the back and a female fan asks him if he'd be going to any more games. "Yes, on Saturday," Göran says, "On my birthday."

The Flyers dominate the second period. Pelle sees only six shots, of which only two are dangerous. Meanwhile, Ron Sutter and Mark Howe overpower Chicago goalie Murray Bannerman and give the team a commanding 4-1 lead. On the Ron Sutter goal, Bannerman skates out of the net to play the puck around the boards. Sutter steals the puck and stashes the puck in the open net. On Howe's tally, the Flyers turn defense into a rapid counterattack. Lindbergh makes a save, and checking forward Lindsay Carson gets the puck to Rich Sutter (Ron's identical twin brother). Howe follows up the rush, taking a drop pass from Sutter and going in alone. The All-Star defenseman gets Bannerman to commit first and tucks the puck into the cage.

During the intermission, Keenan speaks again to the players. This time, his words are calm. Mostly he reminds his team that the Blackhawks still have plenty of time to get back into the game, and the Flyers can't afford to let up now. Pelle once again sits down quietly, as he stares at the floor. Other players appear a bit distracted. Keenan notices the players' wavering attention.

Overall, he's pleased with how the entire team has performed tonight, but he's not about to let his players get too comfortable. He singles out Lindbergh as his target. "Too may rebounds tonight, Pelle. You're getting too far back in the net again. Come on out and challenge the shooter," he says in feigned anger. To drive home his point, Keenan kicks Pelle's equipment, which Lindbergh had set down on the floor in its usual place. Pelle doesn't respond, but gets up from the bench in front of his locker and re-arranges the equipment with a grim look on his face. Keenan says nothing but gives Lindbergh an apologetic nod as he exits.

By this point, Kerstin and Anna-Lisa have left the stands and gone down to the Flyers' family room on the same lower-level corridor as the Flyers' locker room. The ladies take a coffee break and discuss plans for the weekend. Upon entering the family room, Anna Lisa and Kerstin are greeted by veteran defenseman Brad Marsh's wife Patti. "Oh, hi Kerstin. Hello, Mrs. Lindbergh." "Hello," Anna-Lisa says, smiling politely. Patti says something Anna-Lisa can't understand. Pelle's mom smiles again to Patti, and then turns to Kerstin. "*Vad sade hon?*" Anna-Lisa asks Kerstin. Dutifully, Kerstin translates for Anna-Lisa.

The Flyers are simply too much for Chicago to handle. In the first half of the final period, Howe and Kerr score their second goals of the game to blow the game wide open. With the score 6-1, a contingent of fans contentedly makes its way to the exits and hope to get a jump on the traffic.

Pelle yields a powerplay goal to Chicago late in regulation on a shot that goes in off Ron Sutter's skate. Lindbergh has no chance to stop the severe deflection. Otherwise, it's an uneventful period for Pelle in yet another 20 minutes dominated by the Flyers. He finishes with 18 saves on 20 shots. The final horn comes as something of a pleasant surprise to Pelle, who almost never checks the clock during a game. He doesn't like to know how much time is left, because he believes that it distracts his focus from stopping the puck and increases the chance he'll let in a bad goal.

After the horn sounds, Pelle is surrounded by his teammates. Backup goalie Froese lays his glove hand over Pelle's head in a gesture of congratulations, and Lindbergh responds in kind. Winners of nine games in a row, the players are all smiles as they walk up the tunnel to the locker room. "Good game, boys!" says Brad Marsh. "Hell of a job, Pelle."

Players towel the sweat off their faces and remove their soaked equipment. The air is thick and dank. A few players head into the other room to grab a beer while others go straight to the shower. They pass Lindbergh, who remains seated at his locker, still clad in his uniform and all of his equipment minus his mask, catching glove and waffle board. Restlessly, he sits, waits, and stares straight ahead. Suddenly, Keenan enters the room and stands directly in front of his goaltender. Lindbergh looks up.

Keenan, who has already decided to start Froese in the next game and then go back to Lindbergh for the rematch with Edmonton, knew he'd find Pelle sitting in front of his locker. Pelle waits for Keenan. It's another one of the goaltender's little rituals. "Good game tonight, Pelle," Keenan says, as he shakes Lindbergh's hand. "Thanks," Pelle responds.

One year earlier, there was a mini-incident caused by the disruption of the routine. Keenan got caught up in a lengthy discussion with a reporter while Pelle remained seated at his locker for an inordinate period of time. Finally, Kevin Cady, the team's young equipment manager, came over to Pelle and insisted he get changed. "Not yet," Lindbergh insisted. "I have to shake hands with the coach first." "Sorry but we have to pack up the equipment for the next game. We can't wait any longer," Cady said. Lindbergh stayed put over Cady's protest.

Forty minutes passed. By now, Lindbergh was shivering sitting in the cold, sweaty equipment that clung to his body. He sat alone in the locker room. At last Keenan entered the room. He was surprised to see Lindbergh sitting there at all, much less still dressed in his pads and uniform. Lindbergh was annoyed. "Coach, how can you do this to me?" he demanded in a soft voice.

In the outside world, Lindbergh's behavior would seem eccentric and his annoyance misplaced. But in the hockey realm, Keenan knew he was in the wrong. Adhering to this little routine was an easy way to help keep his goalie focused and happy. Ever since then, Keenan has never again forgotten Pelle after a game.

After Pelle showers and changes his clothes, he meets up with Kerstin, Anna-Lisa, and Göran outside the Family Room. By this point, he's already put tonight's game out of his mind. Unlike many players, Pelle never takes the game home with him. His postgame disposition is the same after a win, loss, or tie. Anna-Lisa tells Pelle she's tired and ready to head back to the house.

"OK, but the whole team is going out to eat," Pelle says. "Göran, do you want to come along with me?" "Sure," says Göran. A few minutes later, Pelle says goodnight to Kerstin and Anna-Lisa. Kerstin removes the keys to the Mercedes from her purse. Pelle and Göran wait a moment and then head out to the parking lot to go to dinner at a nearby hotel. As they walk toward Pelle's Porsche, Göran is taken aback. A throng of fans blocks their path and dozens encircle the car, chanting "Pell-lee! Pell-lee! Pell-lee!" " God Almighty, Pelle. There must be at least 200 of them," Göran exclaims in Swedish.

Pelle just smiles, and begins to sign autographs while standing in the cramped space around the car. Many of the people are regulars whom he recognizes from the Coliseum (the club's practice facility in Voorhees, NJ) and the Spectrum. A few wait for him on almost a daily basis. Finally, Pelle and Göran are able to get in the car and pull the doors shut. Göran is still in a state of disbelief. "Is it like this all the time? Every night?" Göran asks. "Yeah," Pelle says, and chuckles at the expression on his brother-in-law's face. "That was bloody unbelievable the way they all chanted your name when they saw you," Göran says.

Pelle Lindbergh

CHAPTER 2
OSKARSHAMN, SWEDEN, 1936

Twenty-year-old sailor Erik Sigurd "Sigge" Lindbergh has time on his hands today. The cargo ship on which he works in the Swedish coastal town of Oskarshamn is not yet set to embark and there's no work needed onboard. He and the other crewmembers have some rare inland time to themselves on this sunny afternoon.

Sigge is small in stature but strong as an ox. The blond-haired young man doesn't have an ounce of fat on his lean frame. These are tough political and economic times in Sweden, as well as the rest of the world, but Sigge has a survivor's mentality. He longs to see the world and make a living in the process; no matter how much backbreaking work he has to do.

He waited for a long time to be able to escape Lotta's home. A child of the farmlands and meadows north of Stockholm, he was born August 7, 1916. Sigge was raised by his maternal grandmother, Lotta, in the village of Roslags-bro, just outside the town of Norrtälje. While the countryside was lovely, the crowded home in which he lived had no running water or electricity and life with Lotta was miserable. Called "snälla mormor Lotta" (sweet grandmom Lotta) by the children, the name was not a term of affection. Lotta was a mean-spirited woman who lacked maternal warmth. Her daughters were sent out to find work, but her young grandchildren lived at her home.

Sigge lacked much in the way of formal schooling, but he made up for it in common sense, work ethic, and ambition. At age 15, he had left Lotta's house for good. He knew there had to be a better life elsewhere and he intended to find out as soon as possible. Sigge wanted to go to Stockholm, where he had a maternal aunt and uncle living in the working-class south side of the city but the young man lacked the money to get there. Working as a hired hand on a nearby farm, he asked the farmer how to get to Stockholm. "Borrow a horse if you want to move to the city," he was told.

Sigge couldn't do that. He had no money and he had nothing of value to trade. The young man could carry all of possessions on his back; however, where there's a will, there's a way. Sigge worked long hours doing odd jobs on the farm until he was finally able to afford to move to his relatives' home on Bondegatan (Farmer Street) in the Södermalm section of Stockholm.

Things were much better at Bondegatan than at Lotta's but Sigge had no skills to find a job, which were in short supply in Stockholm during the Great Depression. To make matters worse, none of the remaining local farms along the Stockholm outskirts needed a farmhand. His Uncle Nisse had some connections that could help. He worked the seas and asked around to see if there were any crews that needed a hardy, powerful youngster who learned quickly and followed directions without griping.

So it came to pass that farm boy Sigge Lindbergh became a weather-bitten sailor as he traveled the seas from Europe to ports of call as far-reaching as South America and Africa. During his time on land at home, he lived at the Sailor's Home (*Sjömanshemmet*) south of central Stockholm. Even as the rise of the Nazis in Germany posed an ever-increasing threat to European sea trade, Sigge was able to find continuous work. He realized that the voyages were becoming increasingly dangerous – even for Swedish ships – but he had no choice in the matter.

Today, at least, Sigge has time to himself in Oskarshamn, which had developed over the centuries from a small fishing village into a bustling port. Casually he walked over to the Pressbyrå, which was similar to an old-fashioned newspaper stand. These stands are invaluable for they sell morning and afternoon newspapers as well as a large assortment of needed items. It is here that he meets 16-year-old Anna-Lisa Carlsson for the first time. A striking-looking girl with dark hair, Anna-Lisa is the daughter of a railroad worker who helped get her the job at the Oskarhamn Pressbyrå. Sigge strikes up a conversation with Anna-Lisa, and lingers at the Pressbyrå as long as possible. An outgoing, social girl with an engaging smile and laugh, young Anna-Lisa makes quite an impression on Sigge. He's smitten.

Whenever he returns to Oskarhamn from one of his lengthy voyages, Sigge heads straight for the Pressbyrå. Several years after their first meeting, Sigge is injured in an onboard accident while the ship is docked in port. Suffering serious burns on one of his legs, he is laid up in the general hospital in Oskarshamn. After he is discharged from the hospital, he takes up residence in a small room located in the center of the town. As soon as he feels up to it, he seeks out Anna-Lisa again. "Let's go see a movie," he says with a smile. She goes.

As friendship turns to love, neither Sigge (age 26) nor Anna-Lisa (age 21) can bear the thought of him leaving her behind to go on another voyage. The year is now 1942 and World War II is raging around Europe. Sweden is considered one of the few non-combatants, although there are a variety of behind-the-scenes political machinations going on for the country to preserve its neutral status. The Swedish government has made significant concessions to Germany; these include importing iron ore for Germany's military use and allowing the Wehrmacht to use Swedish railways to transport German soldiers.

Meanwhile, everyday Swedes like Sigge and Anna-Lisa hear the relentless bad news from Europe on the radio and read about it in the newspapers. They do not live every day with foreign tanks rolling through their streets but they cannot relate much to the politicians, ideologues, or wartime profiteers. They're too busy trying to eke out an existence.

For people like Sigge, job security meant there was work today – there were no guarantees about tomorrow. At the same time, the war was dangerously close to Sweden's doorstep and the thought of the Russians entering its borders was scarcely more appealing than the thought of occupation by the Germans. But to a young couple in love, lack of money and the conflagration of World War II are no deterrents to starting a life together. Sigge and Anna-Lisa are married at the home of the minister who performs a simple ceremony. Afterwards, they serve coffee and sweet rolls.

The couple moves into a tiny one-room apartment at Bondegatan 17 on the southern side of Stockholm. Here, in living space that measures a mere 130 square feet, they start what will become a family with three children. Sigge and Anna-Lisa find the place thanks to his brother, Oskar, who works for Stockholm's biggest morning newspaper.

Early one morning, Oskar tells his brother that he can help them find an affordable arrangement if they rent the space from the newspaper's doorman. After a meeting with the current doorman, the Lindberghs agree to pay the equivalent of $15 per month for rent. Sigge pays the first year's rent in advance with the money he's saved. Despite the cramped space, Anna-Lisa makes their home a charming little place to live. Sigge is just happy that he and his wife have a place of their own.

One year after moving into their apartment, Sigge and Anna-Lisa have their first child, a girl named Ann-Louise. Anna-Lisa works by packing goods at a shipping company and Sigge has been working on demand on a fairly regular basis. The money he earns isn't as good as it had been during his voyages but they manage. Sigge and Anna-Lisa's "make the best of your life's reality" mentality remains essential to their character and is one of the central values they later instill in their three children.

As time passes, Sigge misses the seas and tells Anna-Lisa that he wants to return to his previous line of work. She's not thrilled because the sea voyages have become more dangerous with the war, but he has made up his mind. With Anna-Lisa living in constant fear for her husband's safety, he becomes a crewman on a cargo ship traveling mostly to ports along the Swedish coastline, as well as less frequent trips through the waterways of Nazi-occupied Netherlands and the warring western European nations. This continues for the duration of the war.

Life in postwar Stockholm improves quickly and Sweden remains neutral and stable. Five years after the birth of Ann-Louise, the Lindberghs celebrate the arrival of their second child, a baby girl they name Ann-Christine. Ann-Louise is already an experienced caregiver by the time her mother gives birth to the family's third child while sister Ann-Christine is now 10 years old. On May 24, 1959, Göran Per-Eric Lindbergh is born at Stockholm's Southern Hospital (*Söder Sjukhus*).

Right from the start, the baby is hardly ever called by his formal name. Everyone refers to him as Pelle, which is a common nickname for Swedes named Per. Although he adores his two daughters, Sigge is overcome with joy when he learns that the third child is a boy. He comes to the hospital with a bouquet of red roses for Anna-Lisa and inside the bouquet he has tucked a special present for his newborn son – a green and white pennant with the logo of Hammarby IF, the biggest and most successful athletic club in southern Stockholm. "What's this?" Anna Lisa asks and Sigge beams as he relates, "I signed Pelle up as a member of Bajen today before I came over to the hospital."

Although he's never played organized sports himself, Sigge has become a passionate fan of Hammarby's top soccer team (like most European athletic clubs, Hammarby IF has teams in several different sports – soccer, hockey, and bandy - that range from youth to adult categories). When time permits, he loves to attend games and like almost every supporter of Bajen (as the locals call Hammarby IF), he's learned to despise the team's top cross-city rivals, Djurgårdens IF and AIK. Sigge doesn't even like it when the name of either rival team is invoked in the Lindbergh home.

Anna-Lisa laughs at her husband's admission that he stopped off to register his newborn son as an HIF member before visiting her in the hospital. It's not exactly a romantic gesture, but Sigge is already sharing one of his passions with their son. At least he remembered to bring the bouquet of flowers before showing her the Hammarby IF pennant.

In 1964, Pelle celebrates his fifth birthday. After twenty-two years of living in the one-room apartment on Bondegatan with their children, Sigge and Anna-Lisa move to a bigger place. While they certainly had opportunity to move before, Anna-Lisa liked the small-town feel of the neighborhood, where all of her daughters' friends lived and she and Sigge knew everyone by name. She had wanted no part of the many new suburbs that were developing along the outskirts of Stockholm, but eventually has a change of heart. Other local families are moving, too, and she has seen a newly built apartment complex that she loves.

There's a three-room flat available at Barnängsgatan 2, with plenty of green trees for Pelle to climb and young children with whom he could play. The Sofia Elementary School, located a few hundred yards away, is visible from the living room window of the second story apartment. Besides, it's not as though they'd be moving all the way across town. Barnängsgatan is located in the south side of Stockholm – still in the heart of the Hammarby IF's support base.

To earn extra money, Anna-Lisa takes on an extra job, by working part-time at a small convenience store on Bondegatan. Sigge works at a shipyard while on land and continues to work the seas. Sometimes the voyages force him to be away from home for several months. He finally puts in enough time at sea to be entitled to collect a full pension. Sigge misses Pelle

A young Pelle poses for a photograph with his father [Courtesy Ann-Louise Hörnestam]

terribly when he is away, but the boy is a happy, well-adjusted child. He's a handful for Anna-Lisa – a perpetual motion machine who rarely sits still for two minutes. It seems that every time Anna-Lisa turns around, she finds her young son, clad in his little ski cap, jacket, and trousers, as he runs off in the opposite direction and has made a once-tidy room into a mess. But she can never stay angry for very long. Pelle has an exceptionally sweet disposition. Two years before the Lindberghs moved to Barnängsgatan, Sigge and Anna-Lisa bought Pelle a train set for Christmas. It quickly became his favorite toy, as he loves to make the trains "go fast." With the vivid imagination of childhood, Pelle relishes his dual job as both engineer and station master.

Pelle's favorite playmate, Mikael Nordh, born just four days after Pelle, lives next door. Anna Lisa and Mikael's mother had actually first met in the maternity ward at the hospital. Over the years, Pelle and "Micke" become inseparable and on many nights, Anna-Lisa cooks dinner for both boys before they hurry off to resume their games.

Together, the boys explore the environment around the Sofia School. Both boys have vivid imaginations and soon become obsessed with things that have motors and wheels. It doesn't take long after Sigge and Anna-Lisa get Pelle his first bicycle for the youngster to run off to show it to Micke, who already has a bike. Within weeks, the boys ride side-by-side up and down the street for hours on end, until the sunsets and the reflectors on the spokes of their wheels glow in the dark and warn oncoming cars of their presence.

Pelle and Micke are classmates at Sophia Elementary School and every morning they eat breakfast together before school. Micke is always finished and ready in plenty of time, and invariably waits for Pelle to stop talking long enough to eat and get his books. As a result, they often walk in late for their first class.

As the oldest of the Lindbergh children, Ann-Louise was also the first to bring dates home. Her redheaded boyfriend Göran Hörnestam is a young sailor, like Sigge was back when he met Anna-Lisa for the time in Oskarshamn. Before too long, he becomes Ann-Louise's husband.

One day upon his arrival to the Lindbergh home, he told the other adults there had been a fender bender down on the street, a four-year-old Pelle excitedly shouted, "I wanna see it! Let's go look at the crashed car! Let's go look at the crashed car!" "Yeah, yeah, OK," Göran said. "Come on. Let's look." He took Pelle downstairs. As they got closer to the crash site, Pelle became a bit scared, and gripped Göran's hand tighter and tighter while shutting his eyes. Finally the youngster opened his eyes and looked.

That same year, Göran bought his own car – a Folka. It was a cold winter, and Göran drove with Pelle along the frozen Saltsjöbaden. But they weren't going there to go ice fishing for herring, like most of the other young men Göran's age. They went because Pelle loved to ride in the car. "We took the Folka out on the ice and Pelle sat on my knee and steered with me," Göran recalls many years later. "I hit the brakes so the car would spin on the ice and Pelle let out a victory yell." Pelle begged Göran to do his "car trick" again.

There's one other thing that Pelle likes and that is being out on the ice. He started to learn how to skate as a four-year-old at Nytorg's Park (Nytorg-sparken) in Södermalm located close to the family's first home at Bondegatan 17. Holding onto Sigge's hand, Pelle wobbles unsteadily at first on his double-runner blades but quickly gets the hang of it. Eventually, Pelle starts to tote around a small bandy stick that Sigge himself had made for him. Even at a tender age, Pelle has exceptional balance on his feet, and on skates he darts around bigger, older children. For the family's first Christmas on Barnängs-gatan, Pelle gets his first real pair of skates and homemade shin guards.

Shortly after the family moves to Barnängsgatan, five-year-old Pelle discovers that he can skate directly underneath the balcony in the wintertime. This area becomes Pelle's main playground until he moves away from home to play hockey. The quickest route to the path is by going out the balcony door in the Lindbergh's family room on the second floor, climbing over the guardrail and jumping down to the ground below. As he gets a little older this becomes Pelle's preferred method of exiting the building.

In the fall of 1966, shortly after the school year at Sofia School started for seven-year-old Pelle Lindbergh, Sigge and Anna-Lisa saw a green-and-white advertisement inviting parents to enroll their children at the skating school in Hammarby. The classes are held on the ice bandy rank at Söderstadion. The Hammarby youth coach who received the youngsters was the future Swedish and Finnish national team hockey coach Curt "Curre" Lindström. Even decades later, Lindström vividly recalls the first time he saw seven-year-old Pelle out on the ice, "He was agile on his skates right from the beginning."

One year after signing up for skating lessons, Pelle joins Hammarby's new youth hockey school directed by Lindström. Shortly thereafter, he becomes a goaltender playing on a boy's team with kids a year older than himself. Pelle lacks nothing in the way of self-confidence. At the age of 10 he announces to Lindström that he'll someday become "the best goalie in the world." Decades later the coach recalls, "I remember he was the most damn positive kid about any situation.... He was already full of life."

Sigge and Anna-Lisa become deeply committed to Pelle's hockey life. They pack his suitcase, chauffer him to practice, tote his equipment bag on the subway, attend his away games and tie his frozen skate laces until their fingers turn blue. "Both Sigge and Anna-Lisa came along. Finally, Sigge became our team's equipment manager," Lindström remembers.

CHAPTER 3

FRIDAY, NOVEMBER 8, 1985

Mike Keenan holds the whistle to his mouth. The players cluster in an incongruous semi-circle. Many are standing, some are leaning against their hockey sticks, and a few are kneeling down on one knee. They listen as the head coach instructs them.

The Flyers soundly defeated the Blackhawks the previous night and are now in the midst of a nine-game winning streak. Keenan has put the team through the paces early, and wants to guard against complacency. His preferred method of doing so is to push his players even harder at practice. Keenan knows that when a team is winning on a nightly basis, it's easy for players to start taking shortcuts. The more the Flyers win, the more vehemently Keenan points out seemingly minor flaws. He separates the team into smaller groups to perform drills with the puck, and he has his players skate sprints. It's one of the players' least favorite exercises.

After the formal practice session ends, several players remain on the ice. Among those who remain are Dave Poulin and Pelle, who feels a particularly close bond with Poulin. The team captain has challenged Pelle to a breakaway duel. Poulin, who spent a season playing in Sweden for Rögle BK Ängelstad after graduating from the University of Notre Dame, grins back at Lindbergh. They needle each other after each shot.

Rögle BK was far from a high-profile club in Sweden. Swedish hockey is divided into various levels, with the highest level being the Elite League (*Elitserien*). The next step down in that era was Division 1, followed by Division 2, and so on. Poulin dominated his Division 1 opponents. In 32 games, he racked up 36 goals and 62 points and earned his Swedish teammates' respect. Even with this, he still couldn't help but feel like an outsider at times – a foreign hired hand. The Swedish players were polite to Poulin, but conversed in the locker room without including him in discussions and socialized away from the rink without inviting him. As a result, ever since Poulin made it to the NHL and became the Flyers' captain, he's gone out of his way to make sure every player on the team feels welcomed and included in all team activities, both on and off the ice.

After returning to the locker room, Pelle Lindbergh and some of the other players speak briefly with the beat writers who cover the Flyers for the city's two major daily newspapers as well as a couple of television and radio reporters. The players talk about the club's busy schedule and the importance of not overlooking the game against the Bruins tomorrow in anticipation of the showdown with the Edmonton Oilers the following week.

Even more than the Spectrum, the Coliseum is the Flyers' players second home. It's situated only 15 minutes from Philadelphia, but it's in this building on Preston Avenue and the surrounding environs of South Jersey where much of the players' professional and social lives are centered. The Coliseum consists of two linked buildings with huge white pillars next to the admission area. The pillars are designed to evoke ancient Rome, but it's not particularly convincing. The inside of the building is more impressive. Apart from the hockey rink, the owners have invested in a gym with a swimming pool, a bowling alley, tennis courts, and a restaurant with five bars that, by night, becomes a popular hangout for many of the Flyers' players. Often, players meet up again at night for drinks. On the fifteenth of every month, the players receive their paychecks here, too. Even the walls of the Coliseum are painted in the Flyers' orange and black team colors.

Whenever Keenan is safely out of earshot, it's not at all uncommon for the players to gripe about him. If a practice session doesn't go according to plan, an explosion from their coach is sure to follow. Many of the players think Keenan is crazy. But the club's most respected leaders – Poulin, Mark Howe, and Brad Marsh - first and foremost recognize Keenan's tactics as psychological ploys. As Keenan intended, the team has become a close-knit bunch, as they share the bond of surviving life under the ultra-demanding coach. By comparison, even the Flyers' toughest NHL opponents seem manageable. The key to playing successfully for Keenan is to recognize that most of the things he says and does are designed for effect and shouldn't be taken personally; however, that's often easier said than done.

But among the players, the most infamous surprise Keenan ever had in store for them occurred during his first season as Flyers' coach: the "Christmas Death Skate" of 1984. Early on the morning of December 24, the players arrived at the Coliseum for what they thought would be a light practice before an informal team Christmas party with plenty of pizza and beer and an exchange of gag gifts. The team had recently worked through a four-game losing streak and had won two of its last three games. Everyone was in a good mood. The previous night, Lindbergh and the team won a 7-4 game at home against the Washington Capitals. Apart from a meltdown early in the third period that saw the Caps score two quick goals to trim a 7-2 deficit, Philly controlled most of the game. At the other end of the ice, Pelle turned back 27 of 31 shots to earn the win. Many saves were of the difficult variety, because the play was wide open. Lindbergh had little chance to stop any of the goals Washington scored.

As the players filed onto the Coliseum ice on Christmas Eve morning, they were greeted by several blasts of Keenan's whistle. He ordered the players to start skating end-to-end sprints. The Flyers, hoping to get the drill over with quickly, skated as fast they could. No such luck was to be had, as Keenan kept them skating. The bag skate lasted for more than two hours. By then, the players' legs burned and some dehydrated players wretched and were close to vomiting. No one was excused. Finally, as the players neared the point of collapse, Keenan blew the whistle to end practice. He gathered his team. Most of the players sat, staring straight down at the ice, both out of exhaustion and anger. Keenan moved his piercing gaze slowly across the ice. One-by-one, the players looked up at the coach. At last he spoke. "Always expect the unexpected," he said, "and Merry Christmas."

For his part, Pelle has come to realize that Keenan has faith in him as the starting goaltender. Keenan gave Lindbergh the playing time he's been craving since the Flyers' drafted him six years ago. Pelle usually got the call in must-win games and games against the Flyers' toughest opponents. He also recognizes that Keenan has played a role by showing greater faith in him than had the team's previous coach, Bob McCammon. Years later, Keenan would admit that he tabbed Lindbergh for the tougher games because of the Swede's mental strength and determination – as well as his physical skills – that even many older and more-experienced goaltenders lacked.

Defenseman Mark Howe is arguably the team's best player. At 30, he's also an elder statesman on the club. The son of the legendary Gordie Howe is universally respected in the dressing room, but no one admires him more than Lindbergh, who is the beneficiary of rock-solid play whenever Howe and his defensive partner, Brad McCrimmon, are on the ice. "Mark makes my job easy. It's a pleasure to play goal when you have guys like him and Brad. He's the best defenseman and one of the best players I've ever played with," Lindbergh said on the eve of the 1985 playoff opener.

During the 1984-85 season, Howe posted 18 goals, 57 points, and a plus-51 defensive rating (meaning that he was on the ice for 51 more Flyers goals at even strength and in short-handed situations than he was for opposition even-strength and short-handed goals). Howe's offensive numbers would have been higher, but he missed nine games with torn cartilage near his

clavicle and a rib injury. McCrimmon had 43 points and a plus-52 rating.
Pelle's Vezina Trophy season would not have been possible without their
contributions to his success. Nicknamed "The Beast," McCrimmon takes
opposing scoring chances – much less goals – as a personal affront. He also
has underrated skills with the puck. Like his more famous partner Howe, Mc-
Crimmon has superior hockey sense that puts him a step ahead of most
opposing players.

So far this season, Howe and McCrimmon are on pace to better their
1984-85 output. The duo continues to shoulder an immense ice-time load
while going on to deliver one of the most spectacular seasons the NHL has
ever seen from a pair of defensemen. Howe winds up scoring 24 goals and 82
points and posts a phenomenal plus-85 rating. McCrimmon, meanwhile,
posts a plus-83 rating to go along with 13 goals and 56 points worth of
offensive production. Thus, it's fair to say that during the 30 minutes per
game that Mark Howe and Brad McCrimmon are on the ice together, Philadelphia is the best all-around team in the NHL – including Edmonton.
During the other 30 minutes with other players manning the blueline, the
1985-86 Flyers are still potent offensively but little more than an ordinary
defensive squad.

Flyers players, like those on virtually every hockey team, generally refer
to one another by nicknames. The current team's predecessors from the 1970s
– the Stanley Cup-winning "Broad Street Bullies" – had some of the most
colorful nicknames in the annals of the game, ranging from "Thunder-
mouth," "Ash Can," "Cowboy," and "Sparky" to "Big Bird," "Moose," and
"The Hound." The current Flyers players fall a bit short of their predecessors
when it comes to nicknaming creativity but Lindbergh sports some colorful
monikers. Not counting the name Pelle (a standard Swedish nickname for
Per), Lindbergh goes by a pair of nicknames around the club: "Gump" and
"Tex." The Swede was dubbed "Tex" after a humorous incident that hap-

pened the previous season.

Late in the evening of December 30, 1984, the Flyers were in Los Angeles. The players were tired and after traveling from Washington to Vancouver to Los Angeles and playing three games over a four-day span. A few hours earlier, the Flyers beat the LA Kings by a 3-2 score. After the game, most players were too tired to go out but Lindbergh and teammates Brian Propp and Brad McCrimmon were hungry, so they went out together to grab a bite at a hotel café. The players talked among themselves while waiting for the waitress to take their order.

The waitress, who had been staring at the players from across the room, finally came over, but not to take their food and drink orders. She approached Pelle and said, "Excuse me, but do you mind if I ask you a personal question?" "What is it?" Pelle asked a little apprehensively. "Well, when you talk, you have the most interesting accent. I don't think I've ever heard one like that before." "Really?" the Stockholm native replied. "Yes. Are you from Texas?" she asked.

The "Tex" nickname became a running gag for the remainder of the 1984-85 season. Pelle got a kick out of re-telling the story and entertained teammates by sometimes introducing himself as Tex Lindbergh. He even donned full cowboy regalia and stood in net to pose for a photo shoot for the Flyers' game program. But "Tex" was only an occasional nickname, used when Pelle and his teammates were in a silly mood. More commonly, he went by "Gump," a nickname trainer Dave "Sudsy" Settlemyre gave him in honor of Hall of Fame goaltender, Lorne "Gump" Worsley, the next-to-last NHL goaltender to play without a mask.

During Lindbergh's first North American season with the Maine Mariners, he frequently kidded around and talked shop with Settlemyre. One day, the subject came around to the top goalies in history. Pelle asked Settlemyre whom he thought was the best goalie of all time (predictably, Lindbergh cast his initial vote for Parent, at least among goaltenders he'd studied). Settlemyre thought for a moment, and then launched into a combination history lesson and monologue on Pelle's behalf.

"Jacques Plante was unbelievable and very famous during his career. He's Bernie Parent's idol, by the way, but Plante is a real jerk as a person. Glenn Hall was very good but he always puked before the games. Terry Sawchuk was an amazing goalie but his life was a mess and he died young. Gump Worsley was great but he drank too much." Finally, they decided Worsley, who played in the NHL until he was 45 and was one of the game's most well liked players, was the best of all time. "That's me. I'm Gump," Pelle said, still chuckling.

The conversation was forgotten but a few weeks later, Lindbergh's mask got knocked off during a game and play continued. For a full minute, Pelle was forced to tend goal without a mask before he was able to retrieve his mask at the next stoppage of play. He wasn't scored upon. "Attaway, Gump!" Settlemyre shouted from the bench. The Mariners' players and coaches quickly picked up on the inside joke between Settlemyre and Lindbergh. From that point forward, Pelle is known as "Gump" or "The Gumper."

After practice, he exits the building into the unseasonably warm November weather. He turns the ignition key on the Porsche, flips some music on the radio, and drives home. His relatives and fiancée are waiting for him when he gets there. Pelle and Kerstin have lived in King's Grant for three years. Their home is a big two-story house with attractive hardwood floors. It's furnished with high-end Scandinavian furniture and other decorative touches reflecting their homeland. On the back of the house, there's a private deck overlooking the artificial lake.

Anna-Lisa and Göran have one week left of their visit. Tonight, Pelle and Kerstin are taking everyone out to dinner to celebrate Göran's birthday and tomorrow is a game night. On Sunday, Pelle will have a rare free day without practice or a game. After the Bruins game, the Flyers won't play again for four days until the Oilers come to town. The family makes plans for Sunday. "I think we should go to Atlantic City," Pelle suggests. "Göran, there's a boat show there this weekend and some great boats down below on the ocean. Afterwards we can meet up with Kerstin and Mama." Kerstin and Anna-Lisa's plan for Sunday is more open-ended as Kerstin tries to convince Anna-Lisa to go out shopping with her. Pelle's mother says there are some things she wants to do first at the house.

Whenever she comes to visit, Anna-Lisa inevitably takes over all the housework and cooking. Kerstin has gotten used to it over the course of her relationship with Pelle. There's no use arguing with Anna-Lisa to let them take care of her for a change; Anna-Lisa won't hear of it. Kerstin and Anna-Lisa have grown close over the years, and Kerstin has come to realize that Pelle's mother gets pleasure from being a caretaker for her loved ones. Whenever Anna-Lisa visits the US or Pelle returns to Stockholm, she treats Pelle to his favorite home-cooked meals. His absolute favorite are her potato dumplings (*kroppkakor*) topped with melted butter and lingonberry jam. Other staples are her cabbage pudding (*kålpudding*), potato pancakes served with bacon or other meat on top (*raggmunkar*), and savory meatballs (*köttbullar*) with creamy gravy and lingonberry jam.

Shortly after her arrival in the US, Anna-Lisa asks Kerstin to take her to the supermarket to get the ingredients to make her *kroppkakor*. Pelle sits down and devours them ravenously. "Mama, these are the best," he says. "They have no good ingredients at the markets here in America. They're better when I make them at home," Anna-Lisa complains. "Nonsense, they taste perfect," Kerstin says. Pelle is thrilled that Kerstin gets along so well with his mother, and Kerstin treats Anna-Lisa likes she's her own mother rather than a future mother-in-law.

Kerstin and Anna-Lisa enjoy passing the time by walking around the various malls disbursed around the Philadelphia suburbs. Today, Kerstin arranges with Pelle to meet up with his mother and her for coffee at a shop near a florist. Anna-Lisa is surprised to see her son come in. Behind his back, he holds a small potted plant with beautiful red autumn flowers. "If we're going to drink coffee here, we have to have a flower on the table," he says as he produces the plant and places it on the table. "Pelle, you're not allowed to take that, are you?" Anna-Lisa asks. "Relax, Mama. I paid for it." Anna-Lisa brings the plant back home with her. This is not the only time during Anna-Lisa's trip that Pelle showed up with flowers. The previous week, he made a side trip after morning practice at the Coliseum to buy two bouquets of flowers: one for Kerstin and one for his mother. "Flowers for my girls," he said as he walked in the door.

Pelle's friends have often told him how lucky he is to have Kerstin, and he readily agrees. Recently, Pelle and Kerstin have discussed setting their wedding date for the summer of 1986. Apart from being beautiful and athletic, she's sweet, patient, and practical. Kerstin is much better than Pelle at managing everyday tasks. She keeps the household running while he's off playing hockey.

Göran meanwhile, is loving every minute of being around an NHL team, which he knows is an experience of which the hockey lovers back home could only dream. One morning after breakfast Pelle asked him if he'd like to come along to practice. "How much fun is it to sit by yourself in the stands?" Göran replied. "Yeah, but there's other stuff to do at the rink if you get tired of watching us. There's a restaurant, a whirlpool, and some other things. Come hang out," Pelle replies. So Göran comes along.

On November 2, when Anna-Lisa and Göran saw their second game at the Spectrum (a 7-4 Flyers win over Los Angeles), they witnessed a brawl-filled tilt in which numerous players were ejected. Midway through the first period, with the Flyers leading 1-0, a pair of fights broke out in the Flyers' end of the ice. Philly's top heavyweight, Dave Brown, and the ever-willing Ed Hospodar dropped the gloves with the Kings' Brian MacLellan and future Flyer Jay Wells.

Pelle was the nearest spectator during the brawl. During the lengthy delay to sort out the various penalties, he suddenly pushed his mask up over his head, and turned and found Göran in the stands behind the sideboards. "Göran!" Pelle shouted. "Did you see the blood?!" Pelle winked and then put his mask back on his face.

Two days after the Flyers-Kings game at the Spectrum, Pelle invited Göran to accompany him to New York City. Lindbergh had a meeting with a Swedish businessman who wanted to discuss some potential endorsement deals with him. Göran had a niece named Anette who lived and worked as an artist in Manhattan. Pelle suggested that he arrange to visit his niece the same day. Pelle drove up to Manhattan in Kerstin's Mercedes. They parked the car in a garage between the skyscrapers, and before they split up for the next few hours, Pelle opened up his wallet. "Here's some walk-around money, Göran."

It was a reversal of roles from Pelle's childhood. Göran was now the one staring wide-eyed, overwhelmed by the size of the avenues and the crowds of people. He'd always dreamed of seeing Manhattan from the time he was a boy in Östergötland but had never made it to the US before. Visiting Anette and spending a full day taking in the sights and sounds of the Big Apple was something he'd never forget.

Meanwhile, while Pelle was at the office for his business meeting, he ran into a famous Swedish pop singer, Carola Häggqvist. Hoping to achieve crossover success, she was launching a debut album in America. Pelle asked Häggqvist for an autograph. She signed it, "Good luck between the posts, Pelle – Carola." Pelle showed the autograph to Göran as they drove home. He was impressed. Ann-Louise's baby brother certainly got to meet a lot of famous people. Hell, Pelle himself was famous nowadays.

———————————————

Whenever he has time, Göran does the repair work on the deck that he'd previously promised Pelle he'd do. Unlike his father and Göran, being handy with tools and carpentry is not one of Pelle's strong attributes. If Göran couldn't do it, he'd have had to pay a contractor to do the work. Pelle gladly pays for the materials and lets Göran do his thing.

One afternoon earlier in the week, Pelle brought company to the house. It was one of his American friends – a police officer named Jack Prettyman. Pelle brought Prettyman outside and introduced him to his brother-in-law. "Göran, this is my buddy," he said. Göran noticed the officer's powerful handshake and recognized his face. Pelle had invited Prettyman, his closest American friend outside of the hockey world, to come to the Coliseum as his guest.

Three years earlier, Pelle made Prettyman's acquaintance by chance. Lindbergh noticed that the officer frequently took long walks as he passed by in his car. On one hot day, Pelle lowered the window and asked Prettyman if he needed a lift. "No, thanks," said Prettyman. "I need the exercise." But Pelle insisted. Conversing during the car ride, they hit it off right away. In the time since then, Lindbergh and Prettyman have developed a deep friendship. Pelle and Kerstin are frequent guests at Prettyman's home. Other times, Pelle meets up for lunch with Jack after practice. When there's a break in the Flyers schedule, Jack and Pelle go fishing, play street hockey together, and ride mopeds with Jack's teenage son, Jay. From time to time, Pelle even gets to ride in Prettyman's squad car. Still just a kid at heart, Lindbergh is enthralled the first time he gets to listen to the police radio and sees how to turn on the siren and flashing lights.

Today Pelle plans to introduce his family to another of his non-hockey friends, Dr. Steven Rosenberg. He drives the Mercedes over the bridge to Philadelphia and hits heavy traffic on this Friday afternoon. By the time they arrive at Rosenberg's office in Center City, Pelle is late for his appointment. He hurriedly gets out of the car and goes inside as Kerstin, Göran, and Anna-Lisa wait for him in the car.

Rosenberg, who wears big glasses and an even bigger smile, greets Pelle and leads him in for his session. Rosenberg has been a big help to Pelle over the past year. While Pelle's connection to Rosenberg started out as strictly a therapist-patient relationship, it's quickly grown into a friendship. Lindbergh's self-confidence on the ice was at a low point after a difficult second season in the NHL. He was worried that his job was in jeopardy. A teammate referred Pelle to Rosenberg and told him the psychologist could teach him techniques to improve his focus. One therapeutic technique, that has been particularly effective in helping Pelle to calm some of his hyperactivity and maintain a higher degree of relaxed concentration, has been to create 25-minute positive imagery cassettes that Lindbergh can listen to at his leisure.

After his session with Rosenberg, Pelle joins his family in the car. They're not happy because Pelle was gone much longer than he said he'd be. He apologizes. Pelle then drives over to the hospital to visit his friend "Sudsy" Settlemyre, who is recuperating from surgery. On the way, Pelle tells the clan that he spent much of the time talking to Rosenberg about his unhappiness with the goaltending rotation that Keenan has used of late. He also wanted to get a few things off his chest. He believes he's earned the right to play almost every game, and is not happy that Froese has been tabbed to play two of three games. The Chicago game wasn't really a difficult test for Pelle, but he now faces a five-day stretch of not playing in a game. The meeting with Edmonton follows this series. He's chomping at the bit to play in the rematch against the Oilers and Rosenberg discussed ways to stay focused in the interim. Rosenberg has even encouraged Lindbergh to make a greater effort to get to know the other goaltender. This is something that Pelle has avoided in the past.

Pelle has tried to take it to heart, but he and Froese are competitive by nature and want to be the undisputed starter. The relationship remains a bit awkward. Nevertheless, Froese acknowledges two decades later that Pelle and he had started to make efforts to interact on a more collegial basis. "We started to spend more time together toward the end and I got to know Pelle a little bit more as a person," Froese recalled.

When he finishes talking hockey, Pelle tells Rosenberg that things are otherwise going well in his life. He's mostly satisfied with his play on the ice so far, the club is on a roll, and he's enjoying the visit from Anna-Lisa and Göran, even though he misses his father and wishes he had come along. Pelle also expresses hopefulness that the health of his sister, Ann-Christine, will finally turn a corner for the good. While Pelle was in the midst of a disastrous second year in the NHL, Ann-Christine was diagnosed with cancer and has gone through a hellish course of chemotherapy. The cancer is now in remission and she's feeling better than she has in some time.

Pelle takes the scenic route on the way to visit Settlemyre, by driving through Camden, NJ – one of the poorest and highest-crime areas in the country. "We should lock the doors now," Pelle says and presses the lock button on the driver's side; Anna-Lisa and Göran look at each other. Pelle chuckles and Anna-Lisa sees nothing humorous about it. She's extremely uncomfortable, especially whenever the car stops at red lights. Nothing out of the ordinary happens, but several people standing on the streets and sidewalks stare at the Mercedes and its occupants. Anna-Lisa is relieved when Pelle arrives at the hospital to visit Settlemyre. He and Kerstin go inside and spend about a half hour with him. Before Pelle leaves, Sudsy assures him he'll be back with the team soon. "Talk to you after the game tomorrow night?" Pelle asks. Settlemyre nods and tells Pelle to call him after the game.

After leaving the hospital, Pelle and company head out for dinner in Philadelphia to celebrate Göran's birthday. "Where do you want to go?" Pelle asks his brother-in-law. Göran isn't sure. "How about the seafood restaurant you say is so good?" Anna-Lisa suggests from the back seat. Pelle takes his family to Old Original Bookbinders Restaurant on Front and Walnut Streets in Philadelphia. It's pricey but worthwhile. Pelle orders a good bottle of wine for the table and makes a toast to Göran. "*Skål*," everyone says, as they clink their glasses. After a rocky start, it becomes a fun evening, filled with conversation and laughter. For Pelle, the only thing missing is his dad, Sigge, who is home in Stockholm.

CHAPTER 4

STOCKHOLM, SWEDEN, SEPTEMBER 1969

Ten-year-old Pelle Lindbergh has already decided he wants to be a professional hockey goaltender when he grows up. Accompanied by Hammarby youth team director Curt "Curre" Lindström, Pelle, and the other boys are going to one of their first hockey camps away from Stockholm. He can barely contain his excitement.

Schoolwork has never been much fun for Pelle. He has a very active mind and a vivid imagination, but hates sitting still all day and not being able to talk with his friends during class. He's not disruptive in class or badly behaved, but his mind wanders easily, even when he tries to pay attention. "Pelle wasn't especially interested in his schoolwork, but he managed around it in any case," Anna-Lisa remembers.

It can't be said for certain that young Pelle has a form of attention deficit disorder (little, if anything, is known about the condition in this era), but the boy displays what later would be considered telltale symptoms of ADD. Often, people who have mild to moderate types of ADD develop compensatory behaviors on their own – typically by hyper focusing on a specific task.

Hockey, of course, is something Pelle loves. He has no problem focusing, but the challenge of playing goal effectively is linked to keen hyperawareness of one's positioning and the location of the puck. When he's at the rink, he zeroes in on the details of the game to the exclusion of everything else. Combined with his God-given athletic gifts and strong self-confidence, Pelle already has the makings of a successful goaltender. It's also not surprising that, being a natural adrenaline-seeker, he later proves to be a better game-day goalie as a professional than he is a practice player. In a 1985 interview, he recalls of this period, "I was always the smallest kid when I grew up, and with goaltenders it's the same thing all over the world. The others all say, "Hey, let the little guy stand in goal. But I loved it right from the start."

He starts to transform his bedroom into a hockey shrine, as his own trophies and mementos begin to collect. He's not only the best 10-year-old goalie in the south of Stockholm, he's better than even some of the top goalies citywide – including kids who are a couple of years older. When Lindbergh isn't playing or practicing at the rink, he can often be found organizing pick-up games with his friends on Barnängsgatan. He'll play any chance he can get. It's here where Pelle plots out a life as a professional hockey goaltender, and tells anyone and everyone that it's what he plans to do for a living.

Curre till Pelle: Future Swedish national team coach Curt Lindström recognized Pelle's rare talent from an early age. On October 12, 1970, Lindström inscribed on this photo "Pelle is a goaltender who can make it as big as he wants." [Courtesy Ann-Louise Hörnestam]

He's even has a favorite NHL team: the Philadelphia Flyers. In this era, few Swedish players give the National Hockey League much thought. There's only been one Swedish-born and trained player to play in the NHL, and he didn't fare particularly well. Longtime Tre Kronor (Swedish national team) star forward Ulf Sterner, a supremely talented product of the Forshaga IF development program, had played a grand total of four NHL games for the New York Rangers during the 1964-65 season and never recorded a point. After spending most of the campaign in the minor leagues, Sterner returned home the following season. Four years later, Toronto Maple Leafs defenseman Börje Salming began a 17-season, Hall of Fame career in the NHL that helped open the door for Swedish players to take a shot at playing in the world's top hockey league.

The pre-teenager has chosen the Philadelphia Flyers as his favorite team. It has nothing to do with the third-year expansion franchise's play on the ice. Pelle knows that the NHL's original six teams – Montreal Canadiens, Toronto Maple Leafs, Boston Bruins, New York Rangers, Detroit Red Wings, and Chicago Blackhawks – are more famous than the new clubs. He's heard of the Stanley Cup and knows that Montreal and Toronto have dominated the championships ever since he's been born. But 10-year-old Pelle has never seen an NHL game at this point. So why are the Flyers, who wind up finishing fifth in the weak Western Conference in 1969-70, his favorite? As he later recalls it: "When I was a kid, a few years before the Flyers won the Stanley Cup, I saw a book or magazine – I don't remember which – that had all the [NHL] teams logos on it, and I liked the one for the Flyers the best."

Five years later, Pelle begins to gain a much more deep-seated affinity for the Flyers. In these boyhood days, his connection to Philadelphia's hockey team goes no further than liking to doodle the club's winged "P" rather than paying attention to the lesson in class. His trips with the Hammarby youth hockey team gets him a much-appreciated reprieve from the classroom, as

Lindström takes his group of boys born in 1959 to practice and play in the industrial city of Västerås, located 62 miles west of Stockholm.

Pelle's best friend on the team is Tommy Nilsson (surname Boustedt), who started out as a fellow goaltender, but soon told his parents that he wanted to be a position player. He later made the switch. Had he remained a goalie, he probably would have spent most of his time watching Pelle play. "Obviously, with a goalie like Pelle on the team, we were outstanding," Boustedt remembers years later.

Even after the hockey season ends and the ice melts, the Hammarby team stays together. Lindström arranges for the team to attend a summer camp called "The Children's Island" (*Barnens Ö*) in Granvik, located in Stockholm's northern archipelago. Lindström has been the camp director for many years. "We held training camps outdoors," Lindström says. "The kids got to run around, lifting and shooting pucks at plywood, and some other things of that nature. It was a real fine summer."

Within Stockholm, there are three prominent athletic clubs featuring hockey programs: Hammarby in the south, Djurgården in the picturesque eastern part of the city and AIK based in the Solna district north of central Stockholm. As longtime Hammarby supporter Sigge Lindbergh would readily attest, there's a decades-old rivalry among the three teams.

The Djurgårdens IF athletic club was formed in 1891, and the hockey program was launched in 1922. The rival DIF senior hockey team has already won 16 national championships. AIK, which is an acronym for the Public Athletic Club (*Allmänna Idrottsklubben*), was founded in 1891 in central Stockholm before its home base relocated in 1937 to Solna. The hockey division was created one year prior to Djurgården's. The senior team, which has had more ups and downs than DIF, had won five Swedish championships up to this point. Pelle is nine when the AIK men's team plays unsuccessfully for the Swedish championship for the first time since it won the national crown in 1947.

Pelle's Hammarby athletic club – HIF or "*Bajen*" to the locals – traces its roots back the farthest. Created in 1889, the club was originally an association of rowers. Eight years later, it added other athletic departments and adopted the Hammarby IF name. Historically, the hockey team played in the top national league from 1922 until it was relegated after the 1956-57 season. Bajen was a hockey powerhouse in the earlier years, winning eight Swedish Championships. By the time Pelle was born, the senior team lagged behind both DIF and AIK.

When Pelle is 11, he dons the black and gold AIK jersey to serve as a fill-in goaltender at the Hanviken Cup. AIK's boys' team of 1959-born players didn't have any goalies available, and Lindström agreed that it would be unfair to the AIK kids for the team to play without a goalie, force a position player to attempt to play goal, or forfeit their game. Most of the AIK players already recognize Pelle even before he takes to the ice. News travels fast in the hockey community.

Pelle feels a bit strange playing for AIK, but even Sigge approves under the circumstances. Little do father and son know that, years later, some casual hockey fans would come to identify Pelle more for his stint with AIK in the Swedish Elite League than as a member of the minor-league Hammarby IF Club. As he evolves from local hero into a star professional player, Pelle makes a point of letting those who are uniformed know that his neighborhood and roots are in southern Stockholm, not Solna.

Even those who played against him in his early years comment on how well-liked Pelle was. Even though he was more skilled than the other young players, he never acted cocky or behaved obnoxiously toward the other teams, whether it was on or off the ice. One of the main reasons Pelle was so much better than most of the other young players – especially the goaltenders – was that he was very sturdy and quick on his skates. "He had a clear advantage over the other goalies because he was great on his skates. For years, Sigge had taken him out on the ice to do a little extra skating, and it showed. Many of the other goalies ended up playing goal because they were bad skaters," says close friend Björn Neckman.

Pelle scarcely needs an excuse to play hockey. When he was younger, he even played inside the front lobby of the apartment building, using a miniature stick. Neighbors complained to Anna-Lisa and Sigge about the racket Pelle and his friends made. The boys soon moved their games outdoors. Pelle plays hockey at recess, after school and on the weekends. "He thought these were damn good games, so he really had a blast," Neckman says. "We'd skate the whole time and later played shinny where Pelle would be a position player. We had two nets on the ice and a lot of kids brought along their skates." One of the nets belongs to Pelle. It was a Christmas gift from his parents. Purchased in 1967, Pelle makes use of it until he moves away from home. He stores it near the towel rack in the bathroom of his family's apartment, with his sweat-soaked goalie equipment and uniforms. Anna-Lisa works hard to keep up. "We had the washing machine going constantly," she says.

The Stockholm winters are brutally cold and it gets dark early. Players battle frozen fingers and toes. Their caps, gloves, and scarves get wet from sweat and snow, quickly turning stiff, but the boys play on. Throughout the years, Micke Nordh and Neckman are regulars in the games played in front of the apartment building. Years later, Rolf Ridderwall, Anders Lånström, and other kids from Pelle's Hammarby youth team join in on the bumpy, frozen grass path.

While he'd never want to be anything but a goalie in a real game, Pelle loved to be an attacker in his front yard game, as he unleashed slapshots at the net. "He shot the way a horse kicks," Neckman says. "It wasn't fun to get in the way." It's rarely the boys who end the games, but rather, it's Anna-Lisa calling Pelle in to eat. He often asks if friends can join them and Anna-Lisa never says no.

Pelle's father and mother are very supportive and involved in his hockey life. One of them is almost always there to take him to games, pack and carry his equipment, and brave the biting winter temperatures to watch his games at outdoor rinks. "Good heavens, I can't even count how many hockey trunks we dragged around through the years," Anna-Lisa remembers. "It was packed and carried, then dried and cleaned. And, yes, everything went in the one trunk." Sigge makes some of Pelle's early equipment by hand and becomes an expert at making quick repairs, which is why Lindström makes the elder Lindbergh the team's equipment manager.

Pelle's mother and father become deeply familiar with the location of each and every outdoor rink in greater Stockholm and get to know everyone in the city's hockey community. Even Pelle's sisters Ann-Louise and Ann-Christine get involved by selling raffle tickets at work to raise money for the Hammarby youth hockey program. It's with the aid of the raffle tickets, bake sales, deposits for returning empty bottles, and donations from friends, family, and interested HIF fan club members that Lindström is able to take Pelle's teams on several increasingly ambitious (and expensive) hockey trips.

In early 1971, Hammarby travels to the Soviet Union for a week of hockey training in Leningrad (now St. Petersburg) and Moscow. Lindström makes the arrangements through the Swedish Ice Hockey Federation (*Svenska Ishockey Förbundet*) and a travel agency in Stockholm. Several parents come along, too, including Sigge and Anna-Lisa. Pelle, who is still a few months away from his twelfth birthday, packs a lot of unforgettable hockey memories into his team's week in Russia.

In Moscow, Pelle gets to defend – or at least attempt to defend – penalty shots taken by 30-year-old CSKA (Red Army) and Soviet national team star Anatoli Firsov. The legendary "father of Russian hockey," Anatoli Tarasov – the man who, for all intents and purposes, built the Soviet hockey program from a ragtag collection of amateurs into a world power – serves as a guest instructor for the youngsters. Pelle's most cherished memory from the Russia trip is seeing a young Vladislav Tretiak, who trades in his goalie equipment for a referee's sweater.

Shortly after the Russian trip there is great news. Pelle Lindbergh and Björn Neckman can hardly believe their ears: Many of the NHL's biggest stars are coming to Sweden – and they're coming to the nearby Johanneshov's Ice Stadium, no less. In September 1972, Team Canada comes to Stockholm for two exhibition games against Tre Kronor in preparation for the upcoming Summit Series against the Soviet Union. A local newspaper holds a contest in which the winner gets the opportunity to see Team Canada practice before the exhibitions. Björn wins the contest and brings Pelle along.

In addition, prior to the first exhibition game, Pelle and the majority of Hammarby's '58 Gang get to meet the Canadian players for a mini-ceremony in which the youngsters present Swedish gifts to the Canadians. Several players return the favor by giving the kids hockey presents. Among the players Pelle meets is Bobby Clarke, the 23-year-old burgeoning star center for the Philadelphia Flyers, for whom the Summit Series marks a breakthrough in his career. Pelle's friend, Anders Lånström, receives Clarke's stick as Lindbergh stands nearby.

By now, Pelle plays only sporadically, usually for special occasions, with Hammarby's team of players born in 1959. Lindström prefers to keep him with the 1958 group, and it is with these older kids that he makes his first trip to North America. On November 3, 1972, Pelle and Sigge board a plane at Stockholm's Arlanda Airport bound for Montreal. The trip marks one of the first times a boys' team from Sweden has traveled across the Atlantic to train and play in a tournament against Canadian youth teams. The 13-year-old talks non-stop throughout the flight, he is eager to arrive in hockey's homeland to begin the 10-day, four-destination trip.

Upon arrival in Montreal, the group prepares to board a connecting domestic flight. With an hour to wait to for the next flight, Pelle and teammate Anders Lånström wander off to explore the airport. He and Pelle are so enthralled by taking in all the sights that they lose track of everyone else and get lost. Neither one knows which gate they're supposed to go to – or how to find the information. "We took a wrong turn somehow, and we searched for a long time to find the rest of the group," Lånström remembers. While they're searching for the rest of the Hammarby contingent, they pass a hamburger stand. The boys have some pocket money and they're tempted to sit down and eat. They decide that they'd better find the rest of the group, lest they miss their flight. "But then Pelle saw something he'd never seen before," Lånström laughs. The boys see huge paper cups overflowing with a concoction they've never heard of before in Sweden– a milkshake. They get in line and order strawberry milkshakes, while savoring every messy sip. With half-finished shakes in hand, Pelle and Ankan resume their search. Luckily, they locate the group with a few minutes to spare before it's time to board the flight, and their teammates greet them with saucer-eyes stares.

Hammarby's '58 team plays a total of six games in Sarnia, Aurora, Oshawa, and Forest, Ontario. In each game, they play against older teams of Canadian boys. During the tournament, Sigge and the thirty plus parents accompanying their children on the trip stay at a hotel. The Hammarby players board with local billet families, on a two-and-two basis. On the second and fourth stops on the tour, Pelle and Ankan room together. "Pelle was actually pretty shy at the families' homes, but he loosened up by the end despite the fact they probably thought were exotic because we spoke pretty strange English," Lånström says.

The first game in Sarnia is shown on local television and the stands are filled to capacity with spectators. Hammarby loses every game on the tour except one. In the lone victory, a 5-4 win over Sarnia, Pelle isn't the goaltender. As a special honored guest, 25-year-old Detroit Red Wings rookie defenseman Thommie Bergman joins his younger countrymen.

While in Toronto, the Hammarby boys go to a sporting goods store. With Sigge at his side, Pelle picks out a new catching glove. His dad also tells him to go ahead and buy the jersey he's been admiring since he walked in the store. Most of the other Hammarby boys buy Maple Leafs jerseys, but Pelle picks a Flyers' one instead. Several years later when Pelle is 15, he discovers the play of Bernie Parent – the goaltender who becomes his idol and, later, his mentor and dear friend. In so doing, he fully adopts the Philadelphia Flyers as his favorite club in the NHL.

After the completion of each hockey season, Curre Lindström throws a party for all the Hammarby youth teams. The boys eat finger food, gulp down soft drinks and the top players receive awards. It is not the awards that make a lasting impression on Pelle, but it's the films of the 1974 Stanley Cup Finals that Lindström has rented and shown on a film projector against a white wall. Lindbergh watches Parent lead the Flyers to victory over the favored Boston Bruins to capture the team's first Stanley Cup, which is punctuated by a 1-0 shutout win in the deciding game. That year, Parent also wins the Vezina Trophy as the NHL's best goaltender and the Conn Smythe Trophy as the most valuable player in the playoffs. As soon as the film ends, Lindbergh asks Lindström to play it again. He then wants to see it a third time. All the while, he watches Parent intently.

The following year the Flyers repeat as Stanley Cup champions with Parent duplicating his individual honors from the previous season. With permission from Sigge and Anna-Lisa, Pelle orders super-8 films of the 1974 and 1975 Finals directly from the NHL offices. He plays them over and over. By now, Pelle is consumed by Parent and the Flyers, and he wants to wear a mask exactly like Parent's and wear Parent's Number 1 on his jersey. From the films he's bought, he studies every nuance of the future Hall of Famer's style and mannerisms in net. Moreover, Lindbergh dreams of playing for Parent's Philadelphia Flyers after his hero retires.

"Pelle didn't just say that he'd play in the NHL. He said he'd play just for the Flyers, and this is when we weren't very old," Neckman remembers. "We watched those films from the NHL games at Pelle's home against his white bedroom door. Sigge taught us how the projector worked and afterward we were set. We watched the films for many years, countless times."

Doing homework and studying for exams at school isn't much of a priority for Pelle. On one occasion, Pelle writes a note on a flunked test paper. In huge block letters, it reads, "This means nothing to me. I'm going to be the goaltender for the Philadelphia Flyers." Another time Pelle gets in trouble for not paying attention in English class. When the teacher reprimands him, he retorts by saying, "Calm down. When I'm playing hockey in the United States, I'll learn plenty of English." The English teacher complains to Pelle's parents and Anna-Lisa lets him have it for being disrespectful to an adult. He says he's sorry but Pelle only regrets displeasing his parents. He meant every word he said to the teacher. Some of Pelle's other teachers recognize that he's intelligent enough to excel in school if he applies himself. They remind him that a professional sports career is not guaranteed, even to a top athlete. What's more, they say, sports careers are short while an education lasts a lifetime. The advice goes in one ear and out the other.

Located in an underground storefront, the ISAB hockey shop in Stockholm has been a Mecca for local players and hockey lovers since it opened in 1966. Owned by Ulf Jernspets and Ola Olsson, the business specializes in importing hockey pads from Canada. It's also the only shop in the city that carries *The Hockey News* and magazines such as *Hockey World* and *Hockey Pictorial.* Not surprisingly, Pelle loves to go to ISAB as he's become more and more involved in hockey; Sigge and Anna-Lisa periodically take him there to buy new equipment. When Pelle was not quite 10, Sigge bought him his first goalie skates for 120 Swedish krona (about $25 US at the time). Jernspets remembers the youngster beaming as he held them. "There weren't any special goalie skates available for boys at the time, but we directly imported a pair of tiny junior skates," Jernspets recalls. The gear is expensive, but Sigge and Anna-Lisa are skilled at budgeting and saving to make sure Pelle has what he needs. "We didn't have much money, but somehow we managed," relates Anna-Lisa.

In his earliest years of playing goal, Pelle played without a mask or helmet cage. Eventually Sigge made him a red metallic mask from sheet metal which he wore with a knit red cap on his head for warmth on the outdoor rinks. When he outgrew his original mask, Pelle stored it in his bedroom and switched to a darker mask with a regular helmet over it. Most of the other young goalies wore cages. It's not until a 1975 trip to ISAB that Pelle gets his first proper goalie mask with the protective device. He gasps when he sees one of the other mask designs in the store; it's the model that Parent wears, except that it's gray instead of white. He takes care of the problem by spray-painting the mask white to match Parent's. Shortly thereafter, he adds Flyers decals, which he wears in games for Hammarby and, later, the Swedish national junior team. During the same trip, Sigge also buys Pelle a new Sher-Wood goalie stick, the same type that Bernie Parent uses.

During his teen-age years, Pelle spends considerable time in the central Swedish province of Dalarna. Dalarna is best known as the heartland of traditional Swedish folklore and culture. This area is home to many of Sweden's most enduring symbols, including the ubiquitous hand-painted wooden horse known as the Dala Horse (*dala häst*). It is also well known for its baked goods, especially for crisp breads (*knäckebrod*), which are a Swedish breakfast staple. Dalarna also has one of the world's richest hockey traditions, which

Long before he was drafted by the Philadelphia Flyers, Pelle adopted the Flyers as his favorite NHL team. He sported Flyers logos on his Bernie Parent-style mask in Swedish league games for Hammarby IF and in international play [File photo]

rivals any region in North America or Europe. In Leksand especially, hockey is central to the town's identity. Pelle is among a group from Hammarby's boys team who take summer trips to Leksand in Dalarna for extra hockey training. Even when Pelle becomes too old to attend the camps as a player, he returns as assistant instructor.

Pelle loves the time he spends in Dalarna. Not only are many of the small towns beautiful, but any place where the local pulse beats to the rhythms of hockey is somewhere he feels at home. While in Leksand, he usually stays in the home of Kjell Ahndén, the man who started the summer hockey school program."He was a like a son in our house," Ahndén remembers. "He was very reliable, and he came back every summer."

Pelle's yearly trips to Leksand are the genesis of many lasting friendships. It's in Leksand that he meets Thomas Steen. One year younger than Lindbergh, Steen is a marvelously skilled young forward who is destined to enjoy a distinguished NHL career of his own. The two prodigies first meet in the summer of 1972 and their friendship blossoms over the next several summers. "We became buddies right away, from the first time we met. I'd never met anyone who was as hockey crazy as myself," Steen recalls. "I remember when he came to Leksand after he'd gotten his Bernie Parent mask and leg pads. To him, the Flyers were all that mattered – nothing else. He dreamed a lot about the NHL already by then and lived to go there someday."

After camp each year, the two continue to get together when time permits, both in Leksand and Stockholm. "Most of the time as children, we hung out together in Leksand, but when I was a little older, I visited him in Stockholm and he showed me the city. We did the things teenagers do. We talked about hockey, obviously, but also there was a lot of music and movies and, yes, girls. But it was mostly hockey." Late in Pelle's teen years, when he goes up to Dalarna to help with the hockey school, he and Thomas become roommates. It's the first time Pelle has lived away from home, without being on a trip with his Hammarby youth team.

Another youngster Pelle encounters in Leksand is a boy from the west side of Stockholm who comes to Leksand each summer because his family has a summer home in the town. His name is Per-Erik "Pelle" Eklund. Years later, Lindbergh only vaguely remembers meeting Eklund in Leksand but Eklund certainly has vivid memories of the goalie. "I saw Pelle for the first time when I was 11 years old and hung out at the rink during hockey school, watching from the side boards. He was four years older and we little guys got a good look at which older players were on the way to getting really good. Everyone said Pelle was going to make it big," Eklund says. Years later, the two Pelles become teammates and friends on the Flyers. By that point, Lindbergh is the defending Vezina Trophy winner and Eklund is an NHL rookie. The boys work hard on the ice, and play hard off it. By the time Pelle serves as a camp instructor, he's long since lost interest in chasing frogs. He's much more interested in chasing girls. "They got into a bit of mischief, almost all the time. I don't remember everything but there were a lot of girls in the room, I remember that," says Andersson.

Pelle is offered an opportunity to move to Leksand year-round and join the Leksands IF program while attending the town's high school and boarding with a local family. When the idea is presented to Pelle, the possibilities spin in his head. Going to Leksand means the chance to play for one of the country's most prestigious teams and to be teammates with Steen. "We were interested in Pelle, and we thought he was absolutely on the way to Leksand," Andersson says. "That's what we worked toward, to find the best talents and offer them the chance to go to the hockey school. Sigge was also involved in the discussion and they thought it over for awhile. But it didn't reach the point that we contacted Hammarby (about a transfer). He felt he couldn't leave Hammarby and the south." Instead, Pelle chooses to attend the hockey gymnasium at Gullmarsplan in Stockholm. When push comes to shove, his heart is at home.

Pelle Lindbergh

CHAPTER 5

SATURDAY, NOVEMBER 9, 1985

It's a game day. Tonight the Flyers will go for their tenth straight victory against the Boston Bruins. The Flyers hold a brief morning workout at the Spectrum that lasts just over half an hour. The atmosphere is relaxed and even Mike Keenan is in a good mood. He's pleased with the tempo of yesterday's practice at the Coliseum and feels the club is well-prepared to take on the Bruins tonight. The coach even smiles.

After the morning skate, Pelle goes home for a lunch prepared (as usual) by his mother. Although he knows he's not starting tonight, Pelle heads upstairs to take his customary pre-game nap. Usually, Pelle sleeps for about two hours, and his game-day routine is very important to him. Disturbing his customary nap could throw off his whole evening. He rests peacefully and wakes up shortly after 4:00. Immediately before changing his clothes and leaving to drive back to the Spectrum, Pelle calls up Sudsy Settlemyre, who has been discharged from the hospital today. "We'll see you tonight after the game," Pelle says. "I'll call you after we've eaten dinner and we're on the way out." "Yeah, we'll have to play it by ear," Settlemyre says, exhausted after a painful and restless night's sleep.

Before Pelle leaves the house for a game, he always makes sure to get a good luck kiss from Kerstin. When he was growing up in Stockholm, Anna-Lisa always gave him a peck on the cheek before he left. Now with his mother visiting his home, Anna-Lisa has once again done the honors of sending him off.

As usual, Pelle plans to drive the Porsche to Philadelphia because everyone else will go to the game in Kerstin's Mercedes. When he gets outside, he sees the Mercedes is parked behind his car. "Göran!" he calls out. "Can you back the Mercedes out of the driveway? I have to take out the Porsche!" Two minutes later, Göran backs the family car onto the street. Pelle pulls out behind him, dons a pair of Ray-Ban sunglasses, and takes off. The late afternoon sun still shines over the roof of the house, as Göran pulls back up the driveway and goes inside.

Unlike Thursday, Pelle makes good time today and arrives at the Spectrum with plenty of time to spare. There are long shadows in the parking lot as Pelle steps out and greets some fans that call out to him. Someone snaps a picture. Lindbergh then enters the arena, has a brief chat with Leo (a security guard), and is soon in the dressing room. In getting ready for the game he follows his typical dressing ritual.

Privately, Lindbergh is still a bit upset that he's not starting tonight, but he tries not to let on to his teammates. He still smiles and jokes around, but he's a little more quiet and subdued than normal. He mischievously tosses a roll of tape at teammate Rick Tocchet when he thinks Tocchet is looking the other way. "Yo, Swedish meatball," Tocchet replies wittily. Pelle smirks. "It wasn't me, Spaghetti!"

A player inquires about when Settlemyre will return. "Hey, Gump!" Ron Sutter hollers. "Why don't you fill in for Sudsy tonight? It's not like you've got anything else to do, anyway." Everyone laughs, including Pelle. More tape flies through the air. Such is hockey locker room humor in its tamest form. It's hardly intellectual and it's rarely politically correct but it keeps things loose in what's otherwise a pressure-filled environment.

On the other side of the room, Bob Froese's face is the picture of concentration, because he's starting the game. While "Frosty" is happy to be starting for the second time in three games, he's frustrated by the perception that he's the team's lesser goaltender. Froese has played well in six starts over the course of the season, and believes that he's consistently performed on a comparable level with Pelle when given the opportunity. Froese has recently gone public with his frustrations, by telling the local newspapers that he'd be willing to be traded to another team if it meant he'd get the chance to be a starting goaltender. There are rumors swirling that the Flyers are close to completing a trade that will send Froese to the Los Angeles Kings in exchange for a defenseman.

Pelle certainly wouldn't complain if a newcomer replaced Froese, especially one called up from the farm team. The previous spring, when Froese was out with an injury, the Flyers called up Darren Jensen from the Hershey Bears. Not surprisingly, Lindbergh hit it off better with Jensen than Froese. Pelle even took Jensen out for lunch and passed along some tips – whereas he and Froese have always kept their distance from one another off the ice.

The Spectrum has begun to fill as the minutes tick down until the drop of the opening faceoff. Kerstin, Anna-Lisa, and Göran are nowhere to be seen. Normally, Kerstin drives south on I-295, rides over the bridge, and is in the stands by now, but on this evening, she encounters car trouble. The car breaks down and she's forced to steer off to the narrow shoulder of the highway next to a concrete wall. Kerstin swears as she realizes they're stranded and dusk is rapidly turning into darkness. Göran steps out of the car, lifts the hood and realizes that the oil pan gasket is broken and the car needs to be towed to a repair shop. Anna-Lisa sits in the car, and nervously watches the oncoming cars rush by just a few feet away from her son-in-law and future daughter-in-law. An unpleasant situation is rapidly becoming a dangerous one with insufficient lighting and fast-moving cars. Kerstin and Göran can barely make out the colors of the cars.

Bob Froese skates out to the crease as the Flyers step onto the ice to a big ovation from the 17,380 fans in attendance. Tonight marks the first meeting of the year between the Flyers and Bruins. Boston has always been a tough opponent for the Flyers.

Pelle, who has a white towel draped over his shoulders, takes a loop around the ice and heads to the bench. After the Star Spangled Banner is finished, he sits down. His white mask, catching glove, and blocker lie behind him.

The Flyers get off to a fast start, but are unable to convert an early power play as former Flyers goaltender Pete Peeters denies several good opportunities. The crowd groans as referee Ron Fournier sends Brad Marsh to the penalty box for hooking, and the Bruins' Barry Pederson capitalizes at the 8:40 mark. Just 19 seconds later, the building erupts as Rich Sutter ties the game. Late in the period, Rich Sutter gives Philly a 2-1 lead, with twin brother Ron once again providing the setup. At the 18:22 mark, Boston's Dave Pasin beats Froese to send the teams to the first intermission tied 2-2, despite a 14-7 shot advantage for the Flyers.

Help has finally arrived for Kerstin, Anna-Lisa, and Göran. After an interminable wait on the side of the road, a young couple stops to offer Pelle's family some much-needed assistance. The pair has graciously offered to give the family a lift to the Spectrum and call a tow truck to take the Mercedes to a nearby repair shop. There's no time to wait for the tow truck, because the game would be over by the time they get to the Spectrum. The family leaves the Mercedes on the side of the road, and heads directly to the arena. Upon arrival at the Spectrum, Kerstin, Anna-Lisa, and Göran profusely thank the good Samaritans for all of their help, and rush inside to find that they've missed most of the game. "Pelle's mom was very upset," Kerstin recalls. "The whole night was ruined."

Pelle keeps an unusually low profile on the bench. It's hard to tell if he's still trying to visualize himself in goal or he's reverted to lamenting the fact that he's not playing. Either way, he's not going to complain – not with his teammates dismantling another opponent.

Tim Kerr has put on an electrifying display tonight, single-handedly taking over the game in the second and third periods. Kerr scores a natural hat trick and brings his goal total to 16 tallies in just 14 games and the Flyers take an insurmountable 5-2 lead with fewer than six minutes remaining. Hats litter the ice. Philly puts down the clamps defensively for the rest of regulation by the exceptional work of Dave Poulin, Ilkka Sinisalo, Ron Sutter, Mark Howe, and Brad McCrimmon. The final buzzer sounds. The Flyers have prevailed, 5-2, and outshoot Boston for the game by a 28-17 margin.

The team has now won 10 games in a row and run its overall record to a gaudy 12-2-0. Befitting the Flyers' league-leading record, the club has the league's best goal differential, by allowing the fewest goals to date while scoring more than every team but the Oilers. Pelle hops out on the ice with the rest of his teammates and congratulates Froese with a clap on his helmet. As he leaves the ice, Pelle places his stick on the stick rack and walks up the tunnel to the locker room. All of the players exchange high fives and smiles.

Keenan keeps his postgame address short. He's pleased with the work his club has turned in the last two days, as they culminate a busy stretch of travel, practice and play. The coach announces that there will be no practice tomorrow and the training session set for Monday is strictly optional. The coach's announcement meets with enthusiastic approval, although it doesn't really come as a surprise. Players have heard whispers all day that Keenan planned to give them a day off tomorrow and a voluntary skate on Monday no matter what happened in the game against Boston. By Tuesday, it'll be time to get back to business and get ready to play the defending Stanley Cup champions.

The players had already planned a postgame party in NJ, and now they firm up their meeting plans. With no need for anyone to get up for practice the next day, everyone knows the party will go on to the wee hours of the morning. Pelle's passive expression has given way to his usual pleasant smile, although he's still not as talkative as usual. Goaltending coach Bernie Parent stops by to congratulate the guys and chats briefly with Pelle about the club's winning streak.

Meanwhile, team president Jay Snider walks around shaking hands with the players. Mark Howe has a special message for Snider: "Boss, I've never played on a better team than the one we have here today. It's fantastic." That means a lot coming from Howe, an NHL star at both forward and defense. He's also someone who doesn't sugarcoat his opinions.

Journalists and photographers still circulate around the dressing room as they interview the players. One of the reporters is *Philadelphia Inquirer* hockey writer Al Morganti, who has gotten to know many of the players away from the ice and has become friends with Pelle. Pelle and Morganti greet one another and Morganti declines an invitation to go along. It's a free night for the players, but the writers still have deadlines to beat tonight and work to do tomorrow. "We'll have to do it another day, Gump," Morganti says just before leaving the dressing room. "Yup, I'll see ya," Pelle says.

Pelle himself isn't sure if he really feels like going out tonight. Lindbergh isn't hungry and he feels a bit tired. He changes quickly out of his uniform, showers, and dons the black suit he wore to the arena. "You coming along tonight, Gump?" several teammates ask. "Maybe. We'll see," Lindbergh says. The players continue to propose meeting places. The most common suggestions are the regular hangouts – Kaminski's in Cherry Hill or a nearby Bennigan's with after-hour drinks at the Coliseum. Some players prefer to head straight to the Coliseum.

In the corridor outside the dressing room Pelle meets up with Kerstin. Walking together into the family room to see Anna-Lisa and Göran, Kerstin tells Pelle about the hellish night the clan has had. Anna-Lisa is still upset and wants to go back to the house as soon as possible but there's no way four people can fit in Pelle's two-seat Porsche. Lindbergh calms his mother down and promises to arrange transportation for everybody. He steps out in the hallway to see whom he can ask to drive two of his family members back to his home.

Walking down the corridor, Pelle passes rookie defenseman Michael "Micke" Thelvén. Pelle has been friendly with Thelvén for years. He's a fellow Stockholm native who played for Djurgårdens IF with Thomas Eriksson before coming to the NHL. "Hey, Pelle! How's it going?" Thelvén asks in Swedish. Pelle responds by complaining that he's not getting to play more, because Mike Keenan is making him split the goaltending duties with Bob Froese. "Ah, you can't play 80 games a year, you know," Thelvén says.

Thereafter, they talk about the latest news and gossip about their mutual friends in Stockholm. Before they part, Thelvén asks Lindbergh what he has planned the rest of the night. Pelle replies that he might go out for a few beers with the guys, because the team has four days until the next game. As the goaltender walks down the hallway, he turns and waves goodbye over his shoulder. "Take it easy, Micke. I'll see you!" Pelle says. Thelvén nods back to Lindbergh.

Pelle now calls over to teammate Ilkka Sinisalo. He asks the Finn if he minds driving Anna-Lisa and Göran back to Kings Grant. Sinisalo, who lives near Lindbergh, agrees. Sinisalo, who plans to go out with other team members, asks Pelle if he's decided to come along with the guys to grab a steak and some beer. "No, I'm tired and I don't feel like it," Lindbergh says.

One hour after the game ends, Pelle and Kerstin sit in his Porsche and head for home. It's been a long and stressful day, and it's already after midnight when Pelle turns onto Landings Drive, parks the Porsche in the driveway and turns the key to open the front door. Saturday has turned into Sunday. Anna-Lisa and Göran are back at the house and are ready for bed. Kerstin goes into the kitchen to cook some sausages and macaroni – it's too late in the evening to fuss with anything fancy. Pelle excuses himself to go change his clothes, and soon returns to the kitchen wearing blue jeans and a sweater. He stands beside Kerstin at the kitchen countertop table in front of the window. Pelle has just finished eating when the phone rings.

On the other end of the line is Ed Parvin Jr., who is friendly with many players on the team, including Pelle. Parvin's father is the real estate agent who sold Pelle and other players their houses. The younger Parvin, who works part-time as a bartender at Kaminski's, visited Pelle in Sweden during the previous summer. The two hung out for a week, and Parvin had gotten to meet and party with some of Pelle's old friends in Stockholm. But Pelle hasn't seen Parvin since the start of the season. Parvin was at tonight's game and several players invited him to come along to the postgame celebration. "Hey, Pelle. Do you want to meet up with us?" Parvin asks. Lindbergh says nothing. He looks over at Kerstin, who sizes up the situation instantly. She speaks first. "You go," she says to Pelle, "but I'm going to stay with your mom." He hesitates. If he's going out, he'd like to have Kerstin's company tonight, too, but he makes up his mind. "OK, Eddie. I'm coming," Lindbergh says. "Great! We're at Bennigan's." Pelle hangs up. He still wants to get an early start in the morning for the planned excursion to Atlantic City. "I'm going to look at the sport boats with Göran," Pelle reminds Kerstin. She nods.

Pelle heads upstairs to say goodnight to his mother, who is already lying down in the guest room. He says he's going out for a little while. "This late? Do you really have to go?" she asks. "Yeah. Otherwise the guys will be upset with me. You know how it is, Mama. But I'll be home soon," he says gently. Pelle sees Anna-Lisa is still concerned. He picks up a stuffed animal from a chair near the bed. The item, a blue and yellow octopus, was given to him by a fan at home in Sweden. He tosses it softly onto the bed and says, "Here, take this. Hold onto it until I get back."

Pelle laughs and then kisses his mother. He walks down the steps, retrieves his new leather jacket, and passes by Kerstin, who is putting away a dish. He gives her a hug and a kiss. "It's cool," he says. "I'll just be out for an hour or two." He places a red key ring in his jacket pocket. Usually, if he's planning to meet up with friends, he'll take the Mercedes, which seats more people than the Porsche. But that's not an option tonight, with the Mercedes out of commission. He drives the Porsche to Bennigan's.

Pelle Lindbergh

CHAPTER 6

STOCKHOLM, SWEDEN, SEPTEMBER 1975

When 16-year-old Pelle Lindbergh is away from the hockey rink, he's like most teenage boys. His main preoccupations are music, cars, and girls, although not necessarily in that order. Resourceful kid that he is, Pelle finds a way to parlay his love of music into a way to meet girls.

Pelle and buddy Anders "Ankan" Lånström become disc jockeys. They spin LP records once a week at the *Katarina Ungdomsgård*, a local youth club. Björn Neckman comes to hang out with Pelle, too. "Pelle loved to be seen and I was his lackey," Lånström recalls with a grin. "We went there because there were a lot of girls and the place was a disco on Fridays. They wanted someone to play some records and Pelle was always up on the latest singles. He bought a lot of records, and he knew just the right thing to play. Later, we also played school dances at Sofia."

Pelle and his friends were Magnus Uggla fans before Uggla hit it big nationally with his 1975 album, *Om Bobby Viking.* They went to Nacka (a suburb east of central Stockholm) to see Uggla play with Strix Q, and became big fans. "We bought these old full-length military coats and green scarves at a place called Impo on Gamla Brogatan. We couldn't afford trenchcoats, so we bought military coats, and I remember that they glittered a little. Everyone had them, because Magnus Uggla wore a trenchcoat for a time and then everyone had to have a coat like it," Neckman says.

Apart from their brief foray into the glam-rock scene, the guys look like countless other teenagers of the mid-1970s. They have long hair with sideburns and wear t-shirts or wide-collared print shirts, bell bottom jeans with big belts and matching boots (or, briefly, platform shoes).

Pelle is one of the most popular kids at school, and has a wide circle of friends, both male and female. Pelle's personality is like his mother's in that he loves to talk with just about anyone he encounters. Later as he becomes a professional star, Lindbergh never loses the inquisitive, down-to-earth nature that enables him to connect with people from all walks of life. That's why as an adult, his non-hockey friends span a wide gamut of professions and socioeconomic backgrounds.

His hockey and social calendars are full. Pelle has difficulty saying no to invitations and requests for his time, because he doesn't want to disappoint people. Those who know him best realize that punctuality isn't one of his strong suits, in part because he often becomes engrossed in conversations and loses track of the time. He also packs every day with activity, both on and off the ice. Waking up early in the morning is just about the only thing he doesn't like about hockey. He's only an early riser when he has to be.

If there's a party on the weekend, it's usually at Ankan's home in Nacka. If not, Pelle and his friends either see live music or go to the movies. Among the films of the mid-1970s, they see subtitled versions of American and British movies such as *Jaws* (called *Hajen* in its Swedish release), *Rocky, Taxi Driver,* a re-release of *A Clockwork Orange,* and Swedish films such as *Jack, En Kille Och En Tjej* ("A Guy and a Girl"), and *Drömmen Om Amerika* ("The American Dream").

One of Pelle's classmates and friends at the Gullmarplan's Gymnasium is Thomas Dennerby, a soccer standout for Hammarby who was born the same year as Lindbergh. Apart from sports, the two share a common passion for fast cars. When they're not talking about sports or girls, they're usually discussing their dream cars. Pelle, not surprisingly, gets a huge kick out listening to the 1975 Queen B-side single, "I'm in Love with My Car," from the album *A Night at the Opera*.

One day at Gullmarplan's Gymnasium, Lindbergh and Dennerby hear that a player on Hammarby's senior hockey team has just totaled his car. "He crashed his Fiat on the way to practice. So during lunch break, Pelle and I went to the repair garage in Årsta where the car was. I remember that we saw it must have been a major accident and we couldn't understand how the guy managed to walk away," says Dennerby. The car had been reduced to a twisted pile of scrap metal.

Soccer has never been a huge passion for Pelle but that's not to say he doesn't enjoy playing soccer. In the summers of his teenage years – when he's not serving as an assistant summer hockey camp instructor in Leksand – he dabbles in playing soccer for the Järla IF junior team. It's here where he first befriends Reino Sundberg, a fellow hockey goaltender turned part-time soccer player.

Pelle inherited his love of the Hammarby IF soccer and hockey teams from his father, Sigge. Here, a five-year old Pelle poses in a Hammarby soccer kit. [Courtesy Ann-Louise Hörnestam]

"Pelle was 15 and I was 17 when we first met in Järla," Sundberg remembers. "My first impression of Pelle was that he was curious about everything. He was just 16 years old when he started coming around to our hockey boutique," Sundberg says. At age 17, Sundberg was recruited from the Skuru IK team to play for Djurgården's top team. In the years to come, Sundberg rapidly becomes Lindbergh's best friend in hockey. In Pelle's adult years, Sundberg is his closest confidant apart from his family and fiancée Kerstin.

"Pelle was social and open from the beginning. But the exception was with other goaltenders. The competition was intense, and it was hard to stop it from effecting life off the ice," Björn Neckman says. "I will say that there were only one-and-a-half goalies that Pelle totally accepted, apart from Bernie Parent in Philadelphia. That would be Reino Sundberg and to a certain extent Rolf Ridderwall. With the other goalies, he kept his distance and preferred to avoid them. It was similar pattern later, with the other goalies in North America. They were never good friends with Pelle. He wouldn't allow it."

In Europe, many goaltenders position themselver deeper in the crease than is recommended in North American hockey. On the bigger rink, many goaltenders are concerned about getting caught out of position if a pass comes across to the other side. In North America, where the rink is smaller and the play is more shooting-oriented, goalies are told to come out and challenge the shooter.

One day at practice, Hammarby IF senior team coach Bert-Ola Nordlander notices that Pelle at 17, the youngest player on the squad, is positioning himself a little too far back in the crease. "Perhaps you shouldn't stand so deep in the net," Nordlander says. Lindberg protests, "Do you want me stand further out? I'm cutting down the angle. I want to make saves, you know."

The TV-Puck (*TV-Pucken*) tournament is a rite of passage for the top teenage hockey players throughout Sweden. Dating back to 1959, the annual under-17 competition pits teams from the various provinces (*landskap*) around Sweden against one another. For much of the event's history, every tournament game was broadcast nationally on Sveriges Television. Among the generation of players born in the late 1940s to mid-1950s, TV-Puck featured the likes of Börje Salming, Rolf Edberg, Anders Hedberg, Ulf Nilsson, Thomas Gradin, Kent Nilsson, Roland Eriksson, Stefan Persson, and goaltending standout Christer Abrahamsson. As a Stockholm born and bred player, Pelle Lindbergh becomes part of the winningest team in TV-Puck history, which has won 11 tourney championships between 1973 and 2007. Pelle comes along at the right time. Within Stockholm, Djurgården, and AIK have a stronger collection of players born in 1958 and 1959 than either of Hammarby's teams from the same age group. AIK has the top '58 team in the metropolitan area, while DIF has the best '59ers. TV-Puck alumni from Pelle's generation of players born from the late 1950s to mid-1960s include not only Lindbergh himself but the likes of Thomas Steen, Mats Näslund, Håkan Loob, Tomas Jonsson, Bengt-Åke Gustafsson, and Pelle's future Flyers teammates, Thomas Eriksson and Pelle Eklund. In the decades that follow, the tradition continues with the likes of Nicklas Lidström, Mats Sundin, Peter Forsberg, Markus Näslund, Mikael Renberg, the Sedin twins, Henrik Lundqvist, Nicklas Bäckström, and many others.

In local tournaments, Pelle's teams are usually outmatched and he has little margin for error in goal if his team is to upend either of its two main rivals. This sometimes bothers Lindbergh, who like most top-notch players, is very competitive on the ice. Once he steps onto the ice, his chattiness and happy-go-lucky demeanor disappear until the game is over.

The 1974 tournament, however, was a major disappointment for Pelle and his team. The defending champs from Stockholm were heavily represented by players from AIK and Djurgården's 1958 squads. Fifteen-year-old Pelle served as the backup goaltender.

One year can make a considerable difference and there's no denying the Stockholm squad the gold in 1975. Pelle is the starting goalie on a team that includes the likes of Thomas Eriksson (Djurgården), Håkan Södergren (Djurgården), Peter Ekroth (AIK), Tommy Mörth (Djurgården), and Ulf Rådbjer (AIK). The 1975 Stockholm team quickly becomes a close-knit squad, despite their rival club-team allegiances. In particular, Pelle and Eriksson become good friends, and the close friendship carries through their future days together as Swedish national team and Philadelphia Flyers teammates. He and Pelle finally end up playing for the same side in TV-Puck.

Stockholm tears through the competition in the tournament. Offensively, the squad is dominant and Lindbergh, who stands about 5-foot-6 at this age and is one of the smallest players in the tournament, stands tall in net. He provides nearly impenetrable goaltending in front of a national television audience at a time when TV channel selections are limited in people's homes.

Stockholm breezes through the preliminaries and earns a trip to the playoffs in Västerås. In the semifinals, Pelle limits Medelpad (eastern Sweden, slightly north of center) to a single tally in a 5-1 win. The top player on the other side is future Brynäs IF Gävle and Montreal Canadiens star, Mats "the Little Viking" Näslund. "When I was 15 there was already a lot of talk about Pelle, but I didn't play against him until TV-Puck in the semifinals when we lost to Stockholm. He was extremely good," Näslund says.

In the finals, the Stockholm squad faces defending champion Gästrikland. Lindbergh elevates his game even further and the Stockholm team goes on to win, 5-1. Pelle, who wins the tournament's best goaltender trophy, joins his victorious teammates in a jubilant celebration at center ice as the club whoops it up and poses for pictures. Shortly after this victory, Hammarby IF offers the 16-year-old junior goalie the opportunity to practice and play with its senior team in Sweden's highest minor league.

After celebrating Stockholm's TV-Puck victory in Västerås, Pelle awaits news of which players will be chosen for the Swedish National Under-19 team camps in the cities of Sundsvall and Södertälje. The goalie gets the news he wants to hear that he's been chosen for his first national team experience.

In the days before New Year's Day 1976, the team assembles in Stockholm and flies to Ljubljana, Yugoslavia for a six-nation tournament against Under-20 teams representing Canada and lesser hockey powers. Falun native Tomas Jonsson gets his first chance both to play with Pelle on the ice and to get to know him off the ice. Jonsson reflects, "Pelle made a big impression the first time anyone met him. We'd all heard the talk about him at TV-Puck – that he had amazing reflexes. I remember that the first time we met was when the team got together at the hotel in Stockholm. The biggest impression was that he talked so much Stockholm slang that I couldn't even understand the half of it. I thought that was rather fascinating."

One thing Jonsson understands loud and clear is Lindbergh's preoccupation with playing in the NHL for the Flyers. "Pelle talked non-stop about the United States and that he'd play in the NHL for the Flyers. The rest of us really had no idea about such things. The NHL wasn't as big (in Sweden) as it is today. When Pelle talked about the Flyers, we had no idea what team that was," says Jonsson, who later gets to know of the Flyers all too well after years of Patrick Division clashes between the Islanders and the Flyers.

The Swedish team reaches the finals of the tournament in Ljubljana but drops a one-goal decision to Canada in the deciding game. Two months later, the team heads to Koprivnice, Czechoslovakia for the European Junior Championships, where the Swedes once again come away with silver medals and Lindbergh, who is the youngest player in the tournament, takes the best goaltender award.

Other notable Team Sweden teammates on the trip to Czechoslovakia include: Bengt-Åke Gustafsson and Harald Lückner. The former goes on to have a solid NHL career with the Washington Capitals and later makes history by coaching Team Sweden to gold medals at both the 2006 Olympics and 2006 IIHF World Championships. The latter enjoys a long career in Elitserien with Färjestads BK. After his retirement, he becomes a well-respected head coach for several Swedish clubs, including a championship Modo Hockey team in 2006-07.

In late December 1976, several of the players from the Ljubljana and Koprivnice tournament squads return to Czechoslovakia for the 1977 World Junior Championships in the towns of Zvolen and Banska Bystrica. The goaltending duties are split between 19-year-old Sundberg and 17-year-old Pelle. The tournament is the first World Junior Championships to be sanctioned by the International Ice Hockey Federation and expectations for the Swedish team are high. Unfortunately, the team flops and finishes fifth.

The experienced players look strangely fatigued, and the only ones who impress the NHL talent scouts in attendance are the team's three youngest players – Pelle, Mats Näslund, and Bengt-Åke Gustafsson. Despite the solid reviews for his own play in net, Pelle's first World Junior Championship experience is one he'd just as soon forget. "We played a horrible tournament," Sundberg says. "For the most part, we sat around the room, but together with the rest of the team, we visited a factory where they rolled out train cars."

Pelle enjoyed the factory tour, but it hardly makes the entire trip worthwhile.

In April 1977, Pelle and the junior national team head to Bremerhaven, West Germany for the European Junior Championship. Lindbergh electrifies observers by allowing just seven goals in six games and shutting out a talented Czechoslovakian team in the finals, 4-0. He is a shoo-in for both best goal-tender and tournament MVP honors. Meanwhile, the team in front of him gains enormous confidence as he allows virtually no second-chance opportunities on rebounds. The Swedes get more and more dominant as the tournament progresses, and end up scoring a staggering 58 goals in the six games. Offensively, the Swedish squad is led by Thomas Steen, who has already signed to play in Elitserien for the Leksands IF senior team.

At the end of the year, Pelle faces a considerably tougher challenge when the Swedish junior team heads to Canada for the World Junior Championships. Not only does Team Canada enjoy home-ice advantage, it also has a not-so-secret weapon to deploy in the youngest member of the team, 16-year-old center Wayne Gretzky. The Great One is making his international hockey debut.

Initially, Team Canada officials did not expect Gretzky to make the team. Despite his immediate dominance in the OHA (70 goals, 182 points in 64 games), the Sault Ste. Marie Greyhounds center is thin as a pencil and three years younger than many of the other players in the tournament. But it soon becomes obvious at camp that the kid from Brantford is already leaps and bounds better than even most of the top 19-year-olds in Canadian and international junior hockey. Gretzky makes the team.

Pelle and the other Swedish players have already heard of Gretzky's exploits (such as scoring 378 goals in 85 games as a peewee player), and are eager to see if he's really as skilled they've heard. Needless to say, the Swedes are impressed as Gretzky leads the tournament in goals and displays the ability to make passes that even many professional players can't execute. He can thread passes at will through mazes of sticks and skates, and his ability to read and anticipate plays is staggering.

Sweden's Small Crowns (*Småkronorna*) are coached by Bengt Ohlson, better known as The Fish (*Fisken*). Apart from Pelle, the team has Brynäs IF junior goalie Göran Henriksson. After a strong qualification round, which includes a 6-3 win over the Soviets, the Swedish team runs into Canada in the semifinals. To his tremendous disappointment, Pelle is the backup goaltender in the game against Canada at the Montreal Forum.

In his last junior game for Hammarby immediately prior to the trip to Canada, Lindbergh injures his shoulder after getting hit with a puck. He's still fighting the pain during the World Junior tournament, so Ohlson gives the nod to Henriksson. The goalie equipment of the 1970s was a joke compared to current-day gear, and Lindbergh's injury probably would have been prevented by the more protective armor adopted in later years. "With the shoulder pads we used back then, it could be unbelievably painful to get hit with the puck," confirms goalie Rolf Ridderwall.

Heading into the semis, Canada needs only a tie against the Swedes to advance to the gold-medal game by virtue of a superior goal differential. The Small Crowns need to win the game outright. Led offensively by Bengt-Åke Gustafsson and Dan Hermansson, the Swedes go on to win, and Henriksson's strong play in goal and a crucial shorthanded goal in the second period are the turning points. The Forum crowd and Team Canada are stunned and devastated by the outcome. The Canadians, including Gretzky, fully expected to be playing the Soviets for the gold medal. "I remember that Gretzky and the other Canadians cried after the end of the game," Ohlson says.

Two days later, the Swedes meet the Soviets for the third time in the tournament. On the morning of the game, Pelle tells Ohlson he's feeling much better, but the coach isn't buying it. Pelle sits with a hangdog expression on his face, as he roots for his teammates. As the game progresses, there isn't much for Pelle and the other Small Crowns to cheer about in the finals. The Soviet squad, which includes future KLM line members Igor Larionov and Vladimir Krutov, is simply too deep and too talented. The Russians seize the gold by a 5-2 count and Sweden settles for silver. Several players stare at the ice and wipe away tears at the postgame medal ceremony, and Pelle looks glumly at his medal as though it's made of tin foil. "We had several players with the flu and we were totally powerless against the Soviets. The game was never close," remembers Ohlson.

The 1979 IIHF World Junior Championships (and the 1978-79 season as a whole) marks Pelle's big breakthrough. It's the year that his dreams start coming true before his eyes, but only after the heartache. Now in his final year of tournament eligibility, Pelle is the undisputed number one goalie and is eager to end his international junior career on a positive note.

One of the first things non-Swedes notice is that the Swedish goalie's mask is decorated with the logo of the Philadelphia Flyers, with decals on the sides and one on the crown of the mask. Naturally, the small contingent of Canadian reporters is curious about the decals. In his still-awkward English, Lindbergh explains that Flyers goaltender Bernie Parent is his hero and his mask is a replica of the one Parent wears. Lindbergh then explains that Philadelphia is his favorite NHL team and his practice jersey also has the Flyers logo on it. It reminds him of his long-term goal. "I'm going to play for the Flyers," Pelle adds matter-of-factly.

Lindbergh's proclamation elicts wry smiles from the writers: The Swedish kid's exuberance and self-confidence is admirable but he's naive about the workings of the NHL draft. Lindbergh is not eligible to be picked in the NHL draft until the summer and there's no guarantee that the Flyers have any interest in him. "There was only one NHL scout in the stands at the World Juniors in Karlstad and Karlskroga," Tomas Jonsson says. "Actually, Pelle went and sat on his knee in the hotel lobby. But the rest of us didn't even worry about [scouts] at all." Flyers scout Jerry Melnyk sees Pelle play two games during the tournament. In the era before NHL teams employed European-based scouts, he's one of the few to take the trans-Atlantic flight to attend. He's impressed. It's not just the Flyers emblems on Lindbergh's mask that catches Melnyk's attention but the goalie's skating ability, his economy of motion and ability to prevent rebounds.

Lindbergh shines throughout the tournament. On December 30, 1978, Pelle turns in a performance that earns him his first media attention outside Sweden, for his play as well as his mask. On this day Sweden plays Canada and the gamesmanship starts early. Twenty minutes prior to the opening faceoff, Team Canada officials, trying to get Lindbergh's pads banned for being too wide, file a complaint with IIHF directorate. "We realized that we might be forced to change goaltenders," Ohlsson recalls. Soon the situation is remedied by Team Sweden's equipment manager who tapes down the pads to make them smaller. Canada promptly withdraws the protest, but they've already gotten what they wanted which is to interrupt Lindbergh's prematch preparations and throw off his rhythm. It's a global hockey truism that coaches will do anything to gain an edge – no matter how small. The only problem: Lindbergh's focus isn't disturbed one iota. This game against Team Canada is huge for his team and a tremendous opportunity for him to move a step closer to getting noticed by the NHL.

In the game Pelle is brilliant. Sweden wins 1-0 in a game that saw the Canadians out-shoot and out-chance the Little Crowns. The game includes two lengthy 5-on-3 powerplays for Canada, but Lindbergh has the answer to every forray. When the Canadians buzz around the net, he calmy freezes the puck. Even when there's a deflection, somehow he picks up the trajectory of the puck in the nick of time. Afterwards, team Canada Coach Ernie McLean and the Canadian players and media marvel about the magnificent display of goaltending they've seen. "We lost to an extremely skilled goaltender," McLean says, "and I'm proud of our team. There's no shame to lose a game like this. Give their goalie credit, because he deserves it."

The Canadian writers are also duly impressed by the undersized goalie with the Bernie Parent mask, catlike quickness and breezy self-assurance. For their part, Pelle's teammates have heard all this sort of talk before, and they also know that when Lindbergh is at the pinnacle of his game, he gives them a chance to beat any junior squad in the world. "His certainty and confidence, cockiness, even made him almost seek out challenges on the ice," teammate Tommy Samuelsson remembers. "That meant that position players like us grew as players. We dared to go forward in a whole new way and were able to play much more aggressively."

In the finals, the Swedes once again find themselves playing the Soviet Union. In the training games leading up the tournament, the Swedes laid a pair of lopsided beatings on the Russians, 11-3 and 8-3. Traditionally the Soviets are notorious for looking flat in meaningless games only to overwhelm the same opponents when the games count. They remain an extremely dangerous squad, despite the fact that Sweden needs only a tie to clinch the gold medal. Following the lead of their goaltender and leaders such as Thomas Steen, the Swedes prepare for the game with a high degree of confidence. "Nothing impressed Pelle. He was never nervous, and he only saw positive things when he knew there was going to be a tough game," Ohlson says.

The stands are packed for the game, with a partisan crowd rooting on the Swedes. Pelle bends but doesn't break in net and when Thomas Steen completes a hat trick early in the third period to give Team Sweden a 5-4 lead; everything seems to be in place for Sweden to win its first World Junior Championship gold medal. Even after the Russians tie the score, the Swedes are still sure they'll hang on for the tie they need to win the gold.

Then something unexpected happens. Pelle, who hasn't allowed a single soft goal the entire tournament, suddenly allows a fluttering shot to dribble through his legs in the final two minutes of play. The puck comes in pants-high and squeezes through the small gap between the tops of his pads. Now trailing in the game with time running out, Ohlson pulls Lindbergh for an extra attacker. The Soviets seal the game and the gold with an empty-net goal in the final seconds. Sweden ends up with the bronze.

The loss is devastating to the Swedish players and Pelle and the others sit in the dressing room in silence. Lindbergh wins the tournament's best goaltender award and is named to the tournament all-star team but the honors feel hollow without a gold medal to accompany it. As painful as the defeat is, not one of Lindbergh's teammates blames him for the final game loss. The team would never have gotten to the gold medal game or been in position to win in the third period if not for the goalie.

But Pelle can't help but feel like he's let everyone down, including himself. Later, Sigge Lindbergh puts an arm around his son's shoulders as a gesture of consolation and pride. Sigge has never been a man of many words, and he lets his actions speak of the joy Pelle has brought to him and Anna-Lisa, both for the hockey player and young man their baby son has become. The healing starts immediately for Pelle. Goaltenders need to have short memories to be successful.

For three seasons after his success at the 1975 TV-Puck tournament, Pelle continues to play junior and then senior-team hockey for Hammarby.

At age 17, he made his senior team debut for Hammarby's adult team in Division I. During the 1977-78 season, Lindbergh dresses for his first pro game. By the end of the next season, it's obvious to even casual observers that he's good enough to be a starting goaltender in the Swedish Elite League. "I'm going to be a pro. Nothing else matters," he says to anyone who asked, and some who didn't.

"Pelle was lazy at practice, but in the games, the juice turned on. He was unbelievably fast in his reactions," recalls Bert-Ola Nordlander, the Hammarby IF senior team coach at the time. It didn't take long for Lindbergh to win the respect of Nordlander and his HIF teammates, but at first some of the older Bajen players were wary of the youngster receiving so much playing time. "There were probably a few of the older ones who complained (among themselves) and thought, 'What the hell is this junior kid doing playing in our goal?' But no one said anything, because Pelle was, of course, good in the games," Nordlander says.

Lindbergh plays so well at the World Juniors and for Hammarby IF in 1978-79 that he's invited to compete for a spot on Tre Kronor for the 1979 IIHF World Championships, despite the fact he's never played a single game in Elitserien. Shortly after the World Juniors in Karlstad, the senior national team's new coach, Tommy Sandlin has a conversation with Bengt "Fisken" Ohlson. Sandlin wants input from Ohlson on which young goalies – if any – he thinks are ready for an invitation to try out for the senior team in upcoming Tre Kronor pre-World Championship training games against Czechoslovakia. Both Sandlin and Ohlson agree there's only one clear-cut candidate. "We said to each other that Pelle Lindbergh is better than both Sune Ödling and Reino Sundberg, and the others," Ohlson recalls.

Lindbergh gets the opportunity to play with the national senior B-team, nicknamed the Vikings (*Vikingarna*), in a tournament in Leningrad.

He passes the test with flying colors, and earns a preliminary roster berth on Tre Kronor's World Championship squad. At the recommendation of Ohlson, Lindbergh is joined on Tre Kronor by some of the other rising stars from the junior national team, including Näslund, Jonsson, Gustafsson, and Thomas Eriksson. "We were young but pretty damned ambitious. We were determined to push the older guys on the national team and I remember that Pelle was extremely successful when he had the chance. He really ran with the opportunity," remembers Gustafsson.

Still a month shy of his twentieth birthday, Pelle Lindbergh becomes the youngest goaltender ever to start for Tre Kronor. On April 7, 1979, he makes his senior national team debut in a game against Czechoslovakia in Prague. It's not exactly a sparkling debut, and Lindbergh is hung out to dry throughout the game as Team Czechoslovakia romps, 6-0.

Shortly after the game, Pelle gives everyone a scare. He's exhausted and allowed himself to get dehydrated during the game, and he faints upon arrival at the team's hotel. Bengt Ohlson stands beside him. "In the hotel elevator, Pelle sank down on the floor. He was totally spent," Ohlson remembers. "Pelle was so hellbent on doing his job in the game, and he came from Hammarby where he hadn't been well-trained [conditioning-wise]. Pelle was an incredible talent but he was used to a different tempo and he had almost no energy left for the pace of the national team. [After that] he drank water as soon as he got a chance." Pelle recovers immediately from the fainting spell and the rough first appearance.

He earns a spot on the roster for the 1979 World Championships in Moscow by beating out Elitserien goalie Benny Westblom for the primary backup job. Coach Tommy Sandlin is not especially confident in the team's chances heading into the tournament, and figures a fourth-place finish is realistic. As expected, Team Sweden has little trouble beating West Germany

and Poland in their first two games. That's about as much as Sandlin antici-
pates this version of Tre Kronor to achieve. His main goal is give his players
the experience they'll need to contend for medals in future World Championship tournaments. Wins in the first two games automatically qualify the
Swedes to play in the next year's World Championship, which will take place
in Gothenburg, Sweden. But Lindbergh and fellow recent junior team
graduates have loftier and more immediate goals in mind. Pelle begins the
tournament as the backup to Sune Ödling, who had just won the Swedish
championship with Modo and won the Elitserien best goaltender award.
Ödling plays well in the win over West Germany but has an awful game
against Poland as Sweden blows a 6-1 lead and has to rally late to salvage the
game. Most of the goals go in through the five-hole (the space in between the
goaltender's pads).

Sandlin is unhappy with Ödling's performance, so he goes to Pelle in
the next game. It's a trial by fire, as the opponent is the mighty Soviet Union
playing on their home ice. Lindbergh is opposed by international superstar
goaltender Vladislav Tretiak and faces the prospect of playing against the likes
of Slava Fetisov and the rest of the star-studded USSR squad. The Soviets toy
with the Swedes and pick Pelle apart from point blank range in a 9-3 rout. In
spite of the loss, Sandlin is impressed by Lindbergh's demeanor for he never
stops battling and never looks to the bench for relief.

Two days later, Sandlin goes back to Lindbergh again for another severe
test, the Czechoslovakian team. By all rights, Sweden should lose this game
because the more experienced Czechoslovaks control the majority of the play,
but Lindbergh plays a tremendous game in net and the Swedes skate off with
a 3-3 tie. "Pelle came in and played huge against the Czechs," Tomas Jonsson
recalls. "After that, he stayed in net and played a big part in why things went
really well for our team."

In the next game, Sweden beats Team Canada, 5-3. Although Canada is rarely able to send its best NHL talents to the World Championships, any victory over the Canadians is a big deal. With Flyers scout Jerry Melnyk and several other NHL scouts in the stands, Pelle goes on to help Sweden emerge from the medal round with a bronze medal. It's a significant accomplishment for the undermanned team. "There were many NHL scouts in Moscow and for many of us younger guys, it was our first direct contact with the league. But Pelle, who was the hottest player already knew all about it. He talked a lot with the scouts," Jonsson says.

During Tre Kronor's return trip to Stockholm, most of the discussion focuses on Lindbergh's play. "When we left Moscow, Pelle was the big star," Thomas Eriksson remembers. Pelle has never doubted that he's destined to be picked by an NHL team in the upcoming draft. In this era, the conventional wisdom among European position players who'd made the jump to the NHL is that it takes two years as a national team starter in the World Championships before one is ready for the NHL. Pelle understands, but sees it differently as a goaltender. "There's a longer development period for a goalie. You need to spend a year or two first with the (NHL team's) farm club," he tells friends.

Over the course of his tenure with Hammarby IF's senior team, Pelle's team reaches the playoffs each year but is unable to earn a promotion to Elitserien. On February 28, 1979, Pelle leaves Hammarby IF and his friend Rolf Ridderwall takes over as the full-time goaltender for Bajen until "Roffe" moves up to Elitserien in 1981-82 to play for Djurgårdens IF. Pelle has come to the sad realization that advancing his career to the next step on the professional ladder, and one step closer to the NHL, will require leaving the organization he's been part of (literally) since the day he was born.

After returning from the 1979 Worlds in Moscow, Lindbergh makes a phone call to Curt Lindström. "Pelle called and said he'd never forget the early years in Bajen, and everything he got to experience," Lindström says. Before hanging up, Pelle thanks Lindström personally for everything he's done, and closes by explaining that he thinks the time has come to move on. Arranging the transfer isn't easy. At first, Hammarby IF balks about letting Pelle walk away to join AIK. Pelle meets with Sivert Svärling, the director of Hammarby IF's hockey section, and tells him that the path to the NHL runs through Elitserien, not Division One.

"When Pelle said that he wanted to develop and was hungry to play in Elitserien, there was no reason to stop him. That would have been idiotic," Svärling says. AIK's Norrman and Hammarby's Svärling meet in a hallway at the Hovet rink and have a preliminary dialogue. Svärling says that he understands Pelle's position and he doesn't want to stop him, but the team can't simply let him leave for AIK. Shortly thereafter, they meet again and work out an agreement for AIK to give Hammarby financial compensation. Pelle gets what he wants: a starting goalie spot in Elitserien and he signs with AIK for the 1979-80 season.

Sigge Lindbergh has mixed feelings about his son's decision. As a lifelong Hammarby supporter, it saddens him to see Pelle leave, but he knows how badly his son wants to play in the NHL, and Elitserien is a more challenging level of play than Division I.

On May 24, 1979, Pelle Lindbergh celebrates his 20th birthday. He's anxiously awaiting the NHL draft, which is still over two months away. The summer of '79 is a time of fun and laughter for Pelle. Apart from his friends and local fame on the south side, he finds himself recognized by strangers.

Pelle also begins his compulsory military service over the summer, primarily serving as a nurse. It's immediately apparent that Pelle is about as likely to pursue a career in the military as he is to seek one in academia. He's no lover of field training exercises, nor is he very attentive to his assignment as a nurse. Thomas Eriksson serves in the same unit, working as a fireman. Another of Pelle's hockey buddies, Claes Elefalk, is a fellow nurse. "I wonder if Pelle saw a first-aid kit the whole time," Eriksson chuckles. What's more Lindbergh is very good at talking his way out of the tasks he doesn't want to do. "While the rest of us were slaving in Kungsängen, Pelle was cruising off to Stockholm after lunch," Elefalk adds. Pelle has a built-in excuse: He needs to go train to get ready for the next hockey season. In truth, Pelle does want to prepare for hockey. But, above all, he justs wants to have fun. Good times await him in his life.

CHAPTER 7

SUNDAY, NOVEMBER 10, 1985, 1:00 AM

It's well after midnight by the time Pelle Lindbergh pulls into the parking lot of the Bennigan's bar and grill on Route 73. Bennigan's is a chain restaurant, popular among many of the younger Flyers' players. Before midnight, the parking lot is usually dominated by family cars and parents taking their children out to eat. After midnight, the family cars are replaced by sportier vehicles and a younger adult and college-age clientele. A few miles away, everyone at Lindbergh's home has already turned out the lights and gone to sleep. Pelle parks his Porsche in between two spaces so that no one can park close enough to clip his doors when the he gets out of the car. Anyone who goes in the front door can't help but see the car. It's still parked close enough to the restaurant for people to admire. Pelle is the last Flyers player to arrive. A handful of his teammates are still there, including Thomas Eriksson, Dave Poulin, and the Sutter twins. Ed Parvin Jr. is also there, as well as some of the players' wives. Everyone is in good spirits, but the exhaustion of the team's third game night in four days has begun to take its toll. Eyes are rubbed and yawns stifled.

Most have consumed a couple beers by the time Pelle orders his first. There's conversation and laughter but nothing rowdy. Pelle soon finishes his beer and orders a second. A couple of players excuse themselves to go home. "I'm out of here. See you later, Pelle," says Eriksson, leaving to head home to his girlfriend, Malin. Poulin leaves, too, for he and his wife Kim have a big day planned. He drives his wife home, and then heads to the Coliseum to meet up with the other players who've gone there.

The remaining players head over to the bar, but there aren't enough stools available on this busy weekend night. At the bar Pelle drinks another beer. Patrons later say that none of the players at the bar seems to be especially intoxicated as they discuss moving the party over to the Coliseum's after-hours bar. Pelle finds a telephone and calls up Sudsy Settlemyre, who is at home after being discharged from the hospital. "I'll pick you up soon," he offers. "Everyone has eaten and we're going to the Coliseum." "I'm out," says Settlemyre. "I'm exhausted and I don't feel like going anywhere. Just go ahead. Forget me!"

Pelle offers Rich Sutter a ride to the Coliseum. Having ridden in Pelle's car before, Sutter knows that being Pelle's passenger can be a hair-raising experience. He declines. Parvin, however, gladly accepts a ride with Pelle. He's been partying since right after the game ended in the Spectrum, and is eager to meet up with some of his other friends at the Coliseum. Lindbergh and Parvin climb into the Porsche. It's 2:30 am.

On the way to the Coliseum, Pelle shows Parvin what the Porsche can do. With few cars on the road, he can rev the car's rocket-like acceleration. Driving on Springdale Road, the driver demonstrates to his friend how the car can reach speeds of over 100 miles per hour without even pressing the pedal to the metal. At this point, Pelle is not significantly impaired by the alcohol.

Hockey teams have much in common with fraternities, including the prevailing attitude toward alcohol consumption. Fueled by testosterone, youth, and a false sense of invincibility, there's often a lot of heavy partying among its members. The Flyers' players of this era are no different than any other team. When it comes to drinking and driving, the barometer is often how someone says he feels. The law has a more scientific (and much lower) threshold for defining intoxication. In the everyday world, people are disinclined to intervene if a friend has been drinking, unless he is staggering, slurring his speech, or showing other obvious signs of drunkenness. The Flyers' socializing behavior is the same. Compared with many hockey players, Pelle usually has a healthy relationship with alcohol. During the season, he rarely drinks at all because it makes him feel sluggish at the rink. Hockey is always his biggest concern, and he doesn't deviate from his daily routines.

In the summertime, it's different. He often hangs out with friends and drinks on a fairly regular basis but not to the point of making a fool of himself or not remembering what he did the night before. During hockey season, Pelle usually prefers not to drink. "When I wanted to drink wine, he took a glass of milk," Kerstin recalls. Pelle's teammates in Philadelphia and Sweden tell similar stories. "The thing you have to know about Pelle is that he was a guy who really didn't drink when we went out after a game," says Brian Propp. "When we'd go out after a game and everyone else was drinking beer, he'd order a Coke."

"Pelle was conscientious when it was hockey season," Rolf Ridderwall adds. "I can hardly recall him even tasting a glass of wine. I never saw him party in the winters. Pelle's passion burned for his hockey." It usually takes a special occasion for Pelle to drink more than a rare beer or glass of wine during the season – such as a birthday, Christmas, or a lengthy break in the schedule. What's more, at least when he was at home in Sweden, Pelle never drives if he's had anything alcoholic to drink. Since he's become an NHL star friends see a difference. He still doesn't drink outrageous amounts of alcohol, but he drinks with greater frequency and will drive after having a few beers. His reckless style of driving is usually of more immediate concern than his alcohol consumption.

Kevin Cady remembers, "I can never get out my mind the time I visited Pelle in Sweden and we ordered drinks at an outdoor place. I asked if he was driving and he said, 'Not a chance. There are tough laws here in Sweden.'

There was no other choice and we took a taxi back in the evenings. But it was different in the States. Just like all the others, he drove fairly often when he had beer in his system. He was pulled over a couple of times on routine stops when I was with him, but he knew all the policemen and he was so popular that nothing bad was going to come of it. When we were stopped, I heard officers say, 'Hell, we can't arrest that guy, it's Pelle Lindbergh.' And Pelle just laughed."

The owners of the Coliseum have been very skillful with the paperwork. Opened 10 years ago, they've managed to obtain a special license to serve alcohol after 3:00 am, when the other bars and restaurants are closed. The main argument is that the building is open 24 hours a day and there are often late-night hockey games that go on into the wee hours, by which time it's too late for their clientele to unwind at other establishments. For this reason, the Coliseum has gained a license to serve alcohol to "members and their guests" until 5:00 am. The arrangement has been profitable for the owners and popular among not only the Flyers and recreational hockey players but also any number of people looking for another place to go after last call at other bars and restaurants.

The most popular bar is "Coliseum after Dark" which opens at 1:00 am and closes at 5:00 am. The place often gets packed for the final two hours. On this late night before a lengthy break in the game schedule, there are about a dozen players, wives and girlfriends, players' male friends and assorted male and female patrons at the bar.

It's about 2:40 am when Pelle Lindbergh parks his Porsche in the lot and enters the bar with Parvin. Lindbergh greets his teammates, and quickly settles into a conversation in Swedish with Pelle Eklund. "I couldn't tell that Pelle was drunk in any way; no chance," Eklund says, looking back two decades later. Eklund is actually just about to leave for the night, but stays a little longer to talk with Lindbergh. They stand at the bar and converse.

After two months, Eklund has just started to feel comfortable as a team member. He takes the opportunity to ask Lindbergh how things went during his earliest experiences with the team, in the hopes of getting some useful feedback from the goaltender. "What do you think?" Eklund asks Lindbergh. It's been a whirlwind two months of hockey and culture shock for Eklund. In early September, Eklund and Thomas Eriksson took the same flight from Stockholm and Eklund initially took up residence with Eriksson at his house in Cherry Hill. The next day, Eriksson drove with Eklund to the Coliseum. The Swedes took a light skate and it gave the rookie a chance to meet many of his new teammates. Two days later, Lindbergh arrived and gave him a warm welcome to the team.

Eklund is still going through adjustments off and on the ice. Back in Stockholm, Eklund had become a folk hero among AIK fans but here in Philadelphia, he was just another rookie who needed to prove himself to Mike Keenan, his teammates, and the fans at the Spectrum. Much like Lindbergh, Eklund worked his way up quickly through the ranks of Swedish hockey, and quickly became one of the better players on the team. He possessed a soft finishing touch but strongly preferred passing the puck to shooting it; a trait that would mark Eklund's entire career.

During his short stay with the Flyers thus far, Eklund has marveled at the graceful way Lindbergh handles all the attention he receives from Flyers' fans. He does so with a smile on his face. He can be seen signing every autograph, posing for every picture, and chatting with anyone who wants to talk to him. For his part, Eklund is still able to be relatively anonymous when he leaves the rink. He still feels a little lonely and homesick at times, but is starting to get into the swing of things. "You're managing just fine," Lindbergh tells Eklund. Lindbergh describes some of his own early adjustments to North America. After nearly a half hour conversation, Eklund says goodnight and leaves to go home. "Yup, see ya," Lindbergh says as he stays at the bar. It's now about 3:10 am.

Shortly before Eklund departs the Coliseum, two attractive young female patrons arrive. Cindy Volpe and Kathy McNeal are friends and co-workers who have finished their shifts as cocktail waitresses at one of Donald Trump's casinos in Atlantic City. Both are familiar to the Flyers at the Coliseum. The 22-year-old McNeal dated Peter Zezel for sixth months, while Volpe has gone out with Rick Tocchet. Parvin also briefly dated McNeal, although the relationship never really progressed.

When Eklund leaves, Lindbergh goes over to a table and joins a group that includes Tocchet, Murray Craven, Parvin, Kurt Mundt, and the young ladies. Meanwhile, Tocchet buys Lindbergh a beer. The two talk and laugh about the team's recent play and trade some running jokes from the locker room. Lindbergh also converses with Mundt. After last night's game with the Bruins, he's packed up Pelle's goalie equipment and brought it directly back to the Coliseum. Since he was already in the building, Mundt has joined the group of players that have been at the Coliseum prior to the arrival of the ones who first went to Bennigan's.

Mundt and Lindbergh discuss their respective plans for the practice-free day and briefly talk about the upcoming game with the Oilers. The group continues to drink. McNeil later says that Pelle and the rest of the group drink a pair of B-52s (a layered combination of Kahlua, Bailey's Irish Cream, and Grand Marnier). A receipt shows Pelle also buys two beers at different junctures during the evening. These are the only drinks that he actually purchases.

Lisa Garaguso and Kristina "Tina" Trout, two 19-year-old college students from Glouchester Township, NJ, also sit in the bar. They have not been served alcohol but Trout amuses herself by pointing out several of the different Flyers players to her friend. It's now 4:45 am and the bartenders stop serving as they prepare to close down at 5:00 am. Parvin, who is extremely drunk, asks Pelle if he can go lie down in the Porsche. "Yeah, sure," Lindbergh says, giving Parvin the keys. Parvin goes out to the car and sits down in the passenger seat where he promptly falls asleep.

Lindbergh and his teammates take the conversation outside as the bar finally empties. At about 5:20 am, Lindbergh puts on his leather jacket and walks outside a few feet to the right of Dave Poulin. The goalie shakes hands with the bouncer at the door and says goodnight (for the second time) to Poulin. Later, Poulin and other eyewitnesses say that Lindbergh still seems coherent and shows no outward sign of being too intoxicated to take himself home. The air is cold, with temperatures at the freezing point, but Lindbergh and the others stand outside as they discuss further plans.

Meanwhile, McNeil says she's hungry after working a late night at the casino. Lindbergh suggests that he drive Parvin home to his place in Mount Ephraim, NJ, and then come back with McNeil to meet Tocchet and Craven for breakfast. Tocchet initially asks if he can simply ride along, too, but sees there's not enough room in the two-seat Porsche. It's now shortly after 5:30 am.

Pelle Lindbergh walks to his car with his hands in his pants pockets, and McNeil squeezes into the middle of the car and sits atop the console. Pelle climbs into the driver's side and shuts the door. Parvin continues to slumber in the passenger seat.

Pelle Lindbergh

CHAPTER 8

MONTREAL, QUEBEC, AUGUST 9, 1979

For as long as anyone can remember, 20-year-old Pelle Lindbergh has dreamed of being chosen by the Philadelphia Flyers in the NHL Entry Draft. He doesn't care if other people find it strange that he wears Flyers logos on his mask or that he talks nonstop of becoming the heir apparent to the recently retired Bernie Parent. Lindbergh is firmly convinced that it's his destiny to play for the Flyers. But what if he's chosen by a different NHL team? Pelle's typical response is that he'll cross that bridge if he comes to it.

The Flyers have scouted Lindbergh at the World Junior Championships in Sweden and the World Championships in the USSR, but so have the Atlanta Flames. Atlanta scouts are divided on whether they prefer Lindbergh or former London Knights goaltender Pat Riggin.

It's been an interminably long wait for Lindbergh and other draft hopefuls. The 1979 draft was originally scheduled for June 10 and has been postponed until the second week of August. One of the primary reasons for the time lapse is the need to resolve a dispute over whether underage players (those under the age of 20 in their draft years) should be eligible for the draft. After heated arguments between the league office, team owners, and the Players' Association, the NHL reaches a compromise on the issue. It allows 19-year-old prospects to enter the 1979 draft with a plan to expand the eligibility rules to allow 18-year-olds to enter the 1980 draft. Canadian major junior leagues, which are still the NHL's primary lifeline for developing young talent, balk at this proposal and it takes considerable time to hammer out a compromise. The NHL creates a rule compelling clubs to return underagers to their Canadian junior teams if they do not make the NHL roster out of training camp (a rule that still exists in 2009).

A second key factor in the postponement of the draft is the need to resolve the merger of the NHL and WHA in terms of drafting order and the draft eligibility of underage players who'd played in the WHA in 1978-79. Players must be considered on a case-by-case basis. Ultimately, eight WHA players are declared eligible for the draft and underagers who would otherwise not have been old enough to play in the NHL in 1979-80 receive special permission to enter the NHL immediately. This special dispensation allows Wayne Gretzky, who played in the WHA for the Edmonton Oilers at the age of 17, to stay with the team as it joins the NHL. Finally, on August 9, the teams convene in the conference hall of Montreal's Queen Elizabeth Hotel to hold the draft.

In terms of available talent, the packed-to-overflowing 1979 draft crop has some big advantages over its predecessors, at least from the perspective of the teams. From the players' point of view, it means more competition for attention. Due to the unusually short lead time before the season, the league limits the draft to six rounds and a total of 126 selections. As a result, a slew of players fall through the cracks of the draft and wind up signing with NHL clubs as undrafted rookie free agents. With European hockey still largely a secondary scouting priority for most teams, there are also many good European players who go unselected in 1979.

If he's nervous about the chance of falling victim to the draft-day numbers game, Pelle doesn't show it. As usual, he foresees only positive outcomes. Much to the amusement of his Swedish junior national team comrades, Pelle also hasn't been shy about approaching scouts if they don't come to him first. That's how badly he wants to play in the NHL. It's not the norm for players in this era to attend, especially Europeans, so Pelle is not in

Montreal. In addition to this, the airfare and accommodations would be expensive, and would have to be paid for by the Lindbergh family.

The Flyers own the 14th overall pick of the first round, as well as a pair of picks in the second round (22nd and 35th overall), and one apiece in the third (56th overall), fourth (77th overall), fifth (98th overall), and sixth (119th). In the first round, the Flyers choose Brandon Wheat Kings left winger Brian Propp. It's a slam-dunk of a pick, although some other teams' scouts consider the 20-year-old to be a one-dimensional talent and a bit immature off the ice. The Wheat Kings of this era were one of the most dominating junior teams ever assembled. Propp is the preeminent scoring forward in western Canadian junior hockey, and *The Hockey News* ranked him as the No. 5 prospect for the draft. In 1978-79, Propp set new WHL scoring records for points in a season (94 goals and 194 points in 71 games) and career points (511). He's ready to compete for an immediate spot in the Flyers' NHL lineup.

With the first pick of the second round, the Flyers choose defenseman Blake Wesley, a big (6-foot-1, 200 pound), physical defenseman. By the time the 35th overall pick comes up, Pelle Lindbergh's teammate on the Swedish junior and senior national squads, Tomas Jonsson, has become the first European taken in the '79 draft. The Islanders select him three picks after Philadelphia takes Wesley. There has also been one goalie chosen as the Flames opt for Riggin with the 33rd pick.

Now it's the Flyers turn to choose again. Flyers general manager Keith Allen confers briefly with his scouts and glances at Jerry Melnyk, who has twice come back from Europe with positive reports on a Swedish goaltender he's tracked. From the Flyers table in the conference room, Allen takes the microphone. "Philadelphia selects goaltender Pelle Lindbergh from Sweden," he says.

With so much marvelous talent available in the draft, the Flyers' second-round selection of Pelle is not without its risks. While several position players from Europe had already proven they could make the jump to the NHL's smaller rinks, goaltenders hadn't fared so well. While Lindbergh's talents are undeniable, he and the Flyers would have to be trendsetters if he's to become the team's goaltender of the future. But Allen, nicknamed "Keith the Thief" for his trading and talent-assessment acumen, has complete trust in Melnyk's recommendation.

"We had lost Bernie [Parent] to retirement and we weren't sure what we had in some of the kids we had in the system," Allen recalls nearly 30 years later. "We were looking for a goalie who, in a short time, could match up to the NHL, and Jerry was extremely pleased by what he'd seen in Pelle. We really wanted to have Pelle and we were very happy when we succeeded. He was a major talent and he was fond of the Flyers, too."

When the draft is over, scout Jerry Melnyk makes a pair of long-distance phone calls to Sweden. First, he calls Pelle who is at home in his family's apartment in Barnängsgatan. Upon hearing the news that the Flyers have chosen him, Pelle screams. When Melnyk adds that the Flyers have also drafted Eriksson, the scout is momentarily concerned that the young goalie is about to sponteously combust from all the excitement. "Mama! Papa! The Flyers! The Flyers! The Flyers!" Pelle shouts. "Thomas Eriksson, too! I can't believe it!" It takes Sigge and Anna-Lisa several minutes to calm their son down enough to get a coherent explanation. Both parents are overjoyed and embrace their son.

"It was like a fairy tale. I couldn't believe it when the Flyers picked me," Lindbergh recounted in a 1985 interview. Pelle's next phone call is to Reino Sundberg, who immediately comes over to Lindbergh's house to congratulate Pelle in person. In the meantime, Melnyk calls Eriksson. He, too, is pleased, although his response is considerably calmer than Pelle's impromptu audition for *Flyermania*. Eriksson also receives a phone call from Pelle. The goalie declares that they should go out and celebrate with all their friends at Bäck-ahästen (a popular nightspot on Hamngatan in Stockholm), and the fun goes deep into the night.

The guys at Hovet rink are thrilled for Pelle. He gets mobbed when he comes to the rink to train the next day. Everyone knows how long he's dreamed of this moment. Curt Lindström, who has known Pelle for 13 years at this point, is especially proud to see that his former charge's talents have been recognized. "Pelle was still on cloud nine. He was ecstatic when Phila-delphia had chosen him," Lindström remembers. "He thought it was the biggest damn thing in the world."

Even before the Flyers drafted him, Lindbergh had plenty of motivation to play well for AIK in the upcoming season: He has to show he can succeed in Elitserien before he'll be ready to play pro hockey in the USA. He also covets the starting job on Tre Kronor's 1980 Olympic roster. Statistically, Lindbergh has pedestrian numbers. His 3.44 goals against average and .869 save percentage are right around the league norms of the time. But his fluid athleticism and his ability to protect narrow leads are noticeable even to casual observers.

One of the team's bright spots is a strong bounceback year from forward Bengt Lundholm. The future Winnipeg Jets forward had a breakout year in 1977-78 but slumped offensively the following year. In 1979-80, he rebounds to lead the club in goals (16), assists (16), and points (32). Veteran forward Pär Mårts also has strong offensive year. Meanwhile, the infamous "Black Army" fan club finds a new favorite in the young national team goalie guarding the AIK goal.

"Pelle was a little up and down, but he certainly swung a lot of games our way," AIK coach Parmström recalls. But as Parmström soon discovers (just like his Hammarby coaches had before), Lindbergh isn't particularly motivated at practice. He's always been able to get away with it because he performs well on game nights, but it doesn't sit well with Parmström. At first he's surprised and then he gets angry. The coach seethes whenever he sees Lindbergh playing with the puck on his stick when other players are doing skating drills, or standing around, chatting and laughing while most of the others are working up a sweat…. Pelle could leave his place in the crease in the middle of a heavy scrimmage, and we had to scream at him, 'Get in the goddamn net!' We often had to give him a kick in the ass to get him going at practice. Otherwise, he got bored very quickly. He wanted to have more time to goof around, just doing his own thing, like wanting to act like a position player," Parnström recalls. AIK's veteran players notice, too. According to left winger Mats Ulander, the older players put Pelle in his place on a few occasions. Mårts adds, "Pelle was different. It felt like the whole time he knew that he was with us temporarily, like a stop on the journey he'd planned to the NHL. That was probably the reason why he was pretty much for himself. It was like he was just on a visit and never got to know us. He barely got his feet wet." To the AIK coach and players, the strangest part of Lindbergh's behavior is that the rookie goalie is usually one of the first players to arrive for practice, and is one of the last to leave. He loves being at the rink and the lack of focus is never an issue during a game.

During much of his time with AIK, Pelle prefers to hang out with the equipment manager rather than his fellow players. Equipment manager Roger Andersson, in fact, becomes his closest friend on AIK. "Pelle was calm and wasn't heard from much in the locker room, but he enjoyed being around the team and was always one of the last to go home. He was never in a hurry after practice. When I was done, we'd get together. Then we'd sit and shoot the breeze and not be stressed in any way. We also met outside work," says

Andersson. "For me as an equipment guy, Pelle was never any problem. With Pelle, we had a chat before the season about how he'd want this or how he'd want that. Afterwards, it was smooth sailing the whole season, but he was short so we had to make his new leg pads shorter and clip the pants."

The first leg pads Pelle brings along in Elitserien are light green and look like they've been through a war. It makes no difference to the goaltender that he's warn them since he was a kid and used needle and thread to mend the tears. Pelle and Reino Sundberg often meet up early to go to the "Ice Hockey Repair Technician" (*Ishockeyreperatören*) on St. Eriksgatan, a firm that had its origins as a cobbling shop that started under the same roof. They're there a lot because their equipment always has some sort of problem with it when they play, and It never really holds tight. That happened easily in these days, because all the equipment is made of leather.

Lindbergh has somewhat shorter legs than many other goaltenders, and the first custom-made leg pads he gets are a pair of Brauns. Work starts in the summer of 1979 before the season with AIK. Jan Wallgren, who is the same age as Pelle, works with the goalie on what becomes a multi-year process of assembling and adjusting the pads in puzzle-like fashion, using leather, needle and thread until Pelle has a pair he feels comfortable wearing in a game. "That first pair I cut and tailored to Pelle's legs: Among other things, I remember that he had especially wide legs," Wallgren says. When Pelle returns home in the summer of 1981 after his first season in North America, he explains to Wallgren that he's ordered new pads in the USA, but he's on a long waiting list. So they get back to creating an entirely personalized pair of pads. Pelle always wants them to be tight around the knee cap but wider down near his skates.

"I took basic cardboard and made models of his legs by taking the measurements. Based on the paper models, we built a new pad, where we used light green cow hide and filled it with reindeer hair and treated coconut fiber, so the pad wouldn't suck in too much moisture. The back side of the pads was the traditional felt and shaped around his calf measurement," Wallgren said. Pelle first tests the new pads in the summer of 1979 and is very happy with the initial feel. After continued modifications, he later makes his NHL debut in these pads, but they survive just one winter. He brings them back to Wallgren in the summer of 1982, who finds that the pads haven't held up well.

"We decided that he should start with better quality pads," Wallgren says. Wallgren and Pelle then begin work on the pair of pads that Lindbergh wears in his Vezina Trophy winning 1984-85 season. Wallgren looks long and hard for a wholesaler in Stockholm who carries a certain cloth with brown calfskin. After that, he splits apart the old pads to see where they were breaking down, and proceeds to renovate them so that Pelle has two pairs he can keep with him. To him they're sacrosanct and not to be touched by others. Both in Sweden and the United States, he keeps his pads in the living room. Pelle's pads even have their own name, written out in big capital letters on the side: "GHOST". "I suggested that, because I wanted him to be like a ghost, spooking the opposition," says Wallgren.

Pelle was very particular, too, about his white mask – the most famous part of the equipment he wore, because it was a copy of Bernie Parent's mask. Pelle actually has two different Parent-style masks. The first one is the one his father bought for him at the ISAB shop in Stockholm. But after two seasons in North America, he has a new one custom-made in Canada. During a Flyers' road trip in Toronto, Lindbergh meets with mask-maker Greg Harrison, who makes a mold of the goaltender's face. Harrison then produces the stark white fiberglass mask.

Much like the other equipment of this era, the masks of the 1970s and early 1980s do not offer the same degree of protection as the designs of the 2000s. On one occasion early in his NHL career, Pelle gets hit in the mask by a slapshot from the Islanders John Tonelli. The force of the shot knocks back the mask so hard against the goalie's face that he's left with a pair of black eyes. Even two weeks later, Pelle still looks as though he has been on the losing end of a bar fight. But Lindbergh isn't about to switch to the wire-cage mask and helmets that many other goalies of the 1980s favor. He sticks with the white Parent mask. "I like my mask better than the new ones, because it's more than just a mask. My mask is personal, it's me," he tells the *Philadelphia Inquirer*. Many years later, both Lindbergh's latter-day white mask and Harrison's mold for it are placed on display at the Hockey Hall of Fame in Toronto.

Pelle Lindbergh

CHAPTER 9

SUNDAY, NOVEMBER 10, 1985, 5:30 AM

Dawn is near. Ed Parvin Jr. slumbers in the passenger seat of Pelle Lindbergh's Porsche 930 Turbo; Kathy McNeal sits on the console with her arms on both headrests. The initial plan is for Pelle to drive Parvin home, and return with McNeal to meet up with Flyers' players Murray Craven and Rick Tocchet for breakfast at the nearby Somerdale Diner.

Craven shares a place with Tocchet two blocks away from the Coliseum. Instead of getting breakfast, Craven invites everyone to come back instead for an after-party at his home, but Pelle has already promised McNeal they'd get breakfast. Craven sticks his head in the driver side window and asks a final time, "Gump, do you want to come hang out later?" "Yeah. We'll come later," Lindbergh says, and starts up the car. Lindbergh leans across McNeal and gently shakes Parvin to wake him. He asks the passenger if he wants to come back for breakfast after making a stop at his home. "Breakfast? Yeah, yeah, definitely," Parvin mumbles and turns his body to go back to sleep. Pelle closes the window to shut out the chilly November air, and pulls out of the parking lot. The guard at the door later notes that Lindbergh takes off from the parking lot as he usually does – like he's trying out for Formula One. No one is wearing a seatbelt.

Pelle drives a little more carefully up Fourth Street and navigates the short stretch through the T-shaped intersection at Somerdale Road. From there he turns right and accelerates quickly and flies through the streets of the quiet suburb. The car brakes at a red light near the White Horse Pike. A Chevy Chevette pulls up alongside the Porsche and stops at the red light. Inside are college students Tina Trout and Lisa Garaguso, who had left the

Coliseum at about the same time as Pelle. Trout is the driver and comments that it was a lengthy red light. The girls look into the nearby car as the streetlights above illuminate the dark asphalt. "Look, that's Pelle," Trout says.

Garaguso later tells police that everyone in the Porsche, including Parvin, is awake and laughing. Pelle's hands are on the wheel. McNeal runs a hand through her hair and then places it behind the armrest again. As the light turns green, Trout glances at the large digital clock at the Sun National Bank on the other side of the intersection. It reads 5:37 am "The Porsche took off like a rocket and was suddenly gone," Trout later says. "We hardly blinked."

Somerdale Road remains straight until about three blocks past the White Horse Pike intersection, at which point there's a banana-shaped curve to the right as the road intersects with Ogg Avenue. At the steepest part of the curve is the Somerdale Elementary School with an elevated lawn and its surrounding wall. The small retaining wall measures three-and-a-half feet high, and is the only one along this stretch of road. Car accidents are common at this intersection, and construction crews have widened the roadway to make it safer for cars to negotiate the unforgiving curve.

With his judgment impaired and driving at about 80 miles an hour, Pelle Lindbergh continues to go straight where the road curves. He's only about 10 feet away from the wall when he finally tries to slam on the brakes, but by now it's far too late to stop. The car careens into the area where the steps meet the wall. Upon impact, the driver's side is totaled with the hood and front end getting pushed into Lindbergh's side of the car. The impact is so violent that the car's windshield launches like a projectile and lands 40 feet away. The passenger side crumples against the steps although the driver's side by far takes the heaviest impact. The motor instantly goes silent.

The Chevette arrives moments later. From a distance, Garaguso and

Trout could tell that the Porsche crashed but couldn't determine the severity of the accident until they got closer to examine the scene. They see the left side of the Porsche is demolished beyond recognition and there's no immediate indication that any of the car's occupants are alive. With her heart racing, Trout turns the Chevette around and hurries back to the intersection, where just minutes earlier she and Garaguso had looked on curiously at Lindbergh and his company. There's a 24-hour mini-market and the ladies hurry in, with the hope of finding a telephone they can use to call for help. "There's been an accident! We need a phone!" Trout and Garaguso shout simultaneously. The male cashier is unmoved and unfriendly. "Use a pay phone outside," he says curtly, although there's a phone in the store. The girls rush out out of the store in search of a phone. Forgetting they can dial 9-1-1, they fish for change in their purses and pockets and call for emergency assistance.

David Diaz, a server at the Coliseum, also leaves the mini-mart on his way home after his late shift. Diaz pulls out of the lot and navigates the intersection, as he drives to the Somerdale Road and Ogg Avenue intersection where he, too, sees the horrendous accident scene. Now wide-awake, he gets out of his car and goes over to investigate the nightmarish scene, by approaching the passenger side. He notices immediately that of the three people in the car, only one is moving. Diaz talks to Kathy McNeal, who is screaming and thrashing around. He also looks at Pelle's grotesquely contorted body in the driver's seat. "Hold my hand!" Diaz shouts to a hysterical McNeal. "Help will be here any minute. Just hold my hand until then."

Diaz then tries to concentrate on Parvin, who is lying closest to him. He doesn't appear to be breathing, but Diaz forces his fingers into Parvin's mouth in order to free his airway from his tongue and the blood in his mouth. He recalls that, among others, he had served Ed Parvin at the Coliseum earlier in the evening. Barely two minutes later, the first police car and two ambulances arrive on the scene, and Diaz moves aside as the rescue crew gets to work.

BettyAnn Cowling-Carson is the first rescue worker to look inside the car, and she uses a flashlight to get a closer look. Neither Lindbergh nor Parvin are conscious, but she hears McNeal's screams. "My legs! My legs!" McNeal yells. "I told him to slow down, I told him!" Cowling-Carson also notices that Lindbergh is bleeding from his nose and mouth, and that at least one of his legs is severely fractured. Parvin appears to have suffered severe head trauma, but both men still have a pulse.

More and more rescue vehicles arrive, as rescue workers attempt to free the passengers from the car. The driver's side door is smashed up against the wall and impossible to reach but the passenger door is accessible with pneumatic tools. Working as carefully as possible, the crew lifts the passengers out so they can receive medical attention.

The lights, sirens, and commotion have attracted a crowd of onlookers. Most are nearby residents, standing outside with bathrobes or jackets over their pajamas or nightgowns. It takes just over 10 minutes to place the two passengers on stretchers on the ground. Neckbraces are placed around both Parvin and McNeal, as the ambulance crew rushes them to the hospital. One ambulance takes Parvin to Cooper Hospital in Camden because it has the best head and neck trauma unit in the area. The other takes McNeal to the closest facility, the John F. Kennedy Memorial Hospital in Stratford. Cowling-Carson retrieves a third neck brace and towel as her partner, Billy Lynch, examines Pelle, who is now the only one remaining in the wrecked vehicle. "Forget the collar," Lynch shouts, "His heart has stopped! Hurry! We have to get him out right now!" Working in the cramped space, the crew supports the driver's head and neck as other rescue workers remove Pelle feet-first. Hurriedly, they cut open the driver's leather jacket and perform CPR on the ground. The crew's fast action is successful. Lindbergh's heart starts to beat again, although his breathing is weak. The crew is extremely worried that his heart can stop again at any time. The initial plan is to take Lindbergh to Cooper Hospital, but the crew decides to take him to Kennedy so that he can get more immediate attention. In the ambulance, Pelle's breathing remains shallow, but hooking him up to a machine normalizes his breathing.

Murray Craven and Rick Tocchet have only been home for about twenty minutes when there's a frantic knock at the door. They planned on an after-party, but from the shouts on the other side, something is clearly wrong. Craven opens the door to find an extremely agitated Tina Trout and Lisa Garaguso, who are shouting at the same time. "There's been a horrible accident! It's Pelle Lindbergh! Pelle crashed! We saw it! We saw it! We know where he is! Hurry!"

Tocchet stays behind, while Craven goes with the girls to the accident scene. Still a bit drunk from the evening's earlier festivities, Craven does not panic because he expects to find the Porsche damaged and Pelle a bit shaken up – but nothing serious. The sky starts to lighten as Craven arrives at the scene. He sees an unconscious Pelle Lindbergh being covered with blankets and placed into the ambulance on a gurney. "How bad is he hurt?" Craven asks a police officer. "It's very bad," the officer says. "Will he be able to play hockey again?" Craven asks. "He'll be lucky if he lives," the officer replies.

All at once, the gravity of the situation hits Murray Craven. His face goes ashen as the policeman, who recognizes Craven as one of Lindbergh's teammates, speaks to him. "Would you please come sit in the car so we can talk?" the officer asks. Craven nods and accompanies the officer to the patrol car with flashing blue lights. The policeman presses him for information about the accident. "Do you know where he had been? Were you there? Were all of you drinking? How much would you say Pelle had to drink?" Craven looks pleadingly at the policeman. "I don't want to answer any more questions. I just want to go home," he says. "It's OK. Go ahead," the officer says.

When he gets home, Craven and Tocchet wonder whom they should call. They decide on Brad Marsh. Marsh is one of the team's best-liked and most respected leaders, both on and off the ice. He is known for taking newly-acquired players under his wing and making sure that everyone on the team feels welcomed. With the exception of Dave Poulin, Marsh may be the player to whom Pelle feels the closest among his North American teammates. The veteran defenseman is also good at offering young players advice about off-the-ice decisions. When Craven calls the house, Brad's wife, Patti, answers. Her husband is still sound asleep after the game night at the Spectrum and the post-game celebration at the Coliseum. Patti has difficulty waking him.

Craven next calls Poulin. He and wife Kim are asleep, but the ringing phone on the night table wakes him. "Pelle was in an accident, a horrible accident. He's hurt," Craven says. "What should I do?" "Call Clarkie right now," Poulin says, referring to general manager Bob Clarke. They end the conversation. Night has become morning.

Pelle's close friend, New Jersey police officer Jack Prettyman, took this harrowing photograph of the goaltender's wrecked Porsche after the vehicle was removed from the scene of the fatal car crash [Courtesy Jack Prettyman]

CHAPTER 10

LAKE PLACID, NEW YORK, FEBRUARY 5, 1980

Soldiers in the Swedish army usually need to be excused for the Olympics, so Pelle Lindbergh finds himself caught up in a web of bureaucratic red tape. As expected, he's earned a spot on the Swedish Olympic hockey team and has beaten out William "Wille" Löfqvist for the starting job. Pelle performed well for Tre Kronor at both the Rude-Provo tournament in Prague and the famous Christmas-time Izvestiya tournament in Moscow. That was the easy part for Pelle, compared with the time and effort it takes to secure the necessary clearances and completed paperwork in a timely manner so that he can take leave. With little time to spare, Pelle finally gets clearance.

For young players like Pelle, Thomas Eriksson, Mats Näslund, and Tomas Jonsson, the journey to Lake Placid is more than just a trip for a hockey tournament. "The Olympics were the first time I was over in the US," Eriksson recalls,

> When we got there, we stayed in a newly built prison, which was to be used for prisoners after the Olympics. So there was also pretty good security. We bunked in open cells, and Pelle and I shared one. Lake Placid is a little village in the middle of the forest. The Olympic village became like its own little town with a movie theater, restaurants, and other amusements. There were a few concerts, I remember. But we were never out of the village to do anything special.

Among others, Lindbergh and his teammates mingled with Ingemar

Stenmark, the gold medalist in both slalom and giant slalom skiing. One night, they got a visit from Sweden's King Carl XVI Gustaf, Queen Silvia, and their entourage. "Damn, she was good looking," is how Pelle later reports his meeting with the queen to his family and friends at home.

While the story of Team USA's "Miracle on Ice" at Lake Placid captivates the entire world, and not just the hockey community, the performance of Team Sweden and its goaltender is also one of the tournament's pleasant footnotes. In the opener, played February 12, Pelle holds Team USA at bay for the first 59 minutes as the favored Swedes cling to a 2-1 lead. With American goaltender Jim Craig pulled for an extra attacker, the Americans hold the puck in the zone and a wide-open Bill Baker drives home a shot from the high slot with just 27 seconds left in regulation. At the time, the tie is a disappointment for Lindbergh and the other Swedes. In light of the subsequent events, especially the Americans' historic come-from-behind upset of the USSR and rally to beat Finland in the final game; it became clear that the collection of American collegiate players was a team of destiny. "How could we not admire what they did?" Lindbergh asked rhetorically in a 1984 interview conducted shortly before the next Olympics. "Obviously, it was tough not to win that (first) game after we had the lead so late, but now we look back and see that we were the only team, including the Russians, that USA didn't beat."

Two days after the tie against the Americans, Tre Kronor faces Romania, which had just upset West Germany in the first game. In a tournament that later proves impossible hockey dreams can come true, Tre Kronor isn't about to play Tomte (the Swedish version of Santa Claus) to the Romanian side and has no problem dispatching the overmatched squad, 8-0. Next Sweden gets a somewhat tougher game from the West Germans, but prevails, 4-2. The Swedes then rout Norway, 7-1.

On February 20, Tre Kronor finds itself the underdog against Czechoslovakia. For much of the game, the ice is tilted. The Czechoslovaks fire 36 shots on Lindbergh's goal, many of which are real testers, but the young goaltender keeps his team close. Meanwhile, despite generating just 16 shots for the game, Sweden gets three powerplay goals and a dominant performance from Mats Näslund. Tre Kronor wins 4-2. "I had three assists and Pelle was just sensational in goal against Czechoslovakia," Näslund later recalls. "They had some very dangerous players, including the Stastny brothers, Milan Novy, Jaroslav Pouzar, and Milan Chalupa."

Two days later, on the same day as Team USA's stunning 4-3 win over the Soviets, Sweden takes on Finland. In a see-saw affair, Lindbergh stops 22 of 25 shots. The Swedes get 30 shots for the game, with Finnish goalie Antero Kivelä finding answers for 27 of them. Mikko Leinonen gives the Finns an early 1-0 lead in a first period that sees Finland fire 11 shots on goal to nine by the Swedes. At the 7:06 mark of the second period, Finnish captain Jukka Porvari extends the lead to 2-0. But Tre Kronor's Ulf Weinstock quickly gets the Swedes back within a goal. In the third period, defensemen Tomas Jonsson and Mats Waltin (the Swedes' captain) strike within a minute of one another to give Tre Kronor their first lead at the 6:14 mark. But Leinonen responds just 1:45 later and the teams skate off to a 3-3 tie.

Tre Kronor is now sitting pretty to win a medal, but with two ties on its record, winning the gold is a bit of a longshot. Sweden is about to run into a furious Soviet squad, fresh off the loss to the Americans. Moreover, Sweden also needs to get help from the Finns against Team USA. It doesn't happen. The Russians make mincemeat of the Swedish defense, by scoring in the first 36 seconds of play (Vladimir Petrov) and roaring out to a 4-0 lead by the time the first period is over. Lindbergh is peppered with 15 shots by a team that rarely piles up big shot totals because it looks for wide-open opportunities and otherwise is content to maintain possession of the puck. The middle period is more of the same. Valeri Vasiliev makes it a 5-0 game just 33 seconds after the drop of the first faceoff. Four more goals follow in almost effortless fashion. In the third period, the Russians shut down their engines, and Sweden scores two meaningless goals while getting 13 of their 26 shots in the game. Tre Kronor takes the bronze medal.

Despite the 9-2 drubbing in the final game, Pelle Lindbergh earns widespread acclaim for his play throughout the tournament. In fact, Radio Sweden chooses Pelle as its Swedish athlete of the month for February, 1980, beating out Ingemar Stenmark and other Olympians.

For the first time in his young career, Pelle's fascination with Bernie Parent is mutual. Now employed as the Flyers' goaltending co-coach along with his own childhood idol, Jacques Plante, Parent watches as many of the Olympic hockey telecasts as he can. He catches Lindbergh's performances against Team USA and Czechoslovakia and likes what he sees.

During the Olympics, Pelle is briefly interviewed by American reporters after the game against Team USA. He happily repeats his by-now much-told story about being a Flyers' fan and a Parent devotee. "I thought it was touching that Pelle wanted to come to the Flyers because I was his idol," Parent says today. "But when people compared him to me on the ice, I started to see why (at Lake Placid). Good Lord, we were so alike. It was a beautiful thing to see. Same mask, same equipment, same playing style." But Lindbergh and Parent still have yet to meet face-to-face. "I was really looking forward to meeting him, especially after I hear that I was his role model," Parent says today. As a coachable prospect, Pelle could also be stubborn, too, when it came to suggestions to alter his goaltending style. In later years, Pelle is eager to receive coaching from Bernie Parent, but as a teenager, he is sometimes resistant to receiving goaltending tips from his Swedish coaches.

Shortly after the 1980 World Championships, Pelle clowns around with father Sigge Lindbergh at the family's home in Stockholm. [Courtesy Ann-Louise Hörnestam]

Watching Flyers prospect Lindbergh emerge at the Olympics and seeing the Philadelphia NHL club reel off a record 35-game unbeaten streak are two fleeting bright spots in an otherwise dark and gloomy time in Parent's life. The period from late 1978 to 1980 was an awful time for him. He continues to wear a smile in public during this time although he's fallen into a deep depression after his career ends. He's going through a private hell even though his Flyers' career ended with a stellar 232-141-103 record, 50 shutouts, and 2.42 goals against average. His playoff numbers were equally impressive with his two Conn Smythe Trophies and 2.38 goals against average. Snider promised Bernie a job for life with the Flyers. As he regains control of his life, Parent is able to become the mentor who gently guides Pelle Lindbergh to the summit of the NHL's goaltending heap five years later.

Pelle's first agent as a professional player is Swedish sports attorney Björn Wagnsson who initiates the relationship. He calls both Lindbergh and Thomas Eriksson to offer his services and the players accept. Two weeks after the Olympics, the Flyers contact Wagnsson and let him know the team wants to sign both of his clients. Wagnsson negotiates the same deal for both players: two seasons, plus an option year, paying $80,000 during the 1980-81 season, $65,000 the following year and $70,000 in the option year. "The most important thing for us was that it was a one-way contract, meaning that we didn't have a second (lesser) contract if we played on the farm team," Eriksson recalls.

AIK equipment manager Roger Andersson remembers Pelle's joy when the contract is signed. "Pelle called me and nearly shrieked, 'Listen up, Roger, I've got something to tell you! I'm going to leave AIK, because now I've got my pro contract!" Andersson says.

On Thursday, March 20, 1980, Lindbergh plays his final game for AIK and what turns out to be his final league game in Sweden. Three teams are tied for the fourth and final playoff spots: AIK, Djurgården, and Brynäs IF Gävle. All have 37 points, but AIK holds the tie-breaker on both clubs by virtue of the best goal differential. On this night, Pelle goes head-to-head with best friend Reino Sundberg and Thomas Eriksson as AIK plays Djurgården in front of a sold-out crowd of over 10,000 fans at Johannsehov's Ice Stadium. With a playoff spot and local bragging rights on the line, the game proves to be dramatic and intense. The game is scoreless with just two minutes left in the first period, when AIK is whistled for a penalty. DIF's Dag Bremberg sets up shop in front of the AIK net and gets taken down by Mats Ulander. The referee, however, points to Lindbergh for the penalty.

It's a costy ruling. In this era, there's a rule in Swedish hockey that even goaltenders have to go to the penalty box when called for an infraction. Lindbergh skates angrily to the box, and ice-cold backup Gunnar Leidborg goes to the crease as AIK sends four penalty killers out on the ice. Pelle isn't in the box for long. Djurgården's Hans Särkijärvi promptly scores on Leidborg to give DIF a 1-0 lead.

Lindbergh and Sundberg match each other save for save throughout a tense second period. The 1-0 score holds until midway through the final period when AIK's Bengt Lundholm finally solves Sundberg. In AIK's very next attack, Peter Gradin fires a rising shot that Sundberg either snares just before it gets over the goal line or gloves a fraction of a second after it goes over the line. The referee waves no goal and calls for a face off. In an era long before instant replay review and overhead camera angles, the controversial call will be debated for years between AIK and Djurgården supporters. AIK has one final chance in the waning minutes as Per Mårts beats Sundberg cleanly with a shot from the circle, but the puck clangs off the goal post on the long side. The game ends in a 1-1 tie. As a result, both are AIK and Djurgården are knocked out of the playoffs, and Brynäs goes on to win the championship.

After the game Pelle and Sundberg go out together to one of their favorite Stockholm night spots, Taurus. Hockey season is officially over and summer vacation has begun. Shortly thereafter, both goalies are invited to play for Tre Kronor in a four-team World Championship preparation tournament called the "GT Sweden Cup" at the Scandinavium in Gothenburg. Lindbergh starts three of the four games with Sundberg playing the other. Sweden finishes second to the Soviets in the tournament. The Swedes beat Czechoslovakia as well as a skeleton crew masquerading as Team Canada. The Russians go undefeated.

Pelle plays somewhat reluctantly in the tournament but knows that he has to avoid injury before his first North American training camp. Sure enough, Lindbergh gets hurt and sustains a foot injury. Rather than withdrawing from the tournament, however, he gets around on crutches in between practices and games. He is worried about his foot, but the injury turns out to be nothing more than a deep bruise. Although his foot is sore, no bones are broken, no tendons damaged. Much to his relief, he's OK by the time he reports to the Flyers' camp.

The 1979-80 season is a memorable one for the Philadelphia Flyers because the team is led by a deep forward corps. The top unit remains the veteran LCB line (Reggie Leach, Bobby Clarke, Bill Barber), but it's supplemented by the Rat Patrol (Ken Linseman centering rookie left wing Brian Propp and the rugged Paul Holmgren) and a dynamic two-way checking line anchored by captain Mel Bridgman. During the regular season, the team sets a North American pro sports record of 35 straight games without a loss. The Flyers advance to the Stanley Cup Finals for the fourth time in seven years but lose in a heartbreaking and highly controversial sixth game to the New York Islanders.

The team also receives strong goaltending from rookie Pete Peeters, who plays in the NHL All-Star Game. Peeters initially splits time with veteran Phil Myre, but emerges almost instantly as the better of the Flyers' two goalies. He doesn't make many friends off the ice in his early days, but Peeters is a force to be reckoned with for prospect Pelle Lindbergh as long as the NHLer keeps stopping pucks so effectively.

Shortly after the end of the Stanley Cup playoffs, the Flyers bring Lindbergh and Eriksson over for their first visit to Philadelphia. The team holds a press conference to announce their signings. The players also get to tour the area. With the Flyers' permission, Pelle also brings along Reino Sundberg on the trip.

Over the years, Hall of Fame goaltender Bernie Parent evolved from Pelle's idol to his goaltending coach and close friend. Lindbergh often referred to Parent as "my father in the United States." [Courtesy Reino Sundberg]

On the night before the press conference, Pelle gets to meet Parent for the first time. The legendary goaltender accompanies the team's senior management and playing assistant coach Bobby Clarke when the team takes the Swedish trio out to dinner. Reino Sundberg remembers, "It was a really nice restaurant, and we were dressed in suits. I remember how big it was to us that Bernie Parent was with us as the table. I was as impressed as Pelle." But the first meeting is a tad awkward for Pelle. As gregarious as Lindbergh can be, this isn't the sort of situation where he thrives. He's star-struck looking at Parent, and nearly 30 years later, Parent still remembers the dinner well:

> All of us at dinner that evening understood that these were
> good guys from Sweden. Pelle was shy and he didn't say much in

English, but he smiled a lot and we knew he was a warm and good guy. It was that night where I realized it would great to be in Pelle's company. There was a lot of laughter, I remember. But I still didn't know much about Pelle's hockey, apart from what I saw from Lake Placid. I first got to know Pelle Lindbergh the goalie when he came over here to play.

Pelle always assumed that sports fans in Philadelphia are fond of Parent, but he now gets his first glimpse of just how popular he really is. The Flyers take Pelle, Eriksson, and Sundberg to Veterans' Stadium to see their first baseball game. It's a good year to go for the Philadelphia Phillies are on their way to their third National League championship and first World Series victory and in the franchise's 97-year history. The baseball game itself doesn't make much of an impression on Pelle, it's the reaction of the Philadelphia crowd that becomes etched in his mind. Inside the Vet, Phillies public address announcer Dan Baker introduces Bernie Parent to the crowd. Instantly, the fans stand up and begin to chant "Ber-nie! Ber-nie! Ber-nie!" as they did in the Flyers' Stanley Cup days. Parent smiles and waves to the fans. Near the stadium, there are several cars that still have bumper stickers reading "Only the Lord saves more than Bernie Parent." The decals were extremely popular when the Flyers won their two Stanley Cups, and there are still mid '70s cars that bear the fading bumper sticker.

A few innings later, a small group of people sitting in the section near the Flyers' contingent recognize that the team's newly signed prospect is sitting with Parent and company, and a new chant goes up: "Lind-bergh! Lind-bergh! Lind-bergh!" On this night, it's only a couple people calling out the Swedish goalie's name, but the young goalie is floored by the attention. "These were folks who knew hockey and knew that Pelle had signed with the Flyers. But when they shouted Pelle's name in the stands at the baseball game, he reacted right away. I can still close my eyes and see how surprised and proud he was," Sundberg recalls. Apart from the baseball game, the Swedes also get to tour Philadelphia, and then see the Jersey shore beaches and luxury hotels in Atlantic City. Flyers' captain Mel Bridgman is the tour guide. "It became a several-day vacation," Eriksson remembers.

———————————

Pelle does enjoy going out to pubs, both in-season and over the summer, but rarely drinks alcohol during hockey season. In summer the only difference is in his choice of beverages and the frequency with which he's able to go out. In the 1970s, he took part in a public service campaign to promote responsible drinking. The ads ran in the Hammarby IF game programs at Johannsehov's Ice Stadium.

Most times Lindbergh, Sundberg, and their other friends are regulars at the Bäckahästen on Hamngatan. On Thursday nights, however, they preferred to go to Taurus on Malmskillnadsgatan. "Taurus was pretty damn trendy," Sundberg recalls. "Every Thursday, they had theme nights and there were lots of sports stars there. I remember that Tommy Boustedt used to go hang out a lot there with Stephan Lundh and Håkan Södergren."

As part of the Friday night routine at Daily News, Lindbergh and Sundberg usually shared a table with AIK players Bengt Lundholm, Mats Ulander, and Lars-Erik Eriksson. Even after Pelle makes it to the NHL, this remains a Friday night ritual during the summers. Of course, a big part of the appeal of going to these places is meeting attractive young women. Pelle has never lacked for female companionship, and has had both short-term and longer-term dating relationships.

On Thursday, July 31, 1980, Pelle heads to Taurus and his life changes forever. That evening, the club's Thursday night theme is windsurfing and

Taurus hosts the TWBA (Täby/Blidö Windsurfing) club for dinner and a presentation by the club's most accomplished members. One of them is a young lady named Kerstin Pietzch, who is a member of Sweden's national windsurfing team. After the presentation, she and two of the other instructors sit down with the owner at a round table as Pelle and hockey buddy Anders "Ankan" Lånström go over and sit down next to her.

Pelle has never stood on a surfboard in his life. He's not terribly convinced that what this young lady does is even a sport, but he sure thinks she's beautiful. "Windsurfing? Is there really anything interesting about windsurfing?" Pelle asks her. "It doesn't look especially hard." Kerstin smiles at his cockiness. "Come out to Näsa meadow so you can try it out, then," she says. That's the reply Pelle is hoping to hear. Näsa meadow is where the TWBA is based, and an adjacent jetty leads out to the water. "You got it," he says. I'll be there."

Two days later, early on Saturday afternoon, Kerstin gets a phone call. It's one of her friends at TWBA. "Kerstin, there's a guy named Pelle Lindbergh standing here. He's asking for you. Apparently you promised you'd teach him to windsurf," her friend says. She's both surprised and happy, as she recognized him the other night at Taurus. Knowing that he was a hockey player, she suspected that lots of girls flirt with him. She didn't really expect him to show up at Näsa meadow. Hurriedly, she heads over to meet with Pelle who soon learns that windsurfing is much more difficult than it looks. "It was probably the first time Pelle surfed, because he spent most of the time in the water instead of on the board," Kerstin recalls. "But he didn't give up and he was really interested." He's more interested in Kerstin and convinces her to go with him to a Saturday night party at the BZ club hosted by hockey buddy Mats Ulander.

The next day they agree to meet up again at Näsa meadow for another windsurfing lesson. Pelle is smitten but Kerstin isn't. She's recently ended a lengthy relationship with a boyfriend and isn't interested in anything more than a casual relationship. They're also from different backgrounds for Pelle is a working-class kid from the south side and she's from an upper-middle class family in Täby. "But he wouldn't give up," Kerstin laughs. "Pelle called often and began to show up with flowers. And when he later took me out to a fine restaurant, he bought perfume for me. I started to feel a way I never felt before, and love got its claws in me."

The remaining summer weeks go by and the couple becomes insepa-rable. Both are working toward a goal to which the other can relate. Pelle tells Kerstin about his NHL dreams, while Kerstin is preparing for a spot in the windsurfing world championships in the Bahamas. "Pelle was proud about what awaited him," Kerstin said. "He was counting down the days." Pelle's interest in windsurfing grows, but almost too fast. The same competitive instincts that serve him so well in hockey get him into trouble as a surfer. ""He signed himself up for a competition, and he was in way over his head. I remember that he was in the water most of the time, and was almost getting in the way of the other surfers," she says and laughs again.

Late in the summer, Pelle brings Kerstin along to an end-of-summer party at the Värmdö golf club. Reino Sundberg and Anders Lånström are also there and everyone has a great time. But come early September, there's a problem. The time has come for Pelle to leave Sweden and head to the Flyers' training camp. He's heartsick. "We were very much in love. But when I came into the picture, it got a little complicated for Pelle. He had his hockey, and I didn't want to sit and wait for him the whole hockey season. I was prepared for this to be the end," Kerstin says.

Pelle Lindbergh

CHAPTER 11

SUNDAY, NOVEMBER 10, 1985, 6:30 AM

Murray Craven calls Bob Clarke's home number. The phone rings several times before Clarke's wife, Sandy, picks up. It's a peculiar time for a call and she knows right away that something strange is going on when she hears the player's solemn voice on the other end of the line. "It's Murray Craven," he says. "Is Clarkie there?" "He's not home," she says. "He's out of town." "Please let him know there's been an accident. Gump – Pelle Lindbergh – has been injured and it's real serious." Sandy sighs. "OK. Give me a few minutes so I can try to get hold of him. Wait by the phone."

Several minutes later, the Flyers GM calls Craven from a hotel room in Boston. Clarke is there on a scouting trip. "What do you know about the accident?" Clarke asks. Craven gives the GM all the information he has.

Pelle, Ed Parvin Jr., and Kathy McNeal have been removed from the wrecked Porsche and taken to two area hospitals. A Voorhees policeman studies the crash site and looks at the foreign registration. He radios central headquarters and asks for Jack Prettyman to be contacted, because he knows that Prettyman is a close friend of Pelle's.

Prettyman worked the previous night, has only been home a few hours and hasn't gotten much sleep. He rubs his eyes as he answers the phone. In his line of work, Prettyman has to deal with unpleasant situations. Even upon hearing the most basic detail of the accident, he immediately gets a sick feeling in the pit of his stomach: a red Porsche has been in a one-car accident in Somerdale. He instantly knows the car was either Pelle's or Thomas Eriksson's, but the officer on the other end of the line does not know the driver's identity. "Which hospital?" Prettyman asks as he hurriedly gets dressed.

Prettyman drives over to John F. Kennedy Memorial Hospital, parks and goes in the ambulance entrance. His head is spinning and he is still unsure whether he'll find Lindbergh or Eriksson. He talks to the hospital staff and finds out that the driver and one of the passengers in the car were brought to JFK, but they still aren't sure of the driver's identity. He had to be admitted immediately to receive emergency treatment. Prettyman offers to identify the patient and is accompanied by a nurse. The sight of Pelle lying there critically injured and hooked up to a respirator genuinely horrifies him. He's seen people in this state before, but the apparently lifeless man lying here is a friend. No amount of experience on the force can ever prepare someone for this.

"This is Pelle Lindbergh," Prettyman says to the nurse. Prettyman leaves the room and discusses the situation with another officer. "Me and Pelle are close friends. I'll contact the family," Prettyman says.

Murray Craven calls Dave Poulin for a second time and is still emotionally torn apart. "Didn't you call Clarkie?" Poulin asks. "Yes, but, Dave, you don't understand. This is really bad and we have to do something," Craven says. "I'll try to get hold of Keenan," Poulin says. "Do the Sniders know, too? Where is Gump – which hospital?" "I think they said Cooper," Craven says. They hang up, and Craven and Tocchet leave to try to find Pelle at Cooper Hospital, where the policeman at the crash site had told Craven that Lindbergh had been taken. When they go inside, they ask someone on duty to take them to see Lindbergh. "There's a guy here but I don't think he's a player on the Flyers," the staffer says.

Tocchet and Craven are confused and extremely worried. A doctor asks if they can come identify the unconscious man brought from the crash scene. The man has a fractured skull and has to undergo emergency surgery. Craven can't bring himself to go so he asks Tocchet to go. Tocchet walks down a long corridor with his heart pounding and lips tight. "Do you recognize who this is?" Tocchet is asked. "Yes, his name is Ed Parvin."

Tocchet returns to speak with Craven and informs him that Pelle isn't at this hospital. He's been told that the other two people in the car have been taken to Kennedy. They leave to head for the other hospital.

In the meantime Poulin reaches Keenan on the first try and he relays the information that he's gotten from Craven. "We need to go and find out exactly what the hell happened," Poulin says. Keenan agrees. The men meet up in the parking lot of Kaminski's Ale House and then drive together to Cooper Hospital. They get the same information that Tocchet and Craven have gotten a little earlier. "I have to call the Parvin family. I know them," Poulin says. The Flyers captain makes the most gut-wrenching phone call he's ever made in his life, and tells Ed Parvin's parents that their son is at Cooper undergoing emergency surgery and he and Keenan know nothing of the prognosis.

By this time, everyone in Flyers' management knows of the accident, as do several of the players. As soon as Patti Marsh wakes up Brad, he heads over to Cooper Hospital where he meets the Parvin family huddled with Poulin and Keenan. Marsh is brought up-to-date on the details. "You go over to see Gump," Marsh says. "I'll stay here with the Parvins." Poulin and Keenan leave for Kennedy Hospital.

It's almost 7:00 am and Policeman Jack Prettyman knocks on the front door of Pelle's home in Kings Grant. Göran, an early riser by nature, is already awake and has come downstairs from the second floor. When he answers the door, he sees Prettyman, who was at the house a couple days earlier. The officer is dressed in civilian clothes. He has no idea what's happened. For all he knows, Pelle is asleep in his bedroom.

The difficult conversation is made all that much tougher by the language barrier. "It's about Pelle," Prettyman says slowly. "He's been in a car accident. Where is Kerstin?" Göran speaks very limited English and has trouble understanding Prettyman. He does not immediately reply because he is still filtering the words in his head. "Where is Kerstin?!" Prettyman asks again and much more forcefully. Göran heads over to the steps, calls upstairs loudly and tells Kerstin in Swedish that there's a policeman here to talk to her. As he calls up, he sees Anna-Lisa standing on the top step. "What's happened?" Anna-Lisa asks in Swedish with her eyes wide in fear.

Kerstin, clad in a bathrobe, stands behind Anna-Lisa and then hurries down the steps past her to speak to Prettyman. "Kerstin, Pelle has been in a car accident. It's extremely serious, and he's in the hospital," Prettyman says. "Oh my God," she says. "What'd he say? What's happening?" Anna-Lisa demands urgently. "Anna-Lisa, we have to go with him! It's about Pelle – he's hurt! We have to go to the hospital!" Kerstin shouts as she heads upstairs to throw on some clothes. As Kerstin runs upstairs, Anna-Lisa bursts into tears for she's unable to hold back her own anguish. "Noooo!" she wails. "I was afraid of this! I was afraid of this!"

As he stands waiting for Pelle's family, Prettyman catches a glimpse of a framed photograph in the entry way. It's a black and white photo of a smiling Pelle from the time he played on the Hammarby boys' team. It was taken in the dressing room as Pelle sits up against the wall. He has just lifted his face and noticed the camera. His chin rests in his left hand.

Keenan and Poulin arrive at Kennedy Hospital shortly after Murray

Craven and Rick Tocchet, but before Pelle's family. They present themselves to hospital personnel and Keenan is allowed to go back to where Lindbergh and McNeal are being treated. He sees Pelle hooked up to the respirator. Keenan leans over Pelle and says, "We went through some good times together, didn't we?" A doctor tells the Flyers' coach that Pelle will be undergoing a CAT scan. Keenan asks McNeal what happened but gets no reply. She is breathing on her own and is awake but too groggy to speak. McNeal has a fractured pelvis and likely has damage to her liver, spleen, kidneys, and appendix.

In the meantime, Poulin is escorted to an unoccupied office. Keenan has told him to call as many of the other Flyers players as he can reach. He sits at a desk and begins the excruciating task. Many are still sleeping off their celebration at the Coliseum, and Poulin has a tough time getting them to grasp what's going on. On more than one occasion, Poulin has to repeat the information several times to make others understand the gravity of the situation. Raising his voice, he says, "No, listen to me! You have to come here to JFK Hospital as fast as you can!" He also phones his wife, Kim, with an update. He tells her that he's left messages for some of the players whom he couldn't speak to, and instructed them to call her as soon as they can. Poulin recalls two decades later, "After awhile, I became numb to the phone calls. I focused on making sure I got in contact with everyone, explaining the situation and making sure everybody got to the hospital."

News of the accident has already filtered to the local media. A man identifying himself as a Voorhees policeman has called WIP radio and the station calls Flyers' play-by-play announcer Gene Hart for confirmation. As recounted in Hart's book, *Score! My Twenty-Five Years with the Broad Street Bullies*, the conversation goes as follows: "Gene, this is John Paul Weber at WIP. Do you know anything about Lindbergh being involved in an accident?" "No, why do you ask?" replies Hart. "Someone claiming to be a policeman from South Jersey said he saw his Porsche all smashed up." "I'll call around and check into it,' says Hart. He calls Dr. Ed Viner, the Flyers' team physician. The doctor confirms that there's been an accident and that it's extremely serious. Hart, who'd recently been through bypass surgery, goes over to Kennedy Hospital, where he finds Ed Snider, assistant John Brogan, Keenan, Craven, and Tocchet. Other Flyers' players arrive shortly thereafter. Several are on the brink of tears and look at the ground. Young forward Peter Zezel is already weeping as he enters. He embraces Keenan and buries his head on the coach's shoulder.

Jack Prettyman drives Pelle's family to the hospital in his unmarked police car. Along the way, he tells Kerstin all the details he knows: Pelle's car drove into a wall on Somerdale Road. He's breathing via a respirator, his leg is shattered, other bones are broken, but the policeman doesn't know his prognosis for living. "I thought to myself, there's hope. If anyone can pull through this and be OK, it's Pelle. He just has to," Kerstin remembers. She then turns to the back seat and translates for Anna-Lisa and Göran.

By the time the family arrives at JFK Hospital, Pelle is undergoing the CAT scan. Prettyman presents the family to the attending physicians and the family is led to a waiting room. They see Keenan and ask how Pelle is doing. "It doesn't look good," he says softly. Kerstin asks Keenan a question he can't possibly answer. She wants to know if Pelle will be able to regain a decent quality of life. "Pelle is in God's hands now," Keenan replies. His words are intended to be soothing but they upset Kerstin. She wails in protest and runs out of the building into the parking lot. Keenan calls after her but she ignores him. He follows her outside, but Kerstin cuts him off and says she doesn't want to hear any more. Keenan nods and stands quietly nearby. The sorrow and pain are suffocating in the early morning air.

Philadelphia Inquirer hockey writer Al Morganti has received an early phone call about the accident from an anonymous tipster. "You should go to the hospital," the man says. "He's over at Cooper." Based on this information, Morganti goes over to Cooper, only to discover that Lindbergh has been taken instead to JFK. He gets into his BMW and drives to the other hospital. Fortunately, traffic is light. Morganti is the first journalist to get there and a guard near the entrance stops him. Kerstin notices this and waves him in. "He's OK," she says to the guard. Morganti steps inside and speaks first to Pelle's fiancée. "Kerstin, I want you to know that I'm not here as a reporter. I'm here as Pelle's friend. Is there anything I can do to help?" Morganti and Kerstin take an elevator to the third floor and they go to the waiting room. Anna-Lisa and Göran are already sitting on couches in front of the room's stark white walls.

Time passes and there's still no update on Pelle. The wait is agonizing as everyone sits anguishing over what might be going on. A few minutes after 9:00 am, a doctor enters. He's the orthopedic surgeon who examined Pelle. With Morganti standing nearby, the doctor tells Kerstin in technical terms that Pelle's lower leg has two severe breaks and that he's also suffered a fractured hip and jaw. Although Kerstin speaks fluent English, she's far too upset to concentrate on the terminology. Morganti helps her translate by putting everything in the simplest possible words. "So what type of rehabilitation does Pelle need to do to play hockey again?" the doctor is asked. The doctor frowns and turns to Kerstin. He says nothing for several seconds. "I'm only an orthopedic surgeon. Do you understand or not?" "Understand what?" Morganti asks. "I'm only talking about the broken bones. I have to send in someone else to evaluate the rest," responds the doctor. Before leaving, he tells the family that Pelle is in critical condition and no further information will be available until the neurologist gets the results of the CAT scan. The wait is interminable as the family sits for another hour.

Thomas Eriksson sits in a car with trainer Dave "Sudsy" Settlemyre.

Like several others, they've been mistakenly sent to Cooper Hospital only to be redirected to JFK. Eriksson's mind is still reeling from the news of the crash. Of all the players on the Flyers, he's known Pelle the longest. When Eriksson first heard of the crash, it took several minutes to wrap his head around the idea that Pelle was in the hospital after having just seen him a few hours earlier. The Swedish defenseman shakes his head ruefully as the first teardrops roll down his chin and neck. Trying to compose himself and think positively as he enters JFK Hospital, he sees Keenan near the entrance. The information he gets from the coach quickly dashes his hopes.

Eriksson is brought upstairs to the third floor to wait with Pelle's family. After consoling Kerstin and Anna-Lisa, he briefly excuses himself to call Pelle Eklund. The rookie forward leaves immediately for the 30-minute drive from his new home to the hospital.

Settlemyre remains with Keenan and the players gathered on the first floor. Jack Prettyman waits on the first floor, too. He knows many of the acute-care workers at the hospital and assists Keenan and the other team leaders by becoming the frontline communications link between the Philadelphia Flyers and hospital personnel.

Dave Poulin's next phone call is made to Rich Sutter, who lives just across the artificial lake from Pelle. On several occasions, Rich would hit golf balls over the water from his side of the lake, and aim them at the back of Pelle's house. Lindbergh would then try to return the favor. It has become a running joke. On a daily basis, the Sutters trade good-natured locker room barbs with Pelle about each other's habits and tastes but none of it was ever meant seriously. In reality, both Rich and Ron had grown close to Pelle and Kerstin, and Lindbergh knows that the brothers would be among the first to come to his aid if he ever needed them whether it be on or off the ice. As soon as Rich Sutter hears Poulin's voice, he immediately says, "It's about

Gump, right?" "Yes," Poulin responds. "I'm coming right over. How's he doing?" says Sutter, who has just woken up. "We're waiting to find out," Poulin says. After contacting or leaving messages for every player on the team, Poulin calls associate club personnel, such as assistant trainer Kurt Mundt. "But we saw him just a little while ago," a surprised Mundt says. "He was fine." The suddenness with which life can be irrevocably altered hits Mundt all at once. Just a few hours ago, he was saying goodnight to Pelle. He's still not ready to say goodbye.

JFK hospital is rapidly becoming a morbid circus scene as the morning hours pass. Reports of the accident are all over the local media now and a crowd of concerned Flyers' fans, many of whom are crying, some bearing hastily made "Get well, Pelle" signs and decked out in Flyers jerseys, have begun to gather outside the hospital. Most stand or sit quietly, in their efforts to comfort each other. Several curiosity-seekers attempt to sneak into the hospital past security and they are unceremoniously escorted out.

In the hospital entryway, Mike Keenan speaks briefly to the media, who are then shuffled into the cafeteria to await further updates. "We can only pray he survives," Keenan tells reporters. "Right now, he's playing the toughest game of his life."

It's nearly 10:00 am and Pelle's family members are still awaiting another update on his condition, and are trying to hold onto a sliver of hope that he might pull through. The neurologist enters the room and his face is grim. He says that trauma to Pelle's brain stem has deprived him of the oxygen he needs for cognitive functioning. In simpler terms, he's brain dead but can breathe with the assistance of the respirator.

A nurse enters and approaches Kerstin. She gives Pelle's fiancée a small box containing the gold ring he got after winning the 1980 Olympic bronze medal with Team Sweden, his necklace, and his watch. Until now, Kerstin has felt like she in the midst of a bad dream from which she'll eventually wake up and find Pelle next to her. She now realizes that the man she loves is gone forever. She weeps uncontrollably, and lays her head on Anna-Lisa's knee. Pelle's mother is also crying as she holds onto Kerstin's head and rocks back and forth.

It is early afternoon in Sweden as the country celebrates its version of Father's Day. Pelle's older sisters Ann-Louise and Ann-Christine are visiting Sigge with their children. They drink coffee, dip bread, and chat amiably. Part of the conversation is about Anna-Lisa and Göran's visit to Philadelphia. Sigge talks to Pelle on the phone so often that it's no surprise when the phone rings. They're expecting him to call to wish Sigge a Happy Father's Day and to ask Ann-Christine how she's feeling now that she seems to be winning her battle with cancer. Ann-Christine answers and it is Göran on the other end of the line. "I need to speak to Ann-Louise," he says gravely. Chaos and anguish ensue as the sisters are unsure whether it would better if they stay with their father or take their young children home. Meanwhile, Ann-Louise and Göran's 14-year-old daughter, Anna, are the last to arrive at the Lindbergh's apartment on Barnängsgatan. She's come via subway after hearing what happened. "He can't be left alone," Anna says. The rest of the day is filled with tears and stress. After the initial shock waves, the focus shifts to hurriedly planning a trip to Philadelphia for Sigge to see his son at the hospital. He hasn't renewed his passport and it's Sunday.

CHAPTER 12

STOCKHOLM, SWEDEN, SEPTEMBER 4, 1980

Today is a day that 21-year-old Pelle Lindbergh has worked toward for many years. He's got a plane ticket to fly from Arlanda Airport in Stockholm to the United States to attend his first training camp with the Philadelphia Flyers. He's not standing restlessly in the vestibule of his family's apartment building on Barnängsgatan, with his suitcases in hand. Despite frequent reminders from his mother, he's found reasons to delay the task and hasn't even packed yet.

Two days before Pelle's scheduled departure, the *Aftonbladet* newspaper visited the Lindbergh home. A photographer snapped a photo of him standing in his bedroom, which he's turned into a hockey shrine. In the photo, Pelle stands next to a poster of Bernie Parent and other goaltending legends taped to the door.

Now Anna-Lisa Lindbergh stands in Pelle's bedroom as she packs his suitcases with him looking over her shoulder. "Mama, I have to have that," he says. "And that. And that over there." "Are you going to America? Or am I?" she asks.

Pelle is the first to admit that he's not very well prepared to live away from home for the first extended period of time for he still relies heavily on Anna-Lisa to take care of his needs. To the newspaper writer he remarks,"The hockey will probably take care of itself. That's not really what I'm nervous about. But the thought of cleaning, washing dishes, and taking care of my own household, well, I'm not trained for that. ...I'm beginning to

Pelle received a warm welcome from his family after returning from the 1980 Olympics and World Championships. [Courtesy Ann-Louise Hörnestam]

understand how good I have it at home." When the discussion turns back to hockey and Bernie Parent, Pelle immediately brightens. "It's unbelievable. All these years I've tried to be like him and suddenly we're part of the same club. What a feeling!"

At the Eriksson family's home, Thomas Eriksson is ready to go. Pelle and he meet at the airport. Once Pelle and Thomas check in, their families see them off with a touch of sadness, and even greater pride and optimism. Pelle gives long hugs to Anna-Lisa and Sigge, and an even longer hug to Kerstin. Thomas is waiting for him by the time he finishes his goodbyes. They fly SAS Airlines to New York. The flight itself is smooth, but things get bumpy upon their arrival at JFK Airport. "It became a hassle when we landed at JFK. We hardly knew how we'd change terminals with so much baggage. The guy who helped us gave us a nasty look. We didn't know we were supposed to tip him, and he was probably expecting one," Eriksson recalls.

The duo takes a connecting flight to Boston, where they're met by Flyers' representatives. They check into a Holiday Inn near the training facility in Portland, Maine and two days later, rookie camp gets underway. "Tough start," Eriksson says. "After the first camp it was time for the full preseason camp." Pelle is one of nine goalies and 60 players at Coach Pat Quinn's camp, but Lindbergh isn't bothered by the lack of attention from Quinn. He's decided it will take at least a three-year commitment to get the Flyers' starting job. For now, he needs to be patient. Pete Peeters, coming off an all-star season and a run to the Stanley Cup finals as a rookie, has earned the starting spot. The team also has veteran Phil Myre, who started out the 1979-80 season as the starter, but was outplayed by Peeters. Lindbergh stands little chance of earning a spot on the NHL roster.

Almost immediately, Pelle sees that he's going to have to make positional adjustments to the smaller North American rink. The shots come in faster and players are more likely to shoot from odd angles, as they hope to get rebounds or to sneak the puck in the short side. Attackers are more likely to crash into the goalie or stand directly in front, and try to block the keeper's line of view. With less room behind the net than on international rinks, pucks are more likely to come out quickly in the slot.

Goaltending coaches Jacques Plante and Bernie Parent split the chores of working with the cadre of keepers at the camp. During his stint with AIK, Lindbergh wasn't always the most attentive pupil, but he stands in awe of the two goaltending legends at the Flyers' camp. One of the first pieces of advice that Lindbergh receives from Parent is that he needs to rely less on his reflexes and more on cutting down the angles. They do a lot of work on adjusting his play around the crease. "You're a great skater, much better than me," Parent says to him in their first session together. "You're gonna have no problem moving when you need to, but right now you're back a little too deep. If you come out and cut down the angle a little more, even if the pass goes across, you're gonna have a good chance to recover with the way you move."

Lindbergh also begins the laborious process of improving his puckhandling – a skill that few Swedish goaltenders practiced in this era. Pelle realizes he has some catching up to do, and puts in extra time each day to work on stopping the puck, getting it safely to his defenseman, and quickly getting back in the crease. "It's no big secret how much Pelle respected Bernie Parent. If Bernie had told him to stand on his head, he would have done that," recalls longtime Flyers defenseman Joe Watson.

The team plays its first preseason game on September 15 against the Boston Bruins and both Lindbergh and Eriksson are in the lineup. They're nervous, and it shows. "Damn, what a catastrophe that was," Eriksson remembers. "It was the first time we wore a Flyers uniform and it was a total disaster for both of us." Lindbergh gets beat for seven goals in a 9-2 loss. Eriksson is out on the ice for five of the Bruins goals. The team as a whole plays poorly but the goaltender and defenseman are two of the prime culprits. "We were both lousy and didn't feel very good about it afterwards. But all we could do was pick ourselves up. Although it really couldn't go any worse, things began horribly for us as Flyers," Eriksson says. To the surprise of no one, the Flyers soon assign Lindbergh and Eriksson to the team's American

Hockey League affiliate, the Maine Mariners.

As the season gets underway, Pelle feels homesick and misses Kerstin terribly. He makes almost daily long-distance calls to her in Sweden and the bills quickly become expensive. "Pelle always called collect, because that was the easiest way. In the end, I couldn't pay all the charges, so he sent me home to his parents who paid the difference for him," she recalls.

In October, Kerstin travels to New York with the Swedish wind surfing team on a trip that ultimately took them to the Wind Surfing World Championships in the Bahamas. Pelle asks the Flyers for permission to take a short leave of absence from the Mariners to see his girlfriend. He gets the go-ahead with no hassle, an indication of just how highly the organization regards him and understands that it would take a little time until he got settled. "It felt like a big deal, because it was my first visit to the U.S, and Pelle had hardly seen New York, either. We were up in the World Trade Center and did some other sightseeing," Kerstin says.

After a week in the Bahamas, Kerstin returns to the United States and stays with Pelle in Portland, Maine. She also accompanies the team on one of its road trips and travels by bus from town to town. "My memories are vague about where we went, but I remember we went to Rochester and some smaller towns," she recalls. "It was overcast or snowy and kind of miserable. I was the only woman on the bus. I felt a little out of place, but Pelle was happy and we were in love. He played very well when I was there."

On Thursday, October 30, the Mariners have a road game against the Rochester Americans. Kerstin is in the stands and Pelle has a strong performance in goal. What makes this game notable is the presence of two strangers who will later play central roles in Pelle's life. The opposition head coach, in his first season as a coach at the professional level, is 31-year-old Mike Keenan. Up in the stands, on the opposite end from Kerstin's section, is the Notre Dame Fighting Irish hockey team. Among the Notre Dame players is a 21-year-old junior center by the name of Dave Poulin.

Rochester dominates the game, but Maine wins 5-2. Up in the stands, Poulin and his teammates can't stop talking about the play of Lindbergh, who is making extremely difficult saves look routine. "Honestly, we wondered, 'Who the hell is that goalie? He's ridiculously good," Poulin recalls.

The Maine Mariners are coached by Bob "Cagey" McCammon. He spent his decade-long playing career in the minor leagues with the Port Huron Flags of the International Hockey League. In 1973-74, McCammon retired to become the team's head coach. Three seasons later, he left to take over as the Mariners' coach and guided the team to the Calder Cup. When legendary coach Fred Shero left the Flyers for the New York Rangers after the 1977-78 season, Philadelphia promoted the 37-year-old McCammon to replace Shero. It soon became clear that McCammon wasn't yet ready to coach in the NHL and he lasted only 50 games – posting a 22-17-11 record. He was demoted back to the AHL, and swapped jobs with Mariners head coach Pat Quinn.

In the fall of 1980, an influx of young players arrives. In addition to Pelle and Eriksson, the club features dipsy-doodling forward Ron Flockhart, Lindsay Carson, former collegiate star Mark Taylor, and 1979 second-round pick Blake Wesley. Pelle isn't really all that comfortable yet around any of his North American teammates, because his English skills still need to be polished. "Pelle didn't say much in the beginning," McCammon remembers. "But we noticed quickly that he had good self-confidence. He wanted to play all the time, but I reminded him often that he was only a rookie and he had to be patient. He was persistent, and he became a hell of a good goalie."

For the first few weeks of the season, Lindbergh and Eriksson live in a Portland hotel at the club's expense, which includes food and cleaning services. The stay is extended another two weeks, but the Swedes are told they need to find their own place as soon as possible. "We said, 'What? How do we do that?' We had no idea of how to go about it," says Eriksson. "But fortunately we got help finding some contacts and in the end we found a house we could rent by the beach. As a pro player, you make a good salary, but you have to keep in mind that we were newly arrived from Europe and there was a bit of difference from things at home. We were the last of all the players on the Mariners to find a house." For awhile, Pelle and Thomas have a third housemate – French-Canadian goaltender Sam St. Laurent, who spends a brief stint with the Mariners as the team's third goaltender before returning to the IHL's Toledo Gold Diggers.

The antique, two-story wooden beach house is located on the Prouts Neck peninsula, a seasonal community, with a view of the Atlantic Ocean. Life in the yellow-painted house is quite an experience for the two Swedish rookies. "It was the type of house you see in horror movies, with an empty, wind-swept beach," Kerstin recalls. Neither Pelle nor Thomas know they have to call to arrange for electricity, water, telephones and other daily necessities. They figure it out before too long.

At home in Stockholm, Lindbergh and Eriksson rarely hang out together, but they grow close as teammates and housemates during the season. "We were close friends, but we were very different as people. Pelle was crazy extroverted and spontaneous, but I was a lot more measured and private. When I look back, though, I don't think we ever had an argument, not even once. Sharing a house was never a problem," Eriksson says. Pelle is glad to have Eriksson around, but he misses his friends from home, especially after Kerstin returns to Sweden. To lessen the homesickness, he invites childhood friend Björn Neckman to come visit him in Portland. Björn thought the visit would last about two weeks, but he ends up staying for two years. "That was how it was with Pelle, it was very spontaneous. He didn't ask, he just said ,'Come hang out' and that was that. Pelle was very keen on having someone to help him with daily life in America. He wasn't so good with English in the beginning and there was a lot of paperwork to do, things like insurance and such," says Neckman.

In the early days in Portland, however, Pelle rarely ventures far from the house. One of the first North Americans he befriends is Mariners' trainer Dave "Sudsy" Settlemyre. The two discuss goaltending frequently and debate the merits of different equipment. "I never got him to get rid of all that homemade equipment he got in Stockholm. I tried, because I thought we had better and more protective gear, but Pelle refused," Settlemyre says.

Kevin Cady, the Mariners' assistant equipment manager who later becomes the Flyers' head equipment manager, befriends both players. He laughs when he's asked to compare the two Swedes. "Both were good guys, but as different as two men can be. Pelle was more of a party guy with tremendous self-confidence and Thomas preferred to sit at home by an open fireplace and read a big, thick book," Cady says.

As far as Pelle is concerned, every day is an adventure, a new arena, a new opponent, a new discovery off the ice. The roads are unfamiliar, and he loves to explore. One of the advantage of living in the community after Labor Day is that he doesn't have to deal with slow-moving cars clogging up the lanes.

The restaurants in the States all serve portions that take up the whole plate. And he's never seen a drive-through in Sweden. In a time before hockey players became hyper-aware of their diets, Pelle takes many greasy drive-through meals back with him in his car before the novelty wears off.

With new friends on the Mariners, Kerstin and his family just a phone call away, and Eriksson and Neckman at the house, Pelle feels more and more comfortable in Portland. The adjustment takes longer for Eriksson. "Everything was so different over there, and I was extremely homesick the first year. Not for the hockey's sake, but for everything else I left at home. With Pelle, the adjustment was lightning quick," Eriksson recalls. Hockey, of course, remains the top priority for both rookies. "Our days were very much routine-oriented," Eriksson says. "There was practice, a nap, and a meal on the same schedule almost every day."

But Pelle still feels occasional pangs of longing for home, especially when his Stockholm buddies tease him about everything he's missing. Christmas also presents a challenge and Pelle decides to celebrate a traditional Swedish Christmas or as close to one as he can manage. Swedes hold their primary Christmas celebration on December 24 (*julafton*), and Lindbergh follows the tradition he's grown up with. He has his gift exchange and Christmas dinner with as many Swedish Christmas foods as possible, such as a specially cured ham (*julskinka*), lye-soaked cod (*lutfisk*), and rice porridge (*risgrynsgröt*). Another custom Pelle brings from home is having everyone at the dinner table dip pieces of bread in broth left over after boiling the ham. This ia a tradition known as "a dip in the kettle" (*dopp i grytan*), and becomes an annual ritual throughout his career in the AHL and NHL.

Throughout the rest of the year, Pelle takes whatever little comforts from home he can manage. Kerstin, who is a year older than Pelle, is back home studying. The six-hour time difference limits some of his opportunities to call, so he has to be content with some of the things he's brought along from Stockholm, especially his cassettes of Swedish music and comedy. "You become extremely patriotic when you're living far from home," Neckman explains.

Pelle's accent is a source of amusement and imitation for his Mariners teammates. One day on the bus, he asks teammate Doug Gillen if it would be possible to get some batteries for his newly purchased Walkman. Teammate Greg Adams overhears. "Hey, Gilly, would eet bay poo-si-ble to get some batt-err-ees?" Adams parrots in a mock Swedish accent. Rather than being self-conscious, Pelle laughs along with everyone else. He repeats the question, this time intentionally exaggerating his pronunciation and sending everyone into fits of laughter. In reality, Pelle's English improves quickly. Before long, his charm and sense of humor help him bridge any cultural gaps.

There is a large measure of turnover on an AHL roster over the course of a season but the Mariners have a relatively stable nucleus. They are one of the best teams in the AHL. The Flyers invest more in the upkeep of their farm team, both in terms of on-ice and off-ice resources, than contempory Swedish Elite league franchises spend on their own senior teams. The Mariners dominate the Northern Division, and only the Southern Division leading Hershey Bears have a deeper and more talented lineup.

Pelle has never been a stickler for hard conditioning. His legs are thick and powerful but he more or less eats what he pleases and doesn't enjoy weight training or riding a stationary bike. He stays in shape via lots of game action, but Pelle soon realizes that the marathon-like North American hockey season is much more physically demanding than the season at home. Like every AHL team, Maine plays a schedule based on the NHL model. Including playoffs and preseason, the team can play upwards of 100 games per season. On a typical day without a game, McCammon has the players report for practice at 10 am and remain on the ice for 60 to 90 minutes. Pelle is not above cutting corners at practice. Kevin Cady recalls, "Pelle really hated to practice. He came out at the last moment and took his time putting on his equipment. Often, he'd oversleep."

After practice, Pelle loves to gab with his teammates. By lunchtime, the arena empties and the players are free until the next morning's practice. One of the most popular postgame watering holes for the Mariners players is a place called F. Parker Reidy's Bar and Restaurant. Another is Caps, which is owned by veteran forward Gordie Clark and 30-year-old defenseman, Dennis Patterson. At both places, the prime spots at the bar are reserved for a small group of older players who are regulars.

"Caps was in the vicinity of the rink, and there were a lot of guys on the team who often went directly to the bar after practice and games," Eriksson recalls, "there were guys in the clique who never did anything other than train, play hockey, and sit at the bar. They were more or less alcoholics." Just as he does in Stockholm, Pelle loves to hang out at the hot spots with them. After home games at the Civic Center, many of the players frequent an after-hours nightclub called The Max, which stays open until 5 am and is hopping with a younger crowd in the late night hours. The club does not have an after-hours liquor license, so it allows customers to bring their own booze and beer. One night, the Mariners players elect the rookie goaltender to provide the post-game refreshments.

Lindbergh goes above and beyond the call. With help from Björn Neckman, he buys a full keg of beer and loads it into his car. The owners let him back the car up to the service entrance and set up for the post-game party. Pelle stays out with the group and has a blast, but hardly drinks himself. "That was typical Pelle to get a whole keg for the guys," Neckman says. "But I don't think we had more than two mugs of beer ourselves. We just offered it around and hung out."

On game days, Pelle invariably follows the same routine, and abstains completely from alcohol the night before. He takes a nap at the same time, wakes up at the same time, and eats the same meal - a big steak covered in ketchup and a side of macaroni, usually washed down with a glass of milk. After games, both home and road, Pelle goes out with teammates for dinner.

When the Mariners are on a road trip, they quickly pack up all their equipment and climb aboard the team bus. The trips, sometimes taking up to 15 hours, can be endless and dull. When Pelle wants a little peace and quiet, he listens to his Walkman, although he rarely plays it quietly. His regular selections include Alice Cooper, the Rolling Stones, and Elton John. Every once in awhile, he even reads a book, usually Stephen King or Swedish novels sent from home.

There are two big ice boxes on board the bus, containing beer and soft drinks. During especially long trips, the players may get ham and cheese sandwiches to satisfy their hunger. Otherwise, they have to use some of their $25 a day meal money (it's $37.50 in the NHL). For accommodations, the team usually stays at budget hotels and players room together in twos. Despite the long bus rides and frat-house behavior, players are required to wear suits and ties when traveling. Pelle doesn't particularly understand or like the dress code, but he complies.

In general, McCammon runs a much looser ship than Pelle later experiences under the hyper-organized, hyper-controlling Mike Keenan. McCammon could be very blunt with players. He seems to have a knack for putting his foot in his mouth, but he wasn't intentionally mean-spirited. At least with Maine, McCammon's approach works. The team takes winning seriously, and is usually successful. In the NHL, McCammon does not prove to be nearly as successful.

Early in the season, opposing players attempt to break Pelle's concentration by bumping into him or giving him gratuitous shots with their sticks. The 6-foot-2, 210-pound defenseman Glen Cochrane soon puts a stop to it.

On one occasion, Springfield Indians center Derek Haas intentionally gives Lindbergh a shower by snow-plowing with his skates as the goalie covers the puck in the crease. Even before Pelle can look up and bark at Haas, Cochrane already has the gloves off and pummels the forward with lefts and rights. "Thanks, Cocher," Pelle says after the game. Cochrane winks.

In a 1984 interview, Pelle responds to a question about fighting in hockey, "I leave the fighting to the big guys." In reality, he gets involved in several line brawls during his AHL and NHL career, by going after the opposing goaltender in the midst of numerous battles erupting. The fighting in North American hockey doesn't bother Lindbergh a bit. "I remember that Pelle dropped the gloves a few times with the other team's goaltender," Kerstin says. "He never started a fight, but he got involved a couple times when he was supposed to take his man. It happened."

Pelle's enthusiasm for these situations earned him teasing from those who knew him best. Former *Philadelphia Inquirer* writer Al Morganti says that Lindbergh loved to talk about the fights that happened during a game. "Pelle thought it was as cool as could be. He fought a few times himself, both with the Mariners and later with the Flyers. He could come flying across the ice at the other goalie, and we'd bust his chops about it afterwards. It didn't happen often, but it happened a few times," says Morganti.

By wearing jersey number 1 in honor of Parent, Lindbergh quickly becomes a fan favorite at the Civic Center. "Pelle was almost like a king in Philadelphia later on, but he was 10 times bigger in Portland, where absolutely everyone knew who he was," Eriksson recalls. Every game, the chants of "Pell-lee, Pell-lee, Pell-lee" that will later fill the Philadelphia Spectrum ring out among the 7,000 spectators at the Civic Center. In Philly, Pelle hears his fair share of boos during his horrendous second NHL season. In Portland, no one can remember Lindbergh getting booed even once. "Pelle really connected with the Mariners fans. He was such a charismatic guy in addition to being a tremendous goaltender, and the fans in Maine already knew that they were looking at a guy who was going to go places," Cady says.

Shortly after Pelle and Eriksson moved to Maine, they bought matching Corvettes with their signing bonuses. "It cost us half of our salaries for the year, but it was worth it. Pelle and I both loved sports cars, and it was a dream to get a Corvette," Eriksson recalls. "But we quickly became well-known by the police." On occasion, however, Pelle is unable to talk himself out of trouble. He ends up getting arrested. Both Lindbergh and Eriksson are stopped for speeding by the Portland police any number of times. For Pelle, it's a fairly regular occurrence but he's almost always able to charm his way out

Pelle after getting arrested for his driving habits [Courtesy Kerstin Somnell]

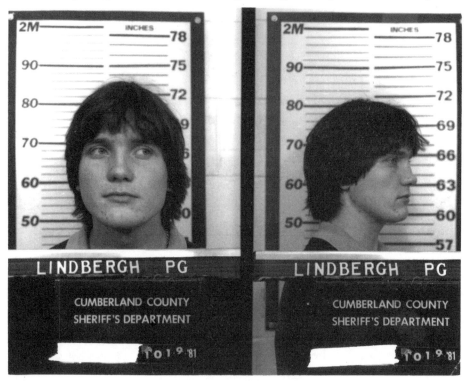

of a ticket, even when he drives 30 or more miles per hour above the speed limit. "The Mariners players, including myself, were able to get away with a warning for speeding. It wasn't like that at home in Sweden, where we were treated like anyone else by the police," says Eriksson. "A lot of the cops were buddies with Pelle, or at least recognized him. He always made friends with police offers, and later hung out with some of them," Neckman remembers.

After some time passes, Pelle's parents are able to visit and stay for two weeks. It's their first trip to the USA. During the trip, the family celebrates Anna-Lisa's 60th birthday together, and Pelle introduces his parents to his teammates. The Mariners players are a little surprised when they meet Sigge. Pelle often described his father to teammates as a "big, strong sailor with broad shoulders, who risked his life doing dangerous work at sea and on the docks." The man they meet is 64 years old, shorter than Pelle, and narrow shouldered. He's nervous and shy around the American and Canadian players. At first glance, the elder Lindbergh even seems frail, although his handshake reveals he's more powerful than he looks.

"Typical Pelle to reel in his teammates like that," Neckman laughs. "But it was actually pretty cool." In Pelle's eyes, Sigge is exactly as he describes him, because he more or less still sees his father the same way he did as a boy. In fact, a big part of what endears Pelle to everyone who meets him is that his world view and perspectives on the people near and dear to him scarcely change over the years. His boyish innocence is never forced or phony. The outgoing Anna-Lisa doesn't understand a word anyone says, but wants to communicate and constantly asks Pelle to translate. But Sigge blushes, sweats, and hardly says a word. In later years, he's perfectly content to keep in touch with Pelle by telephone.

On February 11, 1981, Bob McCammon calls Thomas Eriksson into his office after practice. With a little trepidation, Eriksson follows the coach.

"Pack your bags," McCammon says. "You're going to Philadelphia. The Flyers need you for two games." McCammon goes on to explain that Flyers defenseman Behn Wilson has been suspended, and the club is calling up Eriksson to fill in on the blueline. The following night, Eriksson becomes the first European player to play a regular season game for the Flyers. The Flyers win, 4-3 and Eriksson winds up staying with the big club the rest of the season. He posts one powerplay goal, 10 assists, 11 points, and a plus-four rating in 24 games. He also dresses in every game of the Flyers' first-round playoff victory over the Quebec Nordiques and the first two games of the team's seven-game loss to the Calgary Flames.

"Pelle didn't seem angry at all that I was called up before he was," Eriksson remembers. "He knew he'd get a chance. It was just a matter of when management and the coaches would do it."

Pelle remains with the Mariners the rest of the season. He sweeps all of the AHL's major awards, by winning the Les Cunningham Award as league MVP, the Hap Holmes Award as the league's top goaltender, the Red Garrett Memorial Award as rookie of the year and first-team all-star honors. More importantly, the team advances to the Calder Cup finals after downing Springfield and New Brunswick in hard-fought, seven-game series. In the finals against the underdog Adirondack Red Wings, Pelle sustains a knee injury in the fourth game. He plays through it, but his performance is subpar. "I couldn't stop a thing," Pelle later recounts in a 1985 report aired on Swedish television.

The series is tied two games apiece heading into game five. But Adirondack, two nights after getting crushed by a 10-1 score, downs the Mariners at the Civic Center, 6-4. In the deciding game, the Red Wings prevail, 5-2. On the chartered flight home from the final game in Adirondack, Pelle tries to lighten his dark mood. He asks the flight attendant if he can use the cabin microphone. He proceeds to give a long speech, entirely in Swedish. The speech is a stream-of-consciousness monologue peppered with various swear words. In the back of the plane, Kevin Cady (whom Pelle has taught some Swedish) starts to laugh. Sitting next to Cady is Bruce "Scoop" Cooper, a veteran broadcast statistician, publicist, and game-program feature writer, who was doing some work for the *Portland Press Herald* at the time. "What on earth is he talking about?" Cooper asks. "I know what he's saying. Right now he's talking about the stewardesses," Cady says, translating some of the raunchier words that the smiling Swede speaks to his teammates.

Pelle Lindbergh

CHAPTER 13

SUNDAY, NOVEMBER 10, 1985, 10:30 AM

Amidst the grief over Pelle's hopeless condition, the news on his two injured passengers becomes more encouraging as the day progresses. Kathy McNeal is in serious but stable condition at Kennedy Hospital, and is being operated on to repair a fractured pelvis and damaged liver and spleen. Her post-operative prognosis is good. Over at Cooper Medical Center, Ed Parvin Jr. undergoes a complicated skull operation that takes eight hours. Once it's successfully completed, his life is out of immediate danger.

When Pelle Eklund arrives at the hospital and parks his car, he wades through the chaotic scene outside. He's waved inside, walks past the guard posted at the entrance, and begins to get a sense of the gravity of the situation; it's much more serious than he originally anticipated. He sees Ed Snider and other members of the owner's family, as well as Bob Clarke and Keith Allen, who have just arrived from Boston. As Clarke embraces Eklund, the player knows he's about to receive terrible news. Mike Keenan puts his arm around Eklund and tells him they just found out from team doctor Ed Viner that Pelle will not survive the crash. Eklund's first reaction is one of denial. "I remember thinking that there has to be a way they can help Pelle. There has to be," he recalls.

Nearby, numerous Flyers players stand weeping. Among others, Tim Kerr breaks down as soon as he hears the news, and Ilkka and Carin Sinisalo are both crying as they try to comfort one another. Even the stoic Brad McCrimmon can't hold back the tears. With the help of Jack Prettyman, the entire Flyers contingent is brought to a semi-private waiting room to the left of the entrance. There they can grieve among themselves without onlookers gawking at them.

On the third floor, Kerstin, Anna-Lisa, Göran, and Thomas Eriksson are in the throes of grief. A choked-up Al Morganti feels as though he's intruding as he witnesses their agony and despair, a sight that will forever haunt him even more than the realization that Pelle is gone. Morganti excuses himself, so that Pelle's family and dear friend can be together. He embraces Kerstin, and heads downstairs to join other members of the media and to seek out the comfort of other members of the Flyers' family. Morganti vows never to write a newspaper account of what he witnessed during his time with the family. He told Kerstin that he had come as Pelle's friend and not as a reporter, and stands by it in the years to come. The family placed its trust in him in its darkest hour and he honors that trust.

Bob Froese hasn't heard the news yet because he didn't go out with the others after the game. He was tired and wanted to be able to get up early for church. This morning he has been at church with his wife, Ruth, and sons, Robbie and David. While he's there, he gets a handwritten note from a church official with a message from Kim Poulin: "Call me immediately." When he calls back, he learns that Pelle has a severe leg fracture, but doesn't know that Pelle is brain-dead. He later regrets the first thought that comes to his mind: "I guess this means I'm going to play more now." Later Froese drives to JFK, where he sees Dave Poulin who gets in the car and sits in the passenger seat. "He's dead," Poulin says. When the initial shock subsides, Froese feels horrible for having placed his desire to be a starting goalie ahead of his concern for his teammate's well being.

Anna-Lisa speaks on the phone with Sigge, Ann-Louise, and Ann-Christine. The conversation is short and focuses on how quickly Sigge can get to Philadelphia. With help from Kerstin's mother, Gudrun Pietzsch, and

Thomas Eriksson's mother, Margareta, the family contacts the American Embassy to explain why Sigge needs to travel to the United States. He's granted a special visa. They also arrange for him to turn in his expired Swedish passport for a new one first thing the next morning and then take an SAS flight.

Sigge has a heart condition, which is part of why he hadn't come along with Anna-Lisa and Göran to visit Pelle. He's rarely said much about his health to Pelle, because he doesn't want his son to worry. Anna-Lisa is worried about the strain of traveling overseas, especially under such emotionally-wrenching circumstances. But there's no choice, and time is of the essence.

The doctors tell Kerstin, Anna-Lisa, Göran, and Thomas Eriksson that they can go see Pelle. They're led to the intensive care unit near the waiting room where they've been sitting for the past several hours. Pelle is lying on his back in a bed and is hooked to a respirator. His eyelids are closed and his entire left leg is in a heavy cast. He looks likes he's resting as his family members and Eriksson hold him.

At about the same time, the neurologist meets with the Flyers' leadership to inform them that Pelle's situation is hopeless. When Bernie Parent is informed, he begins to cry. He had still been clinging to the belief that Lindbergh would survive. "It's so unfair. What kind of world are we living in?" he sobs. The mood in the players' waiting room is equally somber. A doctor comes to the room and asks the team leaders which players want to come up to see Pelle one last time. Among those who go up to the third floor are Keenan, Poulin, Parent, announcer Gene Hart, and Sudsy Settlemyre. Tears stream down Settlemyre's face as he feels a wave of anger come over him. "That car," he says to no one in particular. "That goddamn car."

The media coverage continues to intensify, hour-by-hour. The crowd of reporters, cameramen and photographers is moved from the cafeteria to a trailer that functions as a make-shift news room complete with telephones and fax machines. The first press conference is held at 10:30 am and the second at noon. The first report deals only with the bone fractures.

Al Morganti sits in the room. He is aware that the doctors know more than they're saying, but he keeps silent out of respect for Kerstin and Anna-Lisa. He's still trying to come to grips with the term "brain dead" that he heard the doctor say upstairs, and the talk about broken bones seems utterly meaningless in comparison. The events of the day are wearing on Morganti. He feels fatigued and heartsick, but realizes that sooner or later he needs to compose himself enough to write something and meet his deadline at the Inquirer. He does this without revealing any of what he's seen and heard upstairs.

Morganti stays around until the second press conference. Dr. Ed Viner, flanked by Keenan and Flyers' spokesman Rodger Gottlieb, enters the room and approaches the podium, "Pelle is on a respirator and has gotten as much help as possible, but his chances of recovery are practically zero," Viner explains. Keenan says, "It's with deep sadness that I must report that we've lost a person whom everyone loved, and who himself loved life. It's a terrible, terrible tragedy for everyone, first and foremost Pelle's family." Gottlieb adds, "Pelle's mother and girlfriend are grief-stricken. They can't understand the terrible thing that has happened. We share in all of their grief."

Later in the day, there's a third press conference, with Bob Clarke in attendance. Viner reveals for the first time that Pelle, like his teammates, had been out drinking after the game against the Bruins. "But we don't know how much he had to drink or whether it played a role in the accident," Viner says.

The Flyers' leadership admits that it has long been worried about Pelle's love for speed and passion for sports cars. Clarke, who once took a ride with

Pelle, knew first-hand that the young goalie was flirting with disaster. "He liked to drive fast and we told him repeatedly to slow down. But I suppose when you're young, strong, and full of life you think you're invulnerable to everything. I guess it's natural to feel that nothing can ever happen to you," Clarke says.

For his part, Morganti has difficulty accepting the idea that Pelle would drive his Porsche with alcohol in his body. "I've been out with Pelle a lot, and I mean a hell of a lot," he says to a colleague. "The guy pretty much never drank." Someone asks, "Are you just trying to protect him and his reputation?" "No! I'm not protecting him at all," Morganti shoots back. "I really mean that. We sometimes were out three nights a week and had a hell of a good time, but Pelle almost never drank anything – not a drop! He didn't need to."

Kerstin realizes that she and Anna-Lisa can only get privacy in the third-floor waiting room and nearby corridor. If they go down to the first floor, they'll be swarmed with reporters, and Kerstin will be forced to interpret for Anna-Lisa. Later, Kerstin and Anna-Lisa are escorted downstairs by a guard so they can meet with the Flyers' players and their families. Kerstin tries to be strong, and the players' wives and girlfriends come over to hug her and wipe away her tears. They also try to comfort Pelle's mother. Anna-Lisa, who appreciates the outpouring of support, cannot respond, nor does she even know who is who among the people who come to her. She's among strangers in a foreign country.

Everyone in the room is weeping, except Mike Keenan, who feels horrible and offers hugs and soothing words, but doesn't shed a tear. "I couldn't cry. I don't know why," Keenan said in a 1994 *Sporting News* article. He added that when he went through a divorce many years later, he learned that it's OK for a man to cry. He was brought up to believe it was a sign of weakness.

The news of Pelle's crash and hopeless prognosis starts to spread rapidly outside the Philadelphia area. In New York, Pelle's former Tre Kronor team-mate Tomas Jonsson hears the news via a radio report, and informs Swedish teammates Stefan Persson and Anders Kallur. In Winnipeg, Pelle's longtime friend and national team comrade Thomas Steen learns about the accident when he's approached by a TV reporter asking him about his reaction to the news about Pelle. Mats Näslund hears about it in the Montreal Canadiens locker room. He's in denial at first, and is still skeptical about the initial report of alcohol being involved in the accident. "Pelle wasn't drunk," he declares. "He was careful about that."

Hammarby's senior team is on the way home from a road game. Every-one is in good spirits when the team bus stops on the way for the team to get a bite to eat. There's a lot of friendly banter and joking as everyone goes inside. The mood turns somber just minutes later.

Childhood friend and former housemate Björn Neckman goes through a gamut of emotions in a few minutes: disbelief, panic, anger. He's unable to be consoled by his girlfriend and sits on the steps of his apartment, bawling. "Why wouldn't you listen to anyone, Pelle? It was all a big joke to you," he sobs. Later, Neckman speaks to Anna-Lisa by phone, and they cry together.

Reino Sundberg, who is playing hockey in Switzerland for EHC Arosa, doesn't hear the news until late in the evening. He's called by a Swedish reporter who knows how close he is with Pelle. All at once, his world collapses.

CHAPTER 14

STOCKHOLM, SWEDEN, JUNE, 1981

Pelle discovered quickly during the 1980-81 season just how expensive it is to constantly call and send mail back and forth from the US to Sweden. Try as he might, he can't keep in touch with everyone.

One of the first people he catches up with when he returns home for the summer of 1981 is Swedish movie director Jan Halldoff. Two years earlier, Halldoff and Lindbergh met at a Stockholm restaurant called "Kvarnen" (The Mill). The two hit it off quickly. Halldoff discovered the national team goaltender was a real movie buff.

Apart from directing movies, Halldoff is also a screenplay writer. "Pelle, I'm a directing a movie and I think you have the perfect personality to play one of the main roles," Halldoff said. That's all Pelle needed to hear. He immediately arranged to do a test reading for the part of Magnus, a kid from the south side of Stockholm with a promising future in boxing, a girlfriend, and a love for motorcycles. The test reading was done in an apartment on Enskedsvägen. Halldoff had Pelle walk, talk, laugh on cue, and pretend to get angry. He got the part.

In the spring of 1979, after returning from the World Championships, Pelle filmed his scenes for the movie. On one of the first days, he stood outside on seedy Malmskillnadgatan as the director bribed the (real) prostitutes on the street to go away for a little while. It was necessary to shoot a scene with Pelle and professional actresses portraying hookers. If that weren't surreal enough, the real-life prostitutes were upset about being asked to move.

Thinking quickly, Halldoff came up with an alternative to giving them money to go away. "We disturbed the surroundings with our film team, and the prostitutes couldn't work the streets. So we gave them sandwiches to occupy them until we were done. Pelle took it all in stride and did a good job," Halldoff recalls.

To prepare for the role, Pelle took some boxing lessons with the BK Narva boxing club. His excellent balance and lower body power made him effective in sparring sessions despite his lack of height and reach. "Pelle had a damn good time with two scenes in the movie," Björn Neckman recalls. "One was a boxing scene. They had worked out choreography, where Pelle would hit the other guy with a left and then a right, and so on. But Pelle didn't stick to the choreography. He wanted to show off what he'd learned, and he improvised. He ended up tagging the other guy for real. They had to pay the other guy extra."

Pelle wrapped up his scenes fairly quickly and posed for some publicity stills for the movie. The film was released the following year, and premiered in Stockholm on March 7, 1980, shortly after Pelle got back from the Olympics. The movie earned lukewarm reviews and a modest haul at the box office (even by Swedish film standards). Pelle was neither shocked nor disappointed. "He thought the movie turned out so-so," Neckman recalls. "But he had fun." Lindbergh and director/writer Halldoff were friendly long after filming the movie. They got together in the summer of 1981, and every summer to follow.

When Pelle Lindbergh is home during the summer, he lives at his parents' home on Barnängsgatan, but just as frequently stays with Kerstin at her apartment at Storgatan 32 in central Stockholm. He's seldom home for every day and night is packed with activity. He's too social (and restless) to enjoy quiet time at home. "I'd think it's a little tiring to have things happening all the time. But that was Pelle," Kerstin says. "It was like that in the U.S., too. If he wasn't tired after practice, he'd come back and call up his friends at home and say, 'What's up with you?' so that he didn't miss anything. He could talk for hours on the phone when we were over there.

"When we were home in Stockholm for vacation, there were long days spent hanging out with a lot of people, because the sun was still up at night. Pelle could be very charming and romantic when he wanted to be, but we usually went out in groups most of the time." That's not to say Pelle doesn't make time to go out alone with Kerstin, but such nights usually happen spontaneously. "Pelle didn't ponder things. If there was an opportunity and if something sounded like a good idea to him, he'd say 'Why not?' and then he'd do it," explains Thomas Eriksson. "For instance, he ended up seeing an Elton John show and going backstage to meet him because, 'I like Elton John, so of course I'd like to meet him.' It wasn't something planned."

While most find Pelle's live-in-the-moment attitude endearing, he can drive some of his more deliberate (and punctual) friends nuts with his lack of time management. There are plenty of occasions where he gets so engrossed in an activity or conversation that he ends up losing track of time. "Pelle, come on already! We've got to go!" is a common refrain. "Yeah, yeah, just one more minute, OK? I'll be right there."

The same thing happens when he interacts with fans. He holds up the departure of the team bus, because he's signing autographs, posing for pictures, and chatting amiably. But no one close to him could ever stay angry at Pelle for more than a few seconds. "Pelle always attracted a crowd, and it was impossible to not have a good time when he was around," Anders "Ankan" Lånström says. "He brought the party along with him, and he had such a good time. Everything was like a big game to him, and he loved to play, off the ice as well as on." "He was still the same good guy he always was, success never went to his head," adds Stephan "Lillis" Lundh. "He was generous and accessible."

At night, Lindbergh and his contingent of friends hang out at the usual places – Bäckahästen, Martini, Daily News, or Café Opera. In the summer of 1981, like most summers, Pelle drinks his fair share of beer and orders a few gin-and-tonics. But he never drinks and drives, due to Sweden's ultra-strict laws and the zero-tolerance enforcement by the police.

Although he rarely discourages strangers from approaching him in public, there are three groups he generally ignores. The first group is a crowd of uptown types whom he had heard belittle him in the early days. They mocked him when he would tell everyone he would someday make it big and play for the Flyers. Behind his back, they called him "Farmer Pelle" for his wide-eyed naïveté and his working-class dialect that stood out like a sore thumb in some of Stockholm's newer, sophisticated hot spots. As his fame grows, many of these same people try to befriend Lindbergh, only to get snubbed. When they talk to him, he frowns and gives one-word answers. Another group that Pelle is leery of is anyone who tries to ingratiate himself with his friends in order to get close to him. Likewise, he has no interest in interacting with people who hang around him only because they want favors or money.

Lastly, while he never stops enjoying female attention, but he has no time for groupies ("puck bunnies" in North American hockey slang) who come onto him. Once he fell for Kerstin, he knew who he wanted to be with romantically. He isn't about to jeopardize her love and faith in him. If the flirting is innocent, he'll laugh along. But if it's inappropriate, he ignores the person and sometimes even walks away. "Pelle could be extremely generous with his real friends," Neckman says. "But with people who were just hangers-on, he could be ice cold and act almost put out to talk to them. That was often a very clear signal."

Pelle has always had a passion for boating, especially speed boats. Every summer, he and Kerstin attend the annual boating competition at Riddard-fjärden. Lindbergh eventually buys himself a speed boat, and spends many a summer day zipping around on his boat. He's thrilled, too, when he later learns that Bernie Parent is also a boating enthusiast.

He also spends a lot of time with his family. Sigge and Anna-Lisa have bought a small garden plot with a one-room cabin where they spend a lot of time in the summer. The small red cabin is located on Gullmarsplan, adjacent to an old gymnasium. The one-room cabin has a kitchenette and Sigge in particular spends almost all his time there during the summer. "Pelle was all around town during the days, but he knew Sigge loved to go to the cabin, so whenever he had time, Pelle would stop by just to chat with his pappa," Kerstin says.

Pelle confides in his family that he thinks he's ready to push for an NHL spot with the Flyers in the fall – two years ahead of the three-year plan he initially set. Both Sigge and Anna-Lisa shake their heads at their son's restlessness. Lindbergh also spends as much time as possible with sisters Ann-Louise and Ann-Christine and their families. A big kid at heart, he loves getting down on the floor and playing with the kids for hours on end. He also gladly volunteers to take them fishing.

Pelle is very much an old-school hockey player when it comes to his summertime training habits. He gets some daily exercise, but it's rarely strenuous. "Pelle and I mostly played badminton at Eriksdalshallen," recalls Reino Sundberg. "Pelle always won, because he never gave an inch." Apart from badminton, Pelle tries to get in some jogging during the summer. Sundberg also dons boxing gloves on occasion with Pelle for some sparring sessions at BK Narva. Sometimes they opt instead for baseball gloves and have a toss, or Pelle and his friends will get together for a friendly soccer game or street hockey. Whatever the game, Lindbergh plays to win.

Before returning to North America, Pelle volunteers his time to help out at a summer hockey camp in Dalarna. He accepts an invitation from his former national team coach, Bengt "Fisken" Ohlson, to serve as a special guest goaltending instructor. Each year for the remainder of his life, he spends a week at the camp. He usually brings along company. If not Kerstin, he could almost always convince one of his hockey buddies to come along. "He was unbelievably generous with his time to arrange to come and instruct the goalies, and he was enormously popular with the little kids," Ohlson says.

Pelle's social calendar in the summer of 1981 does not yet include visits from North American hockey and non-hockey friends. But with each successive season in North America, he has more and more visitors from the other side of the ocean. There's no dividing line in Pelle's social life for he continues to hang out with his Stockholm friends, while bringing along his visitors. "Pelle was not typical of the Swedish players I knew when I played in Rögle. They were much more reserved and socialized in small, insular groups. Pelle was extremely outgoing," says Dave Poulin. He also points out that while Lindbergh had some expensive tastes, his consumption is neither conspicuous nor obnoxious. "Pelle loved gold watches, big boats and fast cars, but he wasn't boastful about it. He rarely talked about those things in front of strangers. He merely indulged himself in those things when he had the chance," Poulin recalls.

As was the case when he played for AIK, some of Pelle's closest hockey friends in Maine and Philadelphia are the team trainers and equipment managers: Sudsy Settlemyre, Kevin Cady, Turk Evers, and Kurt Mundt. Pelle Eklund recalls,

A few players can be really tough on the equipment guys. There's always something wrong with the equipment, always something that should be done. Pelle caused them no trouble at all. He was easy to work with and treated them like friends. Unfortunately, there are some players who treat them like servants. But Pelle saw them as an important part of the team, and treated them well.

Lindbergh becomes especially close with Cady, who started as a stick-boy with the Maine Mariners and later worked his way up to head equipment manager of the Flyers. Three summers in a row, Lindbergh has Cady come stay with him in Stockholm for six-week periods. Cady recalls his first visit,

Pelle and Björn (Neckman) were supposed to meet me at Arlanda, but naturally they were nowhere to be found. I walked around for a half hour and felt totally helpless. It was my first trip to Europe, and I didn't know anyone. But at last they came forward....When we got out on the beach, the first thing I see are all these incredibly beautiful Swedish women, and most of them are going topless. I could hardly believe it. Pelle cracked up laughing at my reaction. He took my camera, went over to this group of sunbathing girls and asked them if he could take a picture of me with them, because I was an American who had never been on a Swedish beach before. The girls just laughed, and Pelle snapped pictures of me with all of them. He gave all the pretty girls we saw the V-for-victory sign. Typical Pelle: He never saw any problems, only possibilities.

Cady remembers, "Pelle had tremendous self-confidence and it was infectious… Pelle and I spent a lot of time together, especially in the US. We hung out together on regular days, Christmases, and birthdays. He was four years older than me, and I saw him as a big brother."

Lindbergh's relatives, Swedish friends, and North American friends frequently tell stories of how their children gravitated toward Pelle. He's the type of adult who loves to play with toys and invent games. Often, it's hard to tell who's having more fun – the kids or Pelle. Kurt Mundt, for example, relays how his little son, Ryan, adored Lindbergh. "Ryan would play table hockey at the house with Pelle," Mundt says. "They'd have tournaments and Pelle would often let my little guy win."

Lindbergh is very thoughtful in his gift-giving habits, especially for relatives' and friends' kids. He also doesn't forget the elder Mundt, who shares his birthday. "Every May 24, the phone would ring at four in the morning. I knew before I answered who it was. Pelle called from Stockholm and always shouted "Happy birthday!" in the phone," Mundt says.

Jack Prettyman's son, Jay, was a teenager when his policeman father became close with Pelle. He, too, viewed Pelle as a sort of favorite uncle. "Pelle played street hockey with me and my friends and he'd let us use his old equipment," Jay says. "I remember one time in particular when he fired a slapshot that missed the net. The ball broke my bedroom window. "He said, 'Now you see why I'm a goalie,' and laughed. My mom wasn't too thrilled, but Pelle took care of it. He really enjoyed being around our family, because he could just have some fun, mess around, and forget about playing the role of a famous hockey player."

Pelle also has a special knack for bonding with neighbors' kids, both in Sweden and Philadelphia. Robert Burmeister, who was a goalie for the Gladiators of Voorhees boys' team, remembers Lindbergh treating him like a big shot. "My mom lived not too far from Pelle and Kerstin, and when we played street hockey outside her house, I'd wear my Bernie Parent mask. When Pelle saw it, he stopped over. One time (when I was age 11), he came by in his Porsche, stopped, and played with us. I couldn't believe it. He was my idol, and he's playing in our game. He gave me advice to stand up more upright in goal. "Another time, we were invited into his house to get something to drink, because we were all thirsty. He told us we need to drink a lot of water if we're going to play hockey.... "We played our (ice hockey) games at the Coliseum. One game I'm sitting on the bench, and Pelle goes past the box, taps me on the shoulder and he reminds me to stand up more in goal. After that, I went to several Flyers practices to see him play. It ended up with him giving me one of his goalie sticks as a keepsake. That was right before the accident, and was the last time I saw him."

Pelle loves to fill his own home with grown-up toys, both in Sweden and in NJ. He has his model planes, his electronics and all other sorts of other gadgets. Sitting in his driveway, of course, is a sports car. Recalls Jack Prettyman, "I remember one time when Pelle called me late at night. It was after 10 o'clock, and he says, 'Come over, you have to see this new thing I just got.' I figured it had to be important, so I came over right away. When I come over, he shows me this remote-control boat. I could only laugh. He's standing in the dark playing with this boat in the lake behind his house." Al Morganti tells a similar tale:

> Pelle had wonderful toys, and they were always high-tech. I never met someone who had as much fun as Pelle, almost every single day. He got all this outdoor equipment, too. He'd invite me over and we'd shoot bows and arrows or go fishing with harpoons. We'd go out on a raft on the little lake behind his home and try to catch fish with a harpoon. It was totally ridiculous, but we had a lot of fun.

Pelle Lindbergh

CHAPTER 15

SUNDAY, NOVEMBER 10, 1985, 1:00 PM

The Flyers' players, wives and girlfriends have left JFK Hospital and gone to the Coliseum. After speaking at a noon press conference, team doctor Ed Viner goes over to the club's practice facility to privately address the players. Some players, such as Murray Craven and Rick Tocchet, haven't slept in over 24 hours. Standing in the locker room, Viner explains that Pelle is breathing via a respirator because his heart no longer receives any signals from Pelle's brain. Lindbergh no longer has conscious or unconscious use of his brain because it was deprived of oxygen. With tired and bloodshot eyes, he gazes from one person to the next. Many have their heads buried or stare emptily at the wall. Others affix their gaze to his, still with hope for even a sliver of optimism. One of Pelle's teammates asks if "there's any chance he'll live, even if he can't play hockey again." Viner sighs sadly. "You have to understand, there is no chance. Your teammate is dead." "What happens next?" one of the wives asks. "That will be up to Pelle's family to decide," Viner replies softly.

The assembled group remains in the locker room for nearly an hour. There are lots of questions, few reassuring answers and long stretches in which the only sound in the room is muffled sobs. Dave Poulin invites everyone in the room to come to his home in Cherry Hill, so they can all continue to be together for support. Most are able to come.

Before the session breaks up, Mike Keenan gently tells the players that he expects everyone to come to practice tomorrow morning. The session is no longer optional. The team leadership wants everyone together in the environment he knows best, and the coach believes a training session is a good way to set aside the grief for a little while and channel it into something productive. When the room is empty, Keenan, Bob Clarke, and the assistant coaches assemble in the head coach's office. They realize they have to talk business, as much as they don't want to. The all-but-finalized trade sending Bob Froese to Los Angeles will obviously have to be called off, but the team also needs to formulate a plan for a new backup goaltender.

Before the discussion begins, Keenan slumps to the floor in anguish and exhaustion. He hasn't eaten all day and has been a whirling dervish in dealing with doctors and trying to comfort the players. Now that the players aren't around, he permits himself a moment of weakness. "There goes the Stanley Cup," he says gloomily.

As soon as Hershey Bears goaltender Darren Jensen learns the news about Lindbergh, he suspects that he may be recalled to the Flyers. But the thought brings him no happiness under the circumstances. A local newspaper reporter asks him to comment on his status. "I can't think about hockey right now," the goalie says. "I'm just praying for Pelle." Jensen isn't angry at the reporter because he knows the man is just doing his job. The goaltender figures there's a chance that he'll be asked to back up Froese until the team can acquire another goalie. But that discussion needs to wait for a more appropriate time.

Pelle's family remains by his side at JFK Hospital as the respirator beeps rhythmically. At this point, all the clan can do is wait for Sigge to arrive. "I want Pelle to be a person. This isn't living," Kerstin says. Anna-Lisa nods. Gently and carefully, Kerstin pries open one of Pelle's eyelids, but already knows what she'll find. His bright eyes now look glassy. There's no sign of life.

Swedish reporter Gunnar Nordström and photographer Hasse Persson are in New York. Three days earlier, Nordström interviewed Pelle and Persson photographed him with his Porsche for an *Expressen* feature article. Nordström can't help but recall his harrowing ride in the Porsche from the Spectrum to Lindbergh's house in King's Grant. At the time, he felt a little bad for scolding Pelle for driving so fast. Now the conversation and Persson's photographs of Pelle proudly standing next to the car will haunt him for the rest of his life.

Nordström now has to contact Swedish NHL players to get reaction quotes for an article about Pelle's death. He's also been assigned to write a first-hand account from the hospital. The *Expressen* writer and photographer rent a car. With Persson driving down the NJ Turnpike, Nordström writes two articles he needs to submit and prepares notes for the next piece. It's the last thing he'd ever want to be doing on a day like today, but he has no choice.

At the same time, the competing national newspaper *Aftonbladet* is working on a similar article. Before going to the hospital, reporter Bert Willborg and photographer Gerhard Jörén head to the accident scene at the juncture of Somerdale Road and Ogg Avenue. There they find a crowd of people gathered in the pleasant autumn weather, some of whom are wearing replica Flyers jerseys bearing Lindbergh's name and number.

The Porsche has been removed from the scene. All Willborg and Jörén see at first are lovely golden and fire-red leaves blanketing the ground, but it doesn't take long to notice the red paint residue on the corner of the wall or a crack in the cement. There are also tire tracks on the asphalt, very short ones measuring a mere 10 feet, from where Pelle finally tried to slam on the brakes. "This curve isn't especially tricky," Jörén says to his colleague, who later finds out the road was recently widened because it was the scene of many previous accidents.

There are also several curiosity seekers milling around Tomkinson's

Service Station on the White Horse Pike. The ruined Porsche, with the entire left side of the car pushed into the driver's side, rests on a flatbed truck inside the yard. The fence is guarded by a German Shepherd that answers to the name Gretchen.

Bob Clarke sits behind his desk as he talks on the telephone with Glen Sather, the Edmonton Oilers' coach and GM. "Do you want to postpone the game on Thursday?" Sather asks. "I don't know yet. I'll get back to you," Clarke answers. The Flyers' GM talks the situation over with Keenan and telephones the Sniders. They eventually decide to go ahead with the game as scheduled.

Dr. Ed Viner is back at the hospital. He prepares himself for what figures to be an excruciating, but necessary, discussion with Kerstin and Anna-Lisa. Making the situation all the more difficult is the need for Kerstin to translate for Anna-Lisa everything he's about to say. Viner tells them that the family has the option of letting Pelle's situation play out naturally. At some point, he can't say when, Pelle's heart will eventually stop beating despite the presence of the respirator. His heartbeat already stopped once, but it's currently stabilized with the help of the machine. The other choice is to turn off the respirator and have Pelle legally declared dead. If the family wishes, Pelle's organs can be harvested and donated to patients in need of transplants. Doing so could potentially save other people's lives, but it also means racing against time to remove them. Vital organs are only viable for 48 to 72 hours after a person is rendered brain dead. In Pelle's case, his heart, kidneys, lungs, corneas, pancreas and skin are all viable for donation. Viner introduces the family to a doctor representing Kidney One, an organization donation foundation. "The heart has to be transplanted while it's still beating," the doctor explains. "His other organs may shut down unless we prepare them quickly for transplant."

The discussion is extremely upsetting to the family, especially Anna-Lisa. They've hardly had time to wrap their heads around the notion that Pelle is gone forever, and now they're being asked in graphic detail if they consent to him being declared dead and eviscerated. They also realize that there's a window of opportunity to give other people the gift of life, so that Pelle's death at least helps others live. Kerstin and Anna-Lisa ask if they can at least wait until Sigge gets there the next day, so they call all say goodbye to Pelle together. "Yes, of course," the doctor says.

Thomas Eriksson's girlfriend Malin drives a distraught Anna-Lisa and Göran back to Pelle's house at King's Grant and stays with them for support. They're escorted out a side exit in order to avoid the media. Kerstin opts to remain behind at the hospital to sit with Pelle. Thomas Eriksson stands close by.

Kevin Cady learns of the news on TV. He had left the Flyers after the 1984-85 season to return home to Portland, Maine, to pursue a career on the police force. The report on ESPN is a little behind the latest news for it states that Lindbergh is in critical condition. Cady immediately phones the Coliseum and reaches assistant coach E.J. Maguire. "Kevin, Pelle is brain dead," Maguire says. Cady takes the first flight he can get to Philadelphia. He's picked up by Jack Prettyman, who drives him to the hospital. When he arrives, he sees Keenan, who has returned to the hospital. Keenan embraces him and says, "Kevin, we've lost Gump." The coach takes Cady to see Kerstin and Eriksson. Kerstin asks Cady if he wants to see Pelle and he nods solemnly. As Cady looks at Pelle lying on the bed, he appears to be resting peacefully. Cady lets the sorrow take over, leans over and speaks his final words to Pelle. "Thanks for being such a special and good friend, pal," Cady says, as he taps Pelle lightly on the chest.

Borrowing a car from Prettyman, Cady leaves the hospital. He heads over to Pelle's house to see Anna-Lisa. She hugs him and Cady is amazed at the strength she has shown on the worst day of her life. Over the next several days, Cady stays with Tocchet and Craven and spends the entire time with the members of the club. He's back as part of the team.

The Flyers players sit in the living room of Dave Poulin's house. Dave and Kim have served food but no one has eaten a bite. There's a football game on the TV but no one watches it. No one even speaks for they're just glad to have each other. The game is long over by the time everyone leaves to go home. They need to get up for practice in the morning. Among the few players who haven't come to the Poulin house are the Swedes on the team. Thomas Eriksson is still at the hospital with Kerstin, and Pelle Eklund chose to go home to his apartment.

Team president Jay Snider's plane lands in Philadelphia. He had been in Los Angeles for an NHL-related conference and is as distraught as everyone else. The phone call in the morning from his father, Ed, caught him off-guard and left him heartbroken. Apart from Lindbergh's stellar play on the ice, the younger Snider is very fond of the Swedish goalie on a personal level. Three days ago, he was consumed by thoughts of the club's chances of winning the Stanley Cup. Now hockey is the last thing on his mind as he heads straight to JFK Hospital.

Meanwhile, an *Aftonbladet* reporter in Stockholm manages to reach Sigge Lindbergh prior to his departure for the airport. Pelle's father's words are eerily reminiscent of Sudsy Settlemyre's: "That damned car," Sigge says. "But he loved it. It meant everything to him." With a touch of anger and immense pain, the elder Lindbergh also recalls his last phone conversation with his son. "He was so happy and upbeat, yeah, yeah, yeah. He told me how well everything was going. But it looks like everything was too good. Maybe it shouldn't be so good for a person."

Several NHL clubs plan to hold a moment of silence for Pelle before their next games. The Sixers have a game at the Spectrum on this day with the Milwaukee Bucks and they do the same. Ten thousand fans attend, and after the game, Julius Erving expresses his sorrow to the media. "The news has shaken all of Philadelphia. What happened is extremely sad. Now we're all thinking about Pelle, his family, and the Flyers," Erving says.

Kerstin stays at the hospital overnight with Pelle. She's been given a sedative to calm her nerves. Kerstin is now alone in the room, and she cries herself to sleep as a security guard stands watch outside the door.

Pelle Lindbergh

CHAPTER 16

EDMONTON, ALBERTA.
SEPTEMBER 1, 1981

After his dominating rookie AHL season, Pelle Lindbergh is sure that he's a good training camp performance away from winning a job on the Philadelphia Flyers. In Pelle's mind, he's ready for the NHL, and he won't settle for anything less than cracking the Flyers' opening-night roster. Even though their incumbent goalie Pete Peeters has been selected to play in two NHL All-Star games in as many seasons in the league, Pelle believes it's his time.

The first item on Lindbergh's September agenda is the Canada Cup. In late June, Pelle is chosen for Tre Kronor and meets with his teammates at the Carlton Hotel on Kungsgatan. From the start, Lindbergh is certain that he'll be Team Sweden's starting goaltender. The other goalie Peter Lindmark lacks Elitserien experience, although he played very well at the IIHF World Championships. But Pelle is already established on the senior national team, has an Olympic medal to his credit, and is coming off a season in which he led the Mariners to the Calder Cup Finals while sweeping the league's major individual honors.

Lindmark outworked Pelle in the practices leading up to the pre-tournament exhibition games, and coach Ankan Parmström wants to get a look at Lindmark, so he gives him the nod in the training games. Pelle sulks. "It was a little bit of a problem before the trip to Edmonton to start the tournament," Parmström recalls. "But I had Pelle as the first (goalie) when we went over to Canada."

Tre Kronor enters the tournament with high expectations. Parmström fans the flames by introducing the squad as "Sweden's best national team of all-time" when they're presented to media and fans before a soccer game in Stockholm. There are widespread predictions that the Swedes could give the Canadians or Soviets a run for the money to win the tourney.

The Swedes open the tournament against Team USA on September 1. Parmström gives Lindmark the start and the American team upends Tre Kronor, 3-1. The next game is against the Soviets and Lindbergh starts although he is still not in game shape. It is one of his worst performances in years and the USSR prevails, 6-3. "We played a tremendous game against the Soviets," Parmström remembers. "But Pelle was a little shaky and he let in some really shitty goals. We challenged the Russians in every way, and it was our best game of the tournament. But we still lost. As usual, Pelle was very aware that he'd made some mistakes. He'd say, 'I should have had those pucks. This one's on me.'"

Team Sweden bounces back in the next game by blanking Finland, 5-0 with Lindmark in goal. The rest of the tournament is a nightmare as Team Canada beats the Swedes on September 7 by a 4-3 score. Once again, all Pelle can do is watch. Later Team Czechoslovakia hammers Tre Kronor by a 7-1 count in a must-win game for the Swedes. Lindmark starts the game, but gets pulled in the second period after the Czechs' fourth goal. After the final game, Lindbergh sits glowering in the locker room. He's furious at Parmström for starting the other goalie, at his teammates for letting the Czechs freewheel in the offensive zone, and at himself for not playing better against the Soviets. There are many excuses offered after the tournament. These range from an unfavorable travel schedule to questionable officiating. When Pelle is asked by the Canadian media what happened, he has a more succinct analysis. "We sucked," he says.

The Soviets go on to win the tournament, by trouncing Canada in the finale, 8-1. Meanwhile, the embarrassed Swedish team flies back to Stockholm via Paris. By the time he gets back home, Pelle is back to his usual chipper, upbeat self.

A few days later, Pelle departs Stockholm for the Flyers' training camp in Portland. He and Thomas Eriksson have missed the start of camp due to their Canada Cup commitments. Lindbergh works exceptionally hard in camp to catch Pat Quinn's eye and his spirits are high. Not only is he taking his best shot at winning a job, but he's got one of his best friends nearby. The Flyers have invited Reino Sundberg to camp as a non-roster player. Sundberg doesn't know if he has any shot at winning even a minor league spot in the Flyers organization, but he's thrilled to put on a Flyers' jersey and attend camp with Pelle. "It was a tremendous experience, but it was tough for European goalies to get a chance at that time," Sundberg says.

Lindbergh and Sundberg get into several preseason games, and see action against the New York Islanders, Montreal Canadiens and New York Rangers. Sundberg is not offered a Flyers' contract and he's a little disappointed, but not surprised when he considers the competition he's up against (including Pelle). Sundberg winds up playing for Hammarby, and later plays three years in Switzerland.

Pelle meanwhile gives it his all in each of his preseason outings and gives a fine accounting of himself. Nevertheless, he's sent back to the Maine Mariners to start the season. The disappointment is huge. For the first and only time in his North American career, Lindbergh finds it hard to motivate himself to play for the Flyers organization. He feels as though he has nothing left to prove in the AHL. After two weeks of feeling sorry for himself and ignoring advice to be patient, Pelle makes up his mind. If the Flyers aren't going to promote him, he wants to go someplace else. He contacts Keith Allen, who serves as the Flyers and Mariners' GM. "I want to be traded. The way things are right now, I can't stay," he says. Allen is taken aback and asks, "What do you mean?" Pelle responds, "I won't play in Maine anymore. I want to play in the NHL. This needs to be set right, and it has to happen now."

The veteran GM has heard these sorts of things many times before. He's just surprised to hear it coming from Lindbergh. He realizes that Pelle's ambition, youth, and pride are getting the best of him. Allen knows Lindbergh is still very much part of the Flyers' long-term plan. Looking back at the conversation a quarter-century later, Allen says,

> Pelle was extremely disappointed. He thought he deserved a better chance. I had to explain to him that he needed to have patience, and that Pete Peeters had played so well in the NHL that we couldn't just move him out. Those of us in management with the Flyers knew that Pelle had major potential and that he had earned an earlier chance than he got. Pete Peeters wasn't playing bad, and Pelle had to wait. But we felt that Pelle would be our next big goalie after Bernie and he'd be with us five, maybe even 10 years. Pelle was driven by his ambitions and he had exactly what it takes.

After venting his frustration to Allen, Pelle feels better. He doesn't really want to be traded, but he still doesn't want to spend another full year in the minors.

In the meantime, Allen gets an unpleasant surprise from Thomas Eriksson. The defenseman played well the previous season during his call-up to the big club, and the NHL team penciled him into the starting lineup. But after the first game of the 1981-82 season (a 2-2 tie at the Spectrum against the Detroit Red Wings), Eriksson informs Allen and Quinn that he's leaving the team to go back to Sweden. "They were really surprised and not too happy, but they didn't stop me," Eriksson says. "The reason I went home is that I didn't feel ready yet (for the NHL). When I told Pelle I was moving home, he thought it was strange and tried to convince me to stay. But I didn't want to stay for another winter. I was homesick for my lifestyle in Stockholm." Eriksson also harbors a belief that Quinn is a bit biased against European players, although he doesn't confront the coach with his gripes. The defenseman returns to Sweden and signs a contract with Djurgårdens IF. After playing two seasons and winning the Swedish championship in 1982-83, he comes back to the Flyers.

Pelle decides not to re-rent the beach house which he shared with Eriksson and Neckman the previous year. For the first three weeks of the season, he lives in Sudsy Settlemyre's basement, while hunting for a new house. Finally, Lindbergh moves into a smaller house on Woodford Street, which is more centrally located than the beach house. Neckman comes along, too.

Meanwhile, Kerstin has finished her studies and graduated from Stockholm's School of Sport and Health Sciences. She comes to the United States and moves in with Pelle. For public relations reasons, the Mariners aren't thrilled by the news that Kerstin and Pelle are living together. It's not as common in the US in this era as it later becomes, and there's mild concern about projecting a negative public image. "They squawked about it a little because Pelle and Kerstin weren't married. The club thought it was immoral or something. But Pelle and Kerstin got away with it because they were Swedes," Neckman says.

The early 1980s mark the beginning of changing times in hockey. The incorporation of the WHL and the rise of Wayne Gretzky bring about a much more offensive-minded style of play. Scoring rises dramatically and goaltenders struggle to keep up. While many goalies hate the more wide-open style, to Pelle it just means more action. He couldn't care less about his statistics, as long as he makes the saves he needs to make and his team wins. Lindbergh is better equipped than many to handle the changing game because he's an outstanding skater and rapidly improves his puckhandling.

Pelle finds that his North American coaches are more demanding than his Swedish coaches. They're also much more likely to scream at players, and no one could match Mike Keenan when it came to reaming out players on a regular basis. Both Pat Quinn and Bob McCammon, on occasion, could unleash some impressive verbal tirades. For the European players, it took some getting used to. Anna-Lisa witnessed it, both in Portland and Philadelphia. "The coaches could stand by the sideboards during practices and scream a bunch of swear words at certain players," she recalls. As long as the yelling is directed at the entire team, Pelle doesn't mind. He's seen the same thing in Sweden, although with less frequency. "That just rolled off his back," Kerstin says.

But in his early years in North America, Pelle takes offense when coaches single out particular players. It happens to him for the first time early in his second season with the Maine Mariners. Neither Pelle nor the team is playing as well as it had during the previous season, and McCammon reads Lindbergh the riot act in front of the entire club. "Pelle answered back as if someone was angry just at him," Anna-Lisa says. "Afterwards, he'd explain, 'He damn well can't say that to me.'"

When McCammon yells at Lindbergh, Pelle stands up and screams back at the coach. Afterwards, McCammon calls the goaltender into his office. "Don't you ever do that again. If I yell at you in front of the team, I'm yelling because I want to spark the team," McCammon says. "It's not meant against you as a person. You just need to sit and listen." Pelle shrugs. "All right." As he matures, Lindbergh learns not to take such situations personally, but it doesn't happen overnight.

The Flyers get off to a fast start to the season, by jumping out to a 7-0-1 record in their first eight games. But it's an illusion. The club outscores its mistakes in the first couple weeks of the season but is really in utter disarray. The blueline is hurting. Five-time All Star defenseman Jimmy Watson has a chronic bad back and underwent spinal fusion surgery that eventually ends his career at age 30. The team's incumbent top offensive defenseman, Bob Dailey, has knee problems and Eriksson's unexpected departure back to Stockholm further depletes the defense.

Meanwhile, there's a leadership void in the locker room beyond Bobby Clarke. Captain Mel Bridgman held out for a raise and irked Keith Allen and Pat Quinn in the process. Bill Barber's arthritic knee is bothering him, and he got injured at the Canada Cup. The goaltending, too, has also been shaky. Pete Peeters' play slips in his third NHL season, and Rick St. Croix looks more and more like a backup, than a potential starter. The Flyers crash and burn in their ninth game of the year, and are humiliated by Montreal, 11-2. Peeters stops only two of six shots before Quinn pulls him midway through the first period. The Habs then beat St. Croix for seven goals on 37 shots, which begins a stretch of 9 losses in 12 games. Two nights after the Montreal debacle, St. Croix is shaky in a 6-4 win over Pittsburgh.

On Halloween, the Flyers play the Vancouver Canucks at the Spectrum. The Flyers find themselves trailing 4-0 before the first period is even half over. The Flyers crowd takes out its frustrations on Peeters and on defensemen Behn Wilson and Frank Bathe. Peeters goes on to give up four more goals, as he stops just 20 of 28 on the night. The Flyers lose, 8-4. The same evening, Pelle gets a call from Keith Allen. "Pelle, we're calling you up to the Flyers," he says. "Pat Quinn will be starting you tomorrow night in Buffalo. Pack up and go there."

Pelle is giddy and beaming, as he goes to the Civic Center locker room to collect his equipment, but seconds later the smile fades from his face. His equipment is nowhere to be found. Lindbergh searches frantically, wondering if someone is playing a cruel practical joke. But nothing turns up, and no one has seen his pads, glove, blocker, and mask. Lindbergh paces in the hallway, eventually flagging down an arena employee. "Do you know where my gear is?" he asks. "I can't find it anywhere!" "Yeah, Sean borrowed it. He's at the Old Port." Sean is assistant equipment manager Sean McCarthy. He's borrowed Pelle's gear to wear as a Halloween costume at a popular nightclub called the Old Port. Lindbergh speeds over to the club and finds McCarthy dressed in full goalie regalia. In his blocker-hand, McCarthy clutches a beer. One of Pelle's practice sticks is propped up against a bar stool. Ordinarily, Pelle would get a huge kick out of something like this, but not when he needs to get to Buffalo to make his NHL debut. He's friendly with McCarthy but at the moment Lindbergh wants to strangle him. "What the hell do you think you're doing?!" he screams.

On November 1, 1981, Pelle Lindbergh makes his first start as a Philadelphia Flyer. The night he's dreamed of for so many years rapidly turns into a nightmare. It starts with Pelle getting lit up just as badly as Peeters and St. Croix have been of late. Pelle is very nervous before the game, and the Flyers porous defense offers no help as the Sabres jump on Pelle early. Lindbergh stops the first shot he sees, but Tony McKegney collects a powerplay goal at the 3:02 mark to get his club out to an early lead. Pelle battles the puck, but remains unscathed until late in the opening period.

In a disastrous 27-second span, Craig Ramsay scores to make it a 2-0 game. On the next shift, Bobby Clarke gets whistled off for tripping. Just 10 seconds into the man advantage, Yvon Lambert beats Pelle to make it a 3-0 lead for the Sabres. In the second period, the teams trade goals. With Buffalo leading 4-1, Flyers defenseman Bob Dailey raced Buffalo forward Tony McKegney for an icing touch, but never makes it.

Bumped from behind by McKegney, Dailey's skate gets caught in a rut in the ice, he falls backwards into the boards, and shatters both his tibia and fibula. Buffalo goes on to win, 6-2. Meanwhile, Pelle has neglected to drink enough fluid during the game, and he feels increasingly sick as he becomes dehydrated. Both Lindbergh and Bob Dailey end up being taken to the hospital. Pelle receives intravenous fluids and is discharged in the morning to rest in his room at a local Hilton Hotel. The horrific injury to Dailey ends his career.

When Pelle feels better, he joins his new teammates in Philadelphia but his dehydration problems continue. The team doctor leaves it in the hands of Sudsy Settlemyre and Lindbergh to come up with a solution. Settlemyre eventually works out an elaborate fluid-drinking routine with Lindbergh so he can stay hydrated before, during, and after games. Later, Pelle starts to bring a bottle of water out with him on the ice He places it on top of his net and drinks during stoppages of play. The bottle on the net later causes some opponents to gripe, with Glen Sather famously quipping, "What's he want next, a bucket of fried chicken?" It later becomes standard practice for all goalies to have a water bottle on top of their nets. With the hindsight of two decades, it seems strange to recall that it was ever an issue. For Lindbergh, the constant intake of fluids solves a potentially dangerous problem.

But in early November 1981, stopping dehydration isn't the biggest concern for Pelle or the Flyers. Stopping the puck is. On November 5, Pelle backs up Rick St. Croix for a game at the Spectrum against the Rangers. Peeters, incensed to be a healthy scratch, throws a tantrum after the morning skate. Meanwhile, the team defense is nothing short of atrocious and St. Croix has another awful night in net, by letting in a pair of weak goals among the six he gives up on 24 shots.

Two nights later, Pelle gets his second start, as the Flyers play the Penguins in a road game in Pittsburgh's Igloo. It's yet another debacle, as the Flyers give up 45 shots on goal and the Penguins gain the blueline at will. Lindbergh hardly covers himself in glory, either, by getting beaten seven times and leaving out rebounds on shots that he'd normally snap up. Pat Quinn is in a state of apoplexy. To complete the fiasco of the 7-2 loss, Pelle gets dehydrated again and curls up in the fetal position on the bathroom floor of the visitors' locker room after the game. Settlemyre tends to him. "Pelle laid there and vomited and I tried to get water into his system and give him ice cubes to cool him off, because he was burning up. It was awful. Pelle was in really bad shape," Settlemyre recalls.

Five days later, Quinn goes back to St. Croix again. Lindbergh backs up and a sullen Peeters is the third goalie. The Flyers defeat the Hartford Whalers, 5-3, behind a two-goal effort from Paul Holmgren, a goal and an assist from defenseman Behn Wilson, and a pair of helpers by Bobby Clarke.

On November 11, the Flyers announce a major trade. They swap captains with Calgary sending Bridgman to the Flames in exchange for sturdy defenseman Brad Marsh. Lindbergh is sorry to see Bridgman go, because he'd been so friendly and helpful in showing Thomas Eriksson and him around after they were drafted by the Flyers. He soon discovers that the affable Marsh is just as good of a guy as Bridgman, and is a much-needed stabilizing voice both on the ice and in the locker room. Even with new players, the losses continue, and Quinn does not feel that Lindbergh is quite ready for the NHL yet and rotates him between the backup role and the press box. Two weeks later, on December 4, the Flyers send Pelle back to the Mariners.

The entire season so far has been a dud for Pelle. This is certainly not what he dreamed of all those years. Privately, he places most of the blame on Pat Quinn, whom he believes deliberately set him up to fail. He had virtually no time to prepare for his first start as he just went to Buffalo and played. "The conditions weren't right," Reino Sundberg says. "Pelle's experience was orchestrated by the Flyers to take him when he wasn't ready. Because he'd protested that he hadn't gotten a chance, they used him when he wasn't prepared. When he had a couple bad games, they could send him back down in good conscience."

In truth, this scenario is most unlikely. The Flyers were desperately looking for something that would work, and Quinn tried to shake up his team by benching Peeters and St. Croix for Lindbergh. It was undoubtedly risky to throw Lindbergh out there for his first two NHL games at a time when the team was in a state of chaos. Some players would be crushed by this sort of baptism by fire, but Lindbergh isn't crushed. He is a bit paranoid though that Quinn has closed the book on him after two bad starts. He calls Allen again. "If I don't get another chance, I'm going to go home," Pelle threatens. Allen sighs. It's already been a long season, between Bridgman's holdout and trade, Dailey's injury, Peeters' irascibility, Quinn's control issues, defensive problems, Eriksson's departure, and Pelle's impatience. "Pelle, I promise you you'll get another chance. It's two games. We're not giving up on you because of two games. But you have to be patient, OK?" Allen says. "OK," Pelle agrees.

Privately, he's still not convinced. He tells Kerstin that as long as Quinn is the coach, he's probably going to be stuck behind the other goaltenders. "Pat Quinn didn't like European players at that time," Kerstin says. "Pelle always had to play on short notice, and [Quinn] didn't even go over the other team's tendencies with him before the games." Although Lindbergh doesn't trust Quinn, he trusts Allen. Pelle returns to Maine and elevates his game by using a return to the big club as motivation. He hasn't come to America for one bitter cup of coffee.

Maine reels off a winning streak shortly after Pelle's return and he eventually runs his mark to a 17-7-2 record with comparable numbers to his MVP-winning play of his rookie season. The smile returns to Lindbergh's face, for back in Maine he's with Kerstin and is a local celebrity. In Philadelphia, he was shy and quiet and rather overwhelmed by all the upheaval around him on the NHL club. "Going back to Maine was actually a good thing for Pelle. He was better prepared the second time around," recalls Bob McCammon.

During his return to the Mariners, Pelle forms one of his rare friendships with another goaltender, 1980 Team USA Olympic hero Jim Craig. The two first make each other's acquaintance when playing against each other in Erie, Pennsylvania, where Craig tends goal for the Bruins' Erie Blades farm team. Together with Kevin Cady, they go out to eat in the same restaurant adjacent to the arena. Craig and Lindbergh have their Lake Placid experiences in common, but also find they have a lot of other things to talk about. There's a lot of good-natured teasing and laughter. Although Craig's stay with Erie is brief, he and Lindbergh become good friends. Craig even later makes a gift to Pelle of the American flag he famously draped over his shoulders while searching the stands for his father after winning the gold medal.

The two continue to get together whenever they're in the same place. A typical Lindbergh-Craig conversation: "How come I had to put tape over my Flyers logos at the Olympics, but you got to have a shamrock on your mask?" Pelle asks. "Probably 'cause God is Irish, Pelle. That's why." Lindbergh chuckles, "he must be for a bunch of school kids to win the gold like that. We couldn't believe we didn't beat you guys. It was embarrassing." Craig responds "yeah, well, you were the only team that even tied us."

The Flyers temporarily get their ship back on course. In December, the club posts a 10-3-0 mark. Young defenseman Behn Wilson plays the best hockey of his inconsistent career, and wins a spot on the All-Star team. The addition of Marsh is positive, although it's still obvious more help is needed on the blueline. Allen offers St. Croix to the Boston Bruins in exchange for promising young defenseman Brad McCrimmon, but Boston turns down the offer.

Up front, the club makes a major acquisition on January 20, when it acquires 31-year-old star center Darryl Sittler from Toronto. He's added to a formidable group that already includes the likes of feisty Kenny "The Rat" Linseman (92 points, 272 penalty minutes), Brian Propp (44 goals, 91 points), aging Bill Barber (44 goals, 89 points despite chronic knee pain), Bobby Clarke (46 assists in just 62 games played), and promising young forwards Tim Kerr (21 goals, 51 points in 61 games) and Ilkka Sinisalo (15 goals in 66 games of limited ice time).

But there are still problems in goal. St. Croix sputters in big games, while Peeters continues to be strangely inconsistent on the ice and lives up to his nickname, "Grumpy," off the ice. Peeters even gets into a confrontation with a reporter, who accuses the goaltender of physically assaulting him.

The Flyers hit the skids again in late January through February. Over a 22-game span, the club wins only four times, against 12 losses and six ties. Quinn's days as head coach are numbered, although many of the veteran players insist that coaching is not the problem. Two weeks later, with just eight games remaining in the regular season, Pat Quinn is fired. The team promotes Bob McCammon to replace Quinn, just as Quinn moved up to take over for "Cagey" in 1978-79.

On March 2, the Flyers recall Pelle again. For the rest of the season, he rents the house Mel Bridgman vacated when he was traded to Calgary. Kerstin and Anders Lånström come along, too. Lindbergh is sharper and more confident upon his return to Philadelphia, The first game, March 4 against the Rangers, is a bit of a disappointment, even though Pelle plays well and holds a 4-3 lead late in regulation, he lets in a weak goal to Andre Dore with just 2:10 left to play. The Flyers settle for a tie. The rookie waits until March 17 for his next start. The Flyers take on the Rangers again, this time in Madison Square Garden. Nearly two weeks removed from his last game, Pelle is surprisingly sharp. The team as a whole has a bad night, and Lindbergh has little chance to stop four of the five shots that get past him. The Flyers lose 5-2, and get outshot 44-20. In his last game as Flyers' coach, Quinn goes back to Lindbergh the next night after the loss in New York. The Flyers tie Chicago, 4-4, and pull Pelle for an extra attacker in the final minute of regulation. Sittler equalizes the game with just 22 seconds left.

McCammon takes over the next day. He starts Lindbergh in three of the eight remaining games, which includes a home-and-home set with Hartford on March 20 (road) and March 21 (home). Pelle wins both games and draws wide praise for stopping 38 of 40 shots in the first tilt and 41 of 44 shots in the second. The Flyers finish the uneven campaign with 87 points, good for third place in the Patrick Division but a whopping 31 points behind the New York Islanders at the height of its dynastic four-year string of Stanley Cup championships.

The Flyers plays the Rangers in the best-of-five first round series. McCammon announces that Peeters is his starting goaltender and a reporter asks the coach if he's considered Lindbergh, given the rookie's solid play late in the season. "Pelle's time will come," McCammon says.

Peeters is outstanding in the first game of the series and takes first-star honors in turning back 35 of 36 shots. The Flyers win the road tilt, 4-1 and then the walls cave in. The Blueshirts club Philly in the second game, 7-3. In game three, the Rangers nip the Flyers, 4-3, in a game in which the Flyers have an early 3-0 lead, blow it in the second period and head into the final minutes of play tied. Cam Connor's goal with just 1:09 left gives the Rangers the only lead they'll have or need in the game. In game four, Peeters gets pulled after two periods with the Flyers trailing by a 5-2 count. The Rangers add to the lead against St. Croix early in the third period and hold off a late desperation rally by Philadelphia to win, 7-5.

When Lindbergh later looks back at his second year in North America, he considers it to be a disappointment. When he matures and revisits the campaign as an established NHL goalie, he wishes he'd done certain things differently, particularly in the areas of his conditioning and preparation. In an interview with Hockey Night in Canada, he says, "After the Canada Cup, I played terrible hockey with the Flyers in the fall. I was really tired by October and November that season. We had our first training in Sweden for the Canada Cup already in July, and it was really a long year."

On June 9, the Flyers trade Peeters to the Bruins for Brad McCrim- mon. By the end of the summer, the team adds star defenseman Mark Howe in a blockbuster trade with Hartford, and selects veteran Czech defenseman Miroslav Dvorak in the Entry Draft. The path is now clear for Pelle to make it to the big club to stay, and the blueline figures to be substantially im- proved. Pelle has his usual good time during the summer of 1982, but he's chomping at the bit for training camp to arrive.

In Philadelphia now, Pelle Lindbergh is associated with jersey number

31. He'd have rather worn number 1 in Bernie Parent's honor, as he did with Hammarby, AIK, the Swedish Olympic team, and Maine, but Parent's number has been retired by the Flyers. Pelle picks 31, both because it's available and because it least has a number 1 in it.

CHAPTER 17

MONDAY, NOVEMBER 11, 1985

The Flyers players gather at the Coliseum for practice. Originally, Mike Keenan had declared this day an optional skate, and only a couple of players planned to attend with no coaches on the ice. It has now become a mandatory, full practice in the hopes of giving the players something to take their mind off Pelle.

Sudsy Settlemyre has cleared out Pelle's locker, and Kerstin later receives a black equipment bag containing Lindbergh's gear. His nameplate stays in place and Settlemyre places a small Swedish flag (a paper flag that Pelle himself had ordered as a little reminder of home) on the shelf directly above the nameplate.

When the players arrive, one after another pauses to stand in front of Pelle's empty station before heading to his own locker. It becomes a routine that many follow for the rest of the season.

The first practice lasts an hour. It's one of the hardest things everyone on the team, including Keenan, has ever had to do. The coach realizes that it took everything the players had in them to put on their practice uniforms one day after the crash. Before the training session starts, Keenan gathers the team in the corner of the rink. Big, tough hockey players pray together. Bob Froese sinks down to one knee, while Ron Sutter lays his right arm over Pelle Eklund's shoulders.

The Flyers have not yet had a chance to bring up a backup goaltender from Hershey, so Bob Froese, who is suddenly the team's full-time starter, is the only goalie at the practice. The net at the other end of the ice stands unguarded. "When I looked down at the other end of the ice, I really wanted to cry. The permanence of what happened to Pelle truly hit me at that moment. It was very hard to think about hockey," Froese recalls. The first practice is listless. It's enough that everyone is together on the ice.

"Mike was remarkably patient with us," says Mark Howe. "It was a horrible, horrible situation, and he helped keep us all together." Bob Clarke stands by the sideboards, but soon walks over to talk to Jack Prettyman, who is watching from a higher vantage point. "Jack, what we're going to be doing is having some memorials and team gatherings," says Clarke. "I just want to tell you that you're welcome to come. Just let me know. We appreciate everything you've done." In response, Prettyman shakes Clarke's hand.

Back on the ice, the only sounds are of pucks, sticks, skates and ocassional blasts of Keenan's whistle. Afterwards, print, television, and radio journalists in the locker room swarm the players. Much of the attention is focused on Froese. With numerous cameras in his face, the goaltender stares at the ground and speaks softly. Murray Craven appears to be on the brink of tears as a reporter asks him what it felt like to practice on a day like today. "It's the hardest thing I've ever had to do in hockey," he says in a voice barely above a whisper. Over at his stall, Thomas Eriksson seethes. He can't believe the circus atmosphere at the Coliseum, with players having to go out in front of the public eye both on the ice and in the locker room. With questions being fired at him in English by American writers, he turns to the *Expressen* and *Aftonbladet* newspaper writers and says, " *Det som hänt är vidrigt.*" ("What's happened is disgusting.")

Mike Keenan steps out of his office after practice and holds an impromptu press conference. He's surrounded by cameras. "I drove them extra hard today," he says. "I wanted them to vent their emotions into adrenaline after all that's happened. Apart from that, it's important to come back to a normal workday, and this is what we usually do everyday." In reality, Keenan cut the players a little more slack than normal at the first practice, but with each passing day, he instills more and more discipline.

"It was a matter of focus," Howe recalls. "Some of the guys resented it, but Keenan wanted to make sure that when we were at the rink, we kept our minds on hockey. It was tough, but he helped us get through it as a team." Adds Brian Propp, "We really were like a family. Losing Pelle brought us all closer together. That first week was very, very tough. We helped each other pull through it. One thing that made it bearable was knowing how much Pelle loved hockey. He would have wanted us to keep playing."

As the players practice, Kerstin, Anna-Lisa, and Göran are at Kennedy Hospital. They have nothing to do but sit with their grief and wait for Sigge to arrive. Sigge and Kerstin's mother, Gudrun Pietzsch, are en route via an SAS flight to New York. Gudrun has come along both to ensure that Sigge isn't alone and to comfort her daughter in person.

In the parking lot outside the hospital sit a row of news vans representing a variety of TV stations. All that the TV news teams are allowed to do is wait outside until they're invited in for the next press conference. It's also fruitless to try to call inside, even though some reporters try to get in contact with Pelle's family or Kerstin. On one ocassion, Anna-Lisa is taking a walk in the hallway as a receptionist motions to her and hands her the phone. The voice on the other end starts speaking rapid English to Pelle's mother. The only word Anna-Lisa understands is "Hello." "*Hallå, men jag talar inte engelska*," she says and hands the phone back to the receptionist. Flyers' owner Ed Snider witnesses the scene, and is enraged that Anna-Lisa has been bothered as he hollers at the folks at the reception desk.

The previous day Kerstin spoke very briefly with an unnamed Associated Press reporter. She admitted that Pelle's driving habits had been a concern. "I always worried about a car accident, but he laughed at me. He told me not to worry, but I worried," she's quoted as saying.

After the practice at the Coliseum, Mike Keenan invites everyone on the team to come back to his house. They share a long lunch, and a lengthy discussion in the Keenan family room. Everyone comes except Thomas Eriksson, who heads back to the hospital to be with Pelle's family. "Remember all the fun we had with Pelle? All the madness? Let it all out," the coach says. The day before, at Dave Poulin's late-afternoon gathering, everyone was still too stunned and numb to speak. Today, a cauldron of grief, anger, and despair comes bubbling to the surface. "I want my buddy back," says one player, his voice cracking as he breaks down. The tears start flowing again. With the exception of Keenan, mostly everyone in the room cries openly, even the team's tough guys and stoics. "How could he do this to us?" someone else says. "To his family? Goddamn you, Pelle!" A third player whispers, "It could have been me. I drank more than Pelle did the other night. Why him and not me? Hell, it could have been any of us." The players also tell stories about the good times. They laugh as they recall Pelle's affable goofiness, endearing naïveté, boundless energy, and infectious enthusiasm.

When everyone is spent, the discussion turns to more practical matters. The team has to decide what to do with Pelle's locker, and the players offer their input. The Flyers have two locker rooms, one at the Spectrum and one at the Coliseum. Should they leave one, both, or neither of his lockers vacant the rest of the season? Several players want Pelle's equipment to be left at both places. Others want only his nameplate to remain, while a few say it's best if Pelle's locker goes to someone else. Dave Poulin speaks up. "If we leave everything there, can we go forward and focus if the first thing we see every-day is Pelle's equipment?" Silence. "Should we just leave it as a reminder of who we play for, as a way to honor Pelle?" No answer. It's just too soon to decide.

Eventually, the club decides to leave Pelle's space at the Coliseum vacant and to re-assign his spot in the left corner of the Spectrum locker room. At the orders of Mike Keenan, Dave Poulin is later moved to the spot for the rest of the year. It's a wider locker and Keenan says it's befitting of an NHL captain.

The doctors and Flyers leaders approach the podium in the hospital cafeteria for the next press conference. Today's discussion is every bit as unpleasant as the previous day's sessions. "At the point in time when all of the necessary examinations of his brain were done, there was no brain activity and, therefore, Pelle Lindbergh was clinically dead," says Robert P. Wise, the administrative director of John F. Kennedy Memorial Hospital. "The prognosis continues to be incompatible with life," adds Dr. Viner, who spent the night at the hospital. A reporter asks why Lindbergh remains on the respirator if he's clinically dead. "The respirator isn't being used so that he can be rescued to life, it's being used so that his organs should continue to function and therefore can be donated if his family chooses to do so," Wise explains. Dr. Louis Gallo, a staff surgeon at Kennedy, explains what will happen next. "If the family decides to donate his vital organs for transplant, the decision should be made by tomorrow," he says. " We're going to work with the family to decide how far they want us to go in sustaining biological life."

The majority of the discussion focuses on Pelle's alcohol consumption. Tests on Lindbergh's blood serum revealed that Pelle had a blood alcohol level of .024 percent, an amount of alcohol that is more than double the legal limit and close to inducing potentially lethal alcohol poisoning. Dr. Viner and Clarke attempt to make clear that such behavior was rare for Lindbergh. "Pelle was not a drunk," Viner says. "But he did drink too much before the accident. Kids have done this after games for years. I hope that sends a very strong message to student athletes. Pelle made a horrible mistake." Clarke adds, "He hardly ever drank. He didn't have to. A lot of guys get their personality from drinking. Pelle didn't have to."

The Flyers GM is asked if he's made a decision on Lindbergh's replacement on the roster. "You don't replace a Pelle Lindbergh. Goalies like that come along once in a lifetime," he says. "We know what we have to do. It sounds morose, but we're going to have to bring in another goalie. Obviously it's going to be tough on whoever we bring in. There's going to be scars left on a lot of players. As bad as we can all feel, we can't use this as an excuse not to continue." Clarke is also asked about Lindbergh's new contract. Nothing has been signed. If it were not for the accident, today would have been when Pelle officially signed it. The GM is asked what will become of money. "It makes no difference (that nothing is signed). There's an agreement. Obviously, the money will all go to Pelle's family," Clarke says. For a variety of reasons, it's a promise the Flyers are later unable to keep.

The story of Lindbergh's alcohol use on the night of the crash immediately comes to dominate the media coverage and public discussion of the accident. This remains true in the weeks, months, and years to come. A second test of whole blood (rather than blood serum) lowers the blood alcohol reading to a more realistic .017 percent, which is still well above the legal limit and more than enough to impair someone's reflexes and judgment while driving. Those who were at the Coliseum insist that he didn't appear intoxicated before he left, and went lengthy periods of time between drinks.

Five years later, Gene Hart writes in *Score! My Twenty-five Years with the*

Broad Street Bullies, "The people who caused the most pain to the Lindberghs were those who said, 'He was just another drunk driver and it's a good thing he's off the road, so no one else will be killed.' Statements like that were unfair to the memory of this vibrant young man, who, by all accounts of Flyers past and present, was one of the least likely to be involved in an incidence of driving under the influence."

Reporter Al Morganti also uses Pelle's story as a teaching tool. He ocassionally gives presentations to high school hockey players and coaches, in which he shows various pieces of hockey equipment from different eras. At the end, he takes out one of Pelle's game-used jerseys and says, "This belonged to a good friend of mine. It doesn't matter how big a star you are on your team. Don't get in a car if you've been drinking. It's not worth it. Take care of one another." Three images of Pelle Lindbergh are shown: A photo of him smiling, a photo of his wrecked Porsche, and a photo of the memorial at the Spectrum. The message: "It just takes one time to ruin a life."

Expressen reporter Gunnar Nordström has been instructed by his editor to try to arrange an interview with Kerstin and Anna-Lisa. "You known them and you have a good relationship," the editor says. Almost apologetically, Nordström approaches Thomas Eriksson near the hospital entrance. "Is there any chance I can meet with Kerstin or Anna-Lisa for a few minutes?" he asks the defenseman. Eriksson is skeptical but promises to ask. A half an hour later, he returns." No, Kerstin doesn't want to be interviewed yet. It's too soon," he says. "OK. We understand and obviously we respect that," Nordström replies. Eriksson holds up his hand. "Kerstin wants you to come up anyway, totally in private. She feels that Pelle would have wanted you to say goodbye. But you can't do an interview or take any pictures," he says. The reporter and photographer Hasse Persson go up to the third floor with Eriksson, and Kerstin leads them in to see Pelle. Before they go, they give their condolences to Anna-Lisa and Göran. Kerstin says, "You can interview

Anna-Lisa and me tomorrow. But we'll do it at the house, not here." She does the same for the *Aftonbladet* representatives.

Sigge Lindbergh and Gudrun Pietzsch arrive at JKF Airport at 4:48 pm, and Pelle's father is dressed in a jacket with "Hammarby Hockey" emblazoned on the left breast. They're met by Flyers' representative Joe Kadlec and Dr. Jeffrey Hartsell (who has come as a precaution because of 69-year-old Sigge's heart condition). Kadlec and Hartsell lead the Swedes to a private plane belonging to Ed Snider. They take a short flight to a small landing field in Stratford, NJ, where a black limousine, escorted by five police cars, picks them up and drives them to Kennedy Hospital. Upon their arrival, television cameramen and newspaper photographers await them inside the entrance, but Sigge does not want to be seen crying. Before they enter, they're met by the Snider family and other key personnel, who make sure they quickly get up to the third floor.

Anna-Lisa rises from her seat in the waiting room and goes over to husband, who is tired and hardly responds when spoken to. At the same time, Gudrun embraces her daughter. "Does your husband need a sedative?" a doctor asks. Thomas Eriksson translates for Anna-Lisa. "I don't think he wants that. He doesn't like to take pills," she replies. With that Sigge goes in to see Pelle. He looks down at his son in the bed and knows that what happened to him was totally unnecessary. The private, reserved elder Lindbergh anguishes alone.

In the evening, the New York Rangers have a game against the Chicago Blackhawks. The public address announcer asks for a moment of silence in the memory of Pelle Lindbergh. Behind the Rangers' bench, head coach Ted Sator bows his head. It's been a very tough 24 hours for him, too, having coached Pelle as an assistant with the Flyers. "I'll never forget it," Sator says today.

When the Flyers come to New York on December 8, for their first appearance after Pelle's death, many in attendance politely applaud as they step onto the ice for warmups in recognition of how tough it must be to carry on. Once the game starts, the Rangers crowd immediately reverts to hating the Flyers. Matters of life and death transcend sports, at least in the hearts and minds of decent human beings. Years later, Flyers fans at the Spectrum show similar class in giving Mario Lemieux a standing ovation in his first game back after taking leave for treatment of lymphoma.

Kerstin, Anna-Lisa, and Sigge are all agreed that Pelle's organs should be donated. "If Pelle can help others, he does it," Anna-Lisa says. The others nod, but decide to sleep on it overnight just be sure. For the first time, Sigge breaks down and cries in front of everyone else.

When they get back to the house, they find that the Flyers' players wives and girlfriends have sent them food, as they know that neither Kerstin nor Anna-Lisa would feel up to preparing anything. As the night progresses, Kerstin is unable to sleep, and she asks Thomas Eriksson to take her back to the hospital. She spends the night on a cot brought to the waiting room. Later that night, Pelle's heartbeat and blood pressure begin to drop. Fearing that his organs are about to shut down, the doctor's administer powerful medication. His heartbeat stabilizes once again, but time is running out.

Pelle Lindbergh

CHAPTER 18

PHILADELPHIA, PA.
OCTOBER 7, 1982

It's opening night of the Philadelphia Flyers 1982-83 season and Pelle Lindbergh has made it all the way. He has earned a spot on the NHL roster after a solid training camp. All of the dreams, the preparation, the long winters in Sweden and Maine have been leading to this moment. He's in the NHL to stay.

Lindbergh backs up Rick St. Croix in the opening night game against the Quebec Nordiques. He skates out onto the ice to be introduced to the Spectrum crowd with the rest of his teammates. "Number 31, goaltender Pelle Lindbergh!" Lou Nolan, the Flyers' public address announcer intones to polite applause. The Flyers go on to win a sloppily played 9-5 decision over Quebec that saw newly acquired Mark Howe get hit in the face with a puck in his first shift in a Philadelphia uniform, stay in the game, and later score his first Flyers' goal.

Pelle is philosophical about being the backup in the opener. At least it's a step in the right direction after starting the previous season in Maine with little left to prove in the AHL. When Lindbergh departed Sweden for NHL training camp on September 1, he was determined to force Bob McCammon's hand. Even though Pete Peeters had been traded to Boston for defenseman Brad McCrimmon, Lindbergh wasn't taking anything for granted. Despite battling a nasty flu bug, he outplayed St. Croix at camp. Another young goaltender at camp, Bob Froese, also showed promise and the competition pushed Lindbergh to stay focused at practice as well as in games.

The previous night, Pelle got off to a great start in a preseason tilt against the Capitals, by making several outstanding saves. Early in the second period, he gave up a goal he felt he should have stopped. Still upset by the goal, he promptly gave up another. Later Bernie Parent speaks to him about it,

Pelle, I'm gonna tell you something Jacques Plante told me. You've got to forget whatever just happened. Whether it's good or bad, just forget about it. It's gone. I didn't always do that when I was a young goalie, either. You're upset, you're pissed off. You want to crawl under the ice. It's normal. But I learned that the difference between a good goalie and a great one isn't the first goal you give up. It's how you respond to the first goal, and how tough you make it to score the second one.

Coming from some coaches, the words might seem trite. But Lindbergh has such enormous respect for his idol's accomplishments that he later recalls the discussion whenever he endures a slump. Pelle's quest to conquer the mental challenges of NHL goaltending takes him several more seasons to complete. He already knows what he has to do to reach the level he wants to attain, but knowing and doing are two different things.

Pelle and Kerstin move into a townhouse in Cherry Hill, NJ, a short distance from the Benjamin Franklin Bridge. Many of the other players live nearby. NHL rookies are supposed to be seen and not heard, and in his early Flyers' career, Pelle is quiet in the locker room. But it doesn't take too long for his free spirited personality to begin to emerge. It helps that several of his friends from the Mariners, including trainer Sudsy Settlemyre and assistant trainer Kurt Mundt, are now with the Flyers. Likewise, former Mariners defenseman Glen Cochrane is now an established young defenseman on the Flyers. The rest of the greatly improved cast includes the likes of Cookie Dvorak, McCrimmon, and Marsh.

Pelle's favorite part of coming to the practice rink remains his post-practice one-on-one duels with the team's top shooters, especially burgeoning star Brian Propp. He also enjoys challenging speedy Finn Ilkka Sinisalo, dipsy-doodling Ron Flockhart, and one of the team's checking liners, Lindsay Carson.

Off the ice, one of the first things he learns from teammates is that it's unwise to leave valuables unattended in his car at the practice rink at the University of Pennsylvania. There's a good chance they'll be gone by the time he returns. Teammates also suggest Pelle buy a used car to drive to practice every day, rather than risk having his Corvette stolen or vandalized. There has been a recent wave of thefts in the area. The goalie decides to chance it and never has a major problem.

As the early weeks of the season roll by, Pelle's happiness at making the team starts to fade, because McCammon gives St. Croix the lion's share of the playing time. Lindbergh does not get into a game until October 28, when he stops 30 of 32 shots in a 9-2 romp over the Pittsburgh Penguins at the Spectrum. Since St. Croix is not playing particularly well, Lindbergh starts to get frustrated with sitting on the bench every game. He doesn't go to Keith Allen this time, but he privately tells Kerstin and Settlemyre that the only way he can stay sharp is if he plays more often. "Pelle, it'll happen for you," Settlemyre says with a grin. "You know that is just how it goes in the NHL. Keep at it." Bernie Parent and Sigge Lindbergh have similar advice. Pelle knows they're right, but patience isn't one of his virtues. Each day, he wears his usual pleasant smile to the rink, but he stews privately every time Mc-Cammon names St. Croix the starter for the next game.

After the Penguins' game, McCammon starts to give the rookie more opportunities. He goes back to Lindbergh two nights later in Minnesota, Pelle acquits himself well against the Minnesota North Stars, but two goals by Tom

McCarthy send the Flyers to a 3-2 defeat. St. Croix gets the next start, but the goalie is shaky again, and lets in a soft goal to Craig Levie. St. Croix goes long stretches without seeing a shot, and juggles several pucks he sees all the way.

Eleven days later, the Flyers' brass huddles after an ugly 7-2 loss in Buffalo. St. Croix was pulled after two periods with the Flyers trailing 5-1, and Pelle mopped up in the third period. Afterwards, McCammon tells the Philadelphia media that he's going to give Lindbergh an extended opportunity to see if he can take the starting job and run with it. The date is November 10, 1982, exactly three years before Pelle's fatal car crash.

Twenty-four hours after the Flyers' debacle in Buffalo, the hated New York Rangers descend on the Spectrum. The Blueshirts outplay the Flyers early, but Lindbergh yields only a Don Maloney powerplay goal in the first period. In the middle frame, the Flyers come alive. A five-goal outburst whips the Spectrum crowd into a frenzy, and Lindbergh nails down the win in the third period, by stopping 28 of 31 shots in all. Philly prevails, 7-3.

Two nights later, he returns to the crease in a hard-fought 4-3 home loss to Edmonton. Shortly thereafter, Pelle gets another crack at the powerhouse Oilers, and makes 38 saves on 40 shots in a 4-2 Flyers win in Edmonton. Between November 11 and January 4, Lindbergh is nothing short of outstanding. He posts a 15-5-3 record and a goals against average of 2.60. The Flyers soar into first place in the Patrick Division. Lindbergh also records the first two shutouts of his NHL career. On November 27, he makes 22 saves in blanking Los Angeles on the road, 4-0. One week later, Pelle and Penguins goalie Denis Heron duel to a 0-0 tie in Pittsburgh. Lindbergh makes 24 saves, while Heron turns back all 30 Philadelphia offerings. A new chant rises at the Spectrum over the course of the fall. In the same fashion that crowd used to chant Bernie Parent's name, rhythmic calls of "Pell-lee, Pell-lee, Pell-lee" greet every one of the goalie's big saves.

On January 6, 1983, the Flyers have an exhibition game against the Soviet national team. Initially, Lindbergh expected to sit out the contest. St. Croix had only appeared in six games since being replaced as the starter, and was itching to get a chance to play. The game receives widespread local attention. Seven years earlier, the Flyers downed CSKA Moscow (the Red Army team) in a landmark 4-1 victory. The 1976 game also confirmed that the two-time defending Stanley Cup champion Flyers were the top club team in the world. The 1983 contest marks Philadelphia's first meeting with a Russian team since the clash with the Red Army. In Philadelphia, the game is hyped into much more than just a mid-season exhibition game. At the last minute, McCammon tells Lindbergh he's starting the game. Pelle isn't about to say, "No," but he'd prefer to rest while St. Croix gets in some much-needed work. "I'm lousy in these sorts of games," Lindbergh says.

The Russians run roughshod over the Flyers. The famous KLM line of Vladimir Krutov, Igor Larionov, and Sergei Makarov breaks through for a pair of goals. A second period powerplay goal by Mark Howe, set up by Darryl Sittler and Miroslav Dvorak, briefly cuts the deficit to 3-1, but Mikhail Varnakov quickly restores the three-goal cushion. The Soviets prevail, 5-1. Late in the third period, Lindbergh gets his right wrist kicked in a scramble near the net. It still smarts as he leaves the ice after the game, and it gets worse in the dressing room.

Late that night, Kerstin and friend Roffe Alex accompany Pelle to the Penn Sports Medicine Center. Thinking he has a mild sprain, Pelle isn't too concerned, but an x-ray reveals that his hand is fractured. He leaves in a cast up to his elbow. With the fracture Lindbergh misses a month of action. During Pelle's absence from the lineup, the Flyers call up Bob Froese from Maine. McCammon quickly installs Frosty as the starter, much to the dismay of former number-one keeper St. Croix. Shortly thereafter, the Flyers trade St. Croix to Toronto in exchange for veteran backup Michel "Bunny" Larocque.

Pelle suffered a broken wrist in a January 3, 1983 exhibition game between the Flyers and the Soviet Red Army team. This photo was taken at the hospital minutes after his hand was placed in a cast [Courtesy Rolf Alex]

Despite his injury, Pelle is selected to the NHL All-Star Game in Uniondale, New York (home of the Islanders). Mark Howe and Darryl Sittler are also chosen for the game, along with former Flyers' starting goaltender Pete Peeters. When he learns of his selection, Pelle is still unable to touch his right shoulder with his right fingertips. Froese, meanwhile, hits the ground running. On January 8, Pelle sits on his sofa at home and watches the Froese's NHL debut on television. Led by two goals and three assists by Ilkka Sinisalo, the Flyers down Hartford, 7-4.

The Flyers reel off eleven straight wins and Froese goes 11-0-1 in his first 13 appearances, by allowing more than three goals on only two ocassions. While it's true that the team is firing on all cylinders and plays its strongest defense in years, Froese is also in prime form. The Flyers now have an enviable problem: two promising young goaltenders experiencing tremendous NHL success. The situation bothers Pelle, who grows concerned that he'll have to go back to square one to claim the starting job. Privately, he roots for the Flyers to win but for Froese to come back down to earth. It doesn't happen. The previously unheralded rookie earns NHL Player of the Week accolades and shuts out the Rangers at Madison Square Garden. "That really bothered Pelle," Kerstin recalls.

The injury heals more slowly than Pelle expects. In order to get back into the lineup as fast as possible, he works out like a man possessed under the auspices of team physical trainer Pat Croce. Croce recalls, "The worst thing that could happen to player was to get injured. Then he knew he'd get tortured by me. I had my own little 'Club of Pain' where guys could earn medals when they rehabbed after an injury." Croce finds Pelle to be a willing disciple as the two work on exercises to further improve Pelle's cardiovascular conditioning as well as his already exceptional balance and leg strength. "Pelle had the fastest reflexes I've ever seen," Croce says. "I threw tennis balls at him and filmed the saves on video, just because he was absolutely unbelievable at it. He was just as fast and flexible on the ice, too." Lindbergh finally returns to the net on February 5, the last game before the All-Star break. He shuts out the Kings, 2-0, at the Forum.

In the early 1980s, rookie hazing is still common in the NHL. Later replaced by more innocuous welcomes, some of the old-school hazing rituals that endured into the '80s (and beyond that in junior hockey) are downright cruel. When Pelle returns to the lineup from the wrist fracture, he is victim to "The Shave."

The Flyers arrive in Los Angeles a day early and hold practice. After-wards, as Pelle gets undressed in the Forum's visiting locker room, he's quickly surrounded by older players, thrown to the floor and held down.

Pelle screams, thrashes, and kicks, so his mouth is taped shut as players start to shave the hair off the rookie's head. Ordinarily that's where it ends, but the more Lindbergh protests, the more he eggs on the group to take it further. Lindbergh has his head shaved into a severe buzzcut (getting nicked and cut several times), and gets shaved over his entire body. Bob Froese gets similarly butchered.

Pelle is distraught. He has never experienced anything approaching this in Sweden, and is both humiliated and angry. Sudsy Settlemyre remembers, "But even though everyone liked Pelle, they really got him good. He was pretty upset about it. The next day, Pelle continues to keep his shorn head covered." "I laughed hard when I saw him the first time after the shave," Ilkka Sinisalo says. "We were having lunch in the hotel and Pelle comes in wearing this big hat, pulled all the way down. He looked like he wasn't in his right mind."

When the Flyers return to Philadelphia, Kerstin and Roffe Alex pick Pelle up at the airport. He's wearing a stocking cap. When they head home, Pelle tells them he went through "sheer hell" and was especially upset that he was held down and couldn't move. Before long, people around the team get used to seeing Pelle show up in assorted headwear. He does so until his hair fully grows back.

"Pelle was still unbelievably upset over the shave. He bought a bunch of different caps and hats. Months went by before he took them off. He pretended in public like everything was OK, but deep inside he still felt bad about what happened," recalls Al Morganti. Even as his hair grows back, it takes Lindbergh awhile before he begins to trust the other players again. He still resents the way the shave happened. The fact that no one helped him or tried to put a stop to it really gets to him. Kerstin recalls,

After I saw him the first time, Pelle didn't say much more about what happened, but he was very, very down about it. Oddly the weeks before it happened, he told me he thought something would happen. He'd heard about 'The Shave' before, and he was a rookie. If everyone else went through it, he knew he'd also probably get nabbed.

Privately, even the veterans agree that things went too far at the Forum. The 1982-83 rookies are the last in Philadelphia to be subjected to "The Shave." As time goes by, however, Pelle is able to laugh as he recalls what he had to go through to be fully accepted as "one of the guys" by the older Flyers players. Pelle isn't smiling before or after the 1983 NHL All-Star Game. He wears a hat and a suit at the banquet the night before the game. Naturally, people notice and ask him about what happened.

All-Star Games are typically wide-open affairs, with precious little defense played and no physical play. Inevitably, there's at least one goalie that gets picked apart by the highly skilled attackers given free reign in the offense zone. It doesn't help Pelle's chances that this is just his second game back after the wrist injury, and he tends to do poorly in meaningless games under the best of circumstances. He's ripe for the picking. Lindbergh (who didn't take his mask off the entire game, even on the bench) is ripped apart for seven goals as the Campbell Conference beats the Wales Conference, 9-3. Four of them come from Wayne Gretzky in the span of 14 minutes. Pelle is utterly humiliated. "What a nightmare," he says afterwards. "I couldn't have stopped a beachball."

The goalie's sense of humor remains firmly intact; however, and after Gretzky is presented the game MVP trophy and a car, Pelle walks over and shakes his hand. "You owe me half a car," he says. "Huh?" Pelle reminds Gretzky, "You scored the goals, but I let all those pucks get past me!" Gretzky and the nearby media members laugh heartily. "Damn, it was tough out there," Lindbergh says in Swedish. "But there wasn't much I could do about it. I'll be back [to the All-Star Game] and I'll do better next time."

Pelle plays inconsistent hockey after the All-Star break. Froese's momentum is also stalled, and neither goalie is particularly sharp down the stretch. Lindbergh finishes with 2.97 goals against average and .892 save percentage in 40 games, Froese with 2.57 goals against average and .896 save percentage in 25 appearances.

Pelle keeps his eyes on the puck while making a save for the Flyers [Courtesy Kerstin Somnell]

Despite their late-season ups-and-downs, the Flyers cruise to 106 points and a first-place finish in the Patrick Division. At home they're virtually unbeatable, with a 29-8-3 mark (.762 winning percentage) on Spectrum ice.

The Flyers enter

their best-of-five first round playoff series with the Rangers as the favorite. McCammon tabs Lindbergh as the starting goaltender in what proves to be a fiasco for everyone in orange and black. The Flyers can't stay out of the penalty box, the offense goes south, the defense springs leaks and Pelle can't stop anything in goal. Meanwhile, some of McCammon's coaching decisions raise eyebrows, and the Rangers finish off the series with a 9-3 romp at Madison Square Garden. Lindbergh is disappointed by the way his season ends, but realizes that he's created a strong foundation for future success. He's named to the NHL All-Rookie Team after the season.

The Flyers' early playoff exit makes the young goalie available to Sweden for the IIHF World Championships in West Germany. One of the first things the Tre Kronor coaches notice is that Pelle is much more serious in his preparations than he was in the past. "It's because of Bobby Clarke," Lindbergh explains. "He's been a great influence. I watch the way he comes to practice before everyone else and the way he gets ready for every game. I want to do that, too."

Pelle is rejoined on Tre Kronor by Thomas Eriksson. The defenseman informs him that the Flyers have been in contact several times and he intends to return to Philadelphia next season. The two celebrate together by visiting the Porsche factory in Stuttgart, Germany and decide to buy new cars. In Maine, they bought matching Corvettes, and now they choose to get red Porsches.

———————————————

Kerstin leaves Cherry Hill for Sweden shortly before the end of the NHL season. When Pelle joins her in Stockholm, he has a special surprise for his girlfriend, whom he affectionately calls "Kärran." On May 17, 1983, he takes her out to Capri Ristorante, an Italian restaurant at Nybrogatan 15 in Stockholm. "Close your eyes, Kärran," Pelle says. When she opens them, she sees a diamond engagement ring. "I wasn't expecting an engagement at all," she says a quarter century later. "It was romantic and a little old-fashioned. It felt almost like Pelle was becoming Americanized, because it was a really big ring and it was more of an American way to propose. It's not so common for Swedish guys." The couple celebrates their engagement in the sunshine of the Grand Canary Islands, where the Pietzsch family owns a vacation home. Pelle's mom, Anna-Lisa, and Kerstin's mother, Gudrun, also come along on the trip, but Kerstin's father, Werner Pietzsch, rarely has time to travel during the summer because of the demands of his business (he goes in the winter). "Yup, that was really romantic," Kerstin recalls with a laugh. "But we went out on our own a lot, and had time to celebrate ourselves."

Pelle and Kerstin together on the deck of their home in King's Grant [Courtesy Kerstin Somnell]

CHAPTER 19
TUESDAY, NOVEMBER 12, 1985.

At 10:00 am, Anna-Lisa and Sigge Lindbergh meet Kerstin at Kennedy Hospital. During the night, doctors feared that Pelle's organs would shut down, but he has stabilized again. For how long, no one knows.

Pelle's family sits down in a meeting room with the director of Kidney One, and Kerstin utters the hardest words she's ever had to say. "We've decided to donate Pelle's organs," she says. "But we still want to have a chance to say goodbye for the last time, so he has to keep breathing until we've at least had that chance." Dr. Louis Gallo explains that the family will have to do so within a tight time schedule, in order to maximize the chance for successful transplants.

After the discussion of the previous day, Gallo mapped out which of Pelle's organs could be donated matched to qualified candidates, but he still needs to examine them more closely for any damage incurred in the accident. The operation to remove the organs is planned for late in the afternoon into the evening. Ambulances will be stationed in front of the hospital so the organs can be rushed to other hospitals for immediate transplant. There are also logistics to work out with other hospitals to move the transplant patients to operating rooms at specific times.

Pelle's family signs the paperwork consenting for the respirator to be turned off and his organs removed. "That's the last I wanted to know about it," Anna-Lisa says years later. "I wanted [the people receiving Pelle's transplanted organs] to be able to live and to be well. But I didn't want to know anything else about it. It was too painful."

Bob Clarke and Jay Snider discuss for one final time whether to accept the Oilers' offer to postpone the game scheduled for Thursday. Assuming they go ahead with the game, the Flyers also need to decide whether it's more appropriate to hold a pregame memorial ceremony or go ahead with the game as if it were a regular season game.

The Sniders are also taking care of arrangements for a private funeral for Pelle to be held on Wednesday. The Gloria Dei (Old Swedes') Church on Delaware Avenue in Philadelphia seems to be the most appropriate location. There will also be a public memorial ceremony before the next game, and they ask Flyers' play-by-play announcer Gene Hart to direct the ceremony on the ice. It has all come so suddenly. "My God, can you believe we're sitting here planning a funeral?" Jay Snider asks.

Through Poulin, the Flyers players also offer their input on whether to carry on with the game and are grateful that their feelings are considered in the decision. "We talked very frankly about it amongst ourselves," Poulin says. "We had to wonder if we'd be able to focus on hockey, or if it would be disrespectful to Pelle and his family to be out there playing a hockey game so soon. "We also had to consider the aftermath of the game. If we won, could we really feel happy about it under the circumstances? If we lost, was it appropriate to deconstruct the game the way we would if Pelle had been there? There were no clear-cut answers." Ultimately, everyone comes to the conclusion that the best way to honor Pelle's life is to play hockey, because the sport was more than just the Swede's occupation, it was the greatest passion of a person whose very life was driven by the pursuit of his passions.

After practice at the Coliseum, several players go to the hospital to say their final goodbye to Pelle. One player who can't bring himself to go is Pelle

Eklund. "It felt too hard," he says two decades later. "I felt empty and just wanted to try to move on." When the players arrive at the hospital, they go up together to the third floor of the hospital, and stand at the foot of Pelle's bed. Kerstin sits in a chair beside the bed as everyone says his final words, either aloud or quietly. Wiping teardrops from their eyes, they leave quietly. Many of the players have cried more over the last two days than they have at any previous time of their lives. "Most of the Flyers players were still very young guys in there early and mid-20s. In many cases, this was the first time anyone close to them died, including grandparents. So Pelle's death shook them really hard," Al Morganti explains.

Clarke makes several phone calls to other NHL general managers to ask about the availability of backup goaltenders in trade. The Pittsburgh Penguins offer veteran Denis Herron and the Rangers offer Glen Hanlon, but both teams ask for greatly inflated returns because they know of the Flyers' dire straights. Clarke is neither surprised nor offended for such is hockey. He'd probably do the same thing if another team were stuck. He declines the offered trades, and that leaves the GM to consider minor league callups. He decides that it's better to call up a fill-in backup goaltender for Bob Froese rather than disrupt the Hershey Bears' rotation of rookie Ron Hextall and second-year goaltender Darren Jensen. The team has high hopes for Hextall in particular, and it's an awful burden for either to attempt to come up to the Flyers now. Clarke then contacts the Kalamazoo Wings of the International Hockey League and purchases the contract of Mike Bloski, a 23-year-old goaltender who briefly played for Hershey the previous season.

Shortly before noon, the doctors hold their final press conference in the hospital cafeteria. Dr. Ed Viner explains what will happen next. "Pelle's family has decided to donate Pelle's organs, which could potentially save others' lives. From a purely medical point of view, he's been dead since 5:40 am Sunday. The family has accepted the finality of his condition, but they want more private time with him." Viner concludes the press conference by saying; "Out of consideration to the people directly involved in this process, we respectfully ask that all journalists and photographers leave the hospital now. They will have to be coming and going frequently on the last day and should not be disturbed. Thank you." The crowd of roughly 100 journalists and photographers packs up and leaves, and the press trailer is cleared out within the hour.

The Flyers have experienced tragedy before. On May 1, 1977, assistant coach Barry Ashbee (who was a stalwart defenseman on the Flyers' first Stanley Cup team prior to a career-ending eye injury) passed away after battling leukemia. Bob Clarke delivered the eulogy for Ashbee at a memorial service in Toronto before his teammate and friend was laid to rest at Glendale Memorial Gardens in the Toronto suburbs. On this day, Clarke asks Dave Poulin to come to his office after the lunch. The general manager asks Poulin how the team is holding up. "The guys are holding up as well as possible, but it's very hard," Poulin says. Clarke nods. "I know." After a pause, the general manager says, "I want you to give the eulogy for Pelle tomorrow at the funeral. I did it for Barry Ashbee, and it's your turn now as captain to do that for Pelle." "Of course," replies Poulin. "OK," Clarke says. "You're going to have to write something, but you can do that. It'll be good." Poulin nods solemnly, and leaves the office deep in thought. The 26-year-old team leader wonders how to put words to his feelings about his friend whom he and his teammates have so suddenly lost.

As promised, Kerstin and Pelle's family members return to the house in King's Grant to meet with *Expressen* reporter Gunnar Nordström and photographer Hasse Persson. The journalists sit down with Anna-Lisa, Sigge, Kerstin, Göran, Thomas Eriksson, and his girlfriend Malin. Kerstin's mother, Gudrun, brings coffee and biscuits as the family tearfully shares its emotions about their loss and the decision to donate Pelle's organs. "I'm having trouble understanding why this all happened," Sigge says. In response, Nordström asks about the reported level of alcohol in Pelle's bloodstream. "I don't believe that amount," Sigge says firmly. Persson takes several photographs, and when they're finished, Kerstin asks, "Will you come to hear the eulogy tomorrow at the church? It's at one o'clock." "We can't," Nordström says. "Bob Clarke has forbidden all journalists and photographers from coming to the ceremony." "It's OK. I'll talk to him," Kerstin says.

It's late in the afternoon as Sigge, Anna-Lisa, and Göran say their last goodbye to Pelle. They've elected not to be there when the respirator is turned off, but Kerstin remains with her fiancée. Sigge and Anna-Lisa look upon their son's face for the final time. It was twenty-six years and 225 days ago, that Sigge came to Söder Sjukhuset in Stockholm with a bouquet of flowers and a Hammarby IF pennant, as they saw their newborn son together. All of the love, hard work, laughter and everyday ups-and-downs of the intervening years have now come to this. The Lindberghs are in an agony that goes far beyond the tears they shed. Their hearts have been shattered, never to be made whole again. It is several hours later, before the respirator is turned off, that Kerstin has a final moment alone with the man she'd been planning to marry. He lies on a gurney, and is covered by a sheet up to his breastbone. Tearfully, she lays a rose from Anna-Lisa on Pelle's chest.

By 8:00 pm, Dr. Gallo has finished removing Pelle's organs. Five ambulances leave Kennedy Hospital under police escort, and are bound for five different locations. Jack Prettyman leads the escort over the Delaware River to Philadelphia. All of the transplant surgeries are successful.

At Wills Eye Hospital, one of Pelle's corneas saves the eyesight of a year-old girl, and the other cornea is successfully transpla

Institute into a 30-year-old Philadelphia man. Several blocks away, at Thomas Jefferson Hospital, a successful liver transplant is performed on a 30-year-old male Delaware resident. Another success story occurs at Hahnemann Hospital, where a patient who receives both of Pelle's kidneys. And at Temple University Hospital, a 52-year-old Flyers season ticket holder by the name of John Keeler receives Pelle's heart. According to the book *Full Spectrum*, the heart surgeon performing the operation later tells Keeler's wife, Ann, that Lindbergh's heart is "the most beautiful I've ever seen." John Keeler lives five additional years after the surgery.

One hour after Pelle's death certificate is signed at John F. Kennedy Hospital, the Flyers issue a press release. They ask that in lieu of flowers, that people send donations to a cancer fund set up in Pelle's memory. The team informs the public that cancer research is the cause of choice because of the cancer struggle that Pelle's older sister, Ann-Christine, has undergone for the past couple of years. Many people around North America donate to Pelle's memorial fund, and Wayne Gretzky is the only NHL player from an opposing team to openly donate (some other players may have done so anonymously). The Oilers captain gives a generous donation from his own wealth and says it's on behalf of his Oilers' teammates as well as himself. Later in the evening Mike Keenan is approached for a comment on the Lindbergh family's decision to donate Pelle's organs. His response is both sensitive and eloquent. "Pelle's organs are going to save other lives," the Flyers coach says. "It's appropriate. He died making one more save."

Dave Poulin sits upstairs at his home, and composes a eulogy for Pelle. He's worked on it through the night, and it's coming along very slowly. The emotions are still too raw, and the events of the last several days too overwhelming. Alone in the room, Poulin continues to piece together his thoughts. He and Pelle used to call each other "PF" away from the rink. The other players assumed it stood for Philadelphia Flyers or was an inside joke between the two. Instead, the initials stood for "personal friend," a recognition that their bond went beyond just the camaraderie of being teammates. It was the type of friendship that would have carried on long past the end of their careers if Pelle had lived. Poulin remembers a good deal of Swedish from his time living and playing in Ängelholm during the whirlwind 1982-83 season. It was a year that saw him go from planning to quit hockey, to playing in Sweden, to getting a tryout with the Maine Mariners, to being called up to the Flyers and to making an instant impression. He got to know Pelle at the same time.

In recognition of the roots of their first meeting, Poulin peppers the eulogy with several Swedish words and phrases expressing friendship, caring and loyalty. Finally, the main theme of the speech becomes clear to Poulin: "Pelle has experienced more in a short time than most of us will during a whole lifetime." Some time after 3:00 am, a bleary-eyed Dave Poulin finally goes to bed.

Pelle Lindbergh

CHAPTER 20

PHILADELPHIA, PA.
OCTOBER 6, 1983.

It all starts out according to plan, but somehow everything falls apart at the seams over the next six months. The Flyers begin and end the 1983-84 season with games at the Spectrum against the Washington Capitals. The two games serve as a microcosm of the entire season, both for Pelle Lindbergh and the entire Flyers organization.

On opening night of the season (October 6, 1983), Pelle turns back 31 of 32 shots and is named first star of the game in a rousing 4-1 win over Washington. He hears raucous "Pell-lee! Pell-lee! Pell-lee!" chants throughout the game. Already an NHL All-Star and All-Rookie team selection the previous year, Lindbergh and the fans expect great things in his second season. The game also sees Mark Howe tally three points, and Bobby Clarke score in what proves to be the final opener of his career. Brian Propp puts the game away late, while Rick MacLeish scores the Flyers' first goal of the season. Soon enough, the focus is on Lindbergh. "Pelle won this game for us tonight," Howe says to the *Philadelphia Inquirer* afterwards. "We were absolutely brutal in the first period (outshot 10-3) and we were pretty sloppy in the second period, too. Pelle saved our bacon out there until we got going."

Nearly six months later, the Capitals complete a three-game sweep of the Flyers in the first round playoff miniseries. The fans boo throughout the contest and chant for Bob McCammon to be fired. Lindbergh, a frequent target of the Spectrum boo-birds, starts for the first and only time in the series and barely lasts one period. He is chased from the net at 1:52 of the second period with the Flyers trailing 3-0. The Caps go on to win, 5-1. Somewhere between the opening-night accolades and the continued playoff misery, Pelle withstands a season of hell, both on and off the ice.

In the summer of 1983, the Flyers undergo major managerial and infrastructure changes. Ed Snider passes team president duties over to his son, Jay, and the organization moves longtime general manager Keith Allen upstairs into a senior advisory role. The team gives GM duties and head-coaching responsibilities to McCammon, after the Pittsburgh Penguins courted him with an offer of both titles. The Flyers, also, promote skating instructor Ted Sator to a full-time assistant coaching role behind the bench. It was Sator who recommended Poulin to the Flyers during the previous season, and he was also the one who convinced the club to draft Pelle Eklund in the eighth round of the 1983 NHL Entry Draft. Despite lacking a first round pick, the '83 draft crop proves to be one of the deepest in Flyers history, producing the likes of Peter Zezel (2nd round, 41st overall), Derrick Smith (3rd round, 44th overall), and Rick Tocchet (6th round, 121st overall) as well as Eklund.

The club also announces a change in AHL farm teams. One of Jay Snider's first decisions as club president is to sell the team's interest in the Maine Mariners to the NJ Devils. The team opts to share an affiliation with the Springfield Indians in Springfield, Massachusetts with the Chicago Blackhawks. In the following season, the Flyers begin a decade-long affiliation with the Hershey Bears that ends in 1996 when the Flyers establish the Philadelphia Phantoms franchise to play in the Spectrum after the NHL team moves to a new arena across the parking lot. And finally, the Flyers make the Coliseum in Voorhees, NJ their new training rink. The facilities are much nicer, safer and more convenient than those of the Class of 1923 Arena at the University of Pennsylvania.

Training camp and the preseason go fine, and Pelle could hardly have scripted the start of the regular season any better. Two nights after his stellar opening-night performance against Washington, Lindbergh backstops the Flyers to a 6-3 win in the Montreal Forum. Poulin leads the way with a goal and an assist, while Ron Sutter scores the second goal of his NHL career. McCammon goes right back to Pelle the next day in Pittsburgh, and Swede turns back 28 of 29 shots in a 7-1 Flyers romp. Lindbergh goes on to rack up an 8-1-1 record in October, by allowing three goals or fewer in eight of his starts. He wins NHL Player of the Week award for the first week of the season and is runner-up for Player of the Month honors.

Then something unexpected happens: Pelle Lindbergh goes into a horrible November slump that continues to get worse over the next several months before it finally gets better. The slide begins on November 3 at the Spectrum. Coming off yet another strong performance in his previous start (a 3-1 win in Pittsburgh in which he stops 25 of 26 shots), Lindbergh takes a 4-3 lead into the third period against Los Angeles. Thus far in the season, the Flyers have been virtually automatic in closing out games they've led after two periods. But Pelle gives up a weak goal to Brian MacLellan at the 2:42 mark. Rather than getting refocused, Lindbergh lets the mistake bother him. He fumbles the next shot fired his way and is saved by Bernie Nicholls who hits the post on the rebound. Midway through the period, MacLellan scores again to give LA the lead, 5-4. Lindbergh gets a tap on the pads and some words of encouragement from Brad Marsh, but he's still upset over the turn of events in the period and his self-confidence sinks. Two shifts later, Charlie Simmer scores to make it a 6-3 game. A late Doug Crossman tally for Philly isn't nearly enough. After the game, McCammon shrugs off Pelle's third-period implosion as a simple bump in the road. "Give the other team credit," he says. "They were the better hockey team in the third period....Maybe Pelle would have liked to have had a couple of those back, but we didn't pick him up."

Two nights later, the Flyers go to St. Louis for a date with the Blues. A pair of Ilkka Sinisalo goals and single tallies by Rich Sutter and Darryl Sittler stake the Flyers to a 4-1 lead early in the second period, but the rest of the game is a virtual carbon copy of the Los Angeles game. After stopping 11 of the first 12 shots he faces, Lindbergh gives up three goals in quick succession after giving up a preventable Wayne Babych score. With the score now 4-4, Brian Propp restores the lead with a late period powerplay goal. The teams trade goals early the third period, as Rob Ramage re-ties the game and Bill Barber puts Philadelphia back ahead yet again. But Lindbergh can't slam the door with clutch saves. Midway through the final period gives up even-strength goals spaced just 1:23 apart. The Flyers go down, 7-6.

A third straight loss follows on November 8. The Flyers outshoot the New York Islanders on a two-to-one basis, but suffer several breakdowns and go down to a 4-1 defeat. As the month of November progresses, McCammon gives Bob Froese increased playing time. Meanwhile, Bernie Parent tries to give Lindbergh a pep talk and help him adjust his mechanics (Lindbergh has gotten beaten twice in his last start by dropping his shoulder). Parent says, "I've been there myself. I had a game once in Toronto where I think I gave up eight or nine goals. You see all this grey hair? That game almost turned my hair black again. Just calm down. Better times will come."

After an ugly 5-5 tie against the Minnesota North Stars, Pelle appears to make progress in his next two starts. Unfortunately the hopeful signs disappear in a brutal performance against Calgary. The Flyers win by an 8-5 score, but Pelle is pulled after the first period. Brian Propp and burgeoning sniper Tim Kerr rescue Pelle and the team with an offensive explosion. The more Pelle struggles, the more McCammon turns to Froese, who doesn't quite match his performance of January 1983, but plays more reliably than Lindbergh in the late fall and winter. Even a 29-save shutout against the woeful NJ Devils in the Flyers' last game before Christmas does little to lift Pelle's spirits. "I got lucky tonight," he says afterwards to the *Philadelphia Inquirer*. It's not false modesty, for four of Lindbergh's next five outings are horrid. The Rangers put six goals past him on December 30, and right after New Years, Pelle lasts just one period (stopping six of 10 shots) in a 7-6 win over Winnipeg.

Three nights later, the Capitals pump home a barrage of goals past the beleaguered keeper in a 7-1 win. Ironically, Lindbergh's frequent Tre Kronor teammate Bengt-Åke Gustafsson does most of the damage, by scoring five goals. "It was just a game where everything was going my way. Pelle did absolutely nothing wrong in that game," Gustafsson recalls. "The puck bounced the right way every time I shot it. One was a two-on-one rush, another one bounced off the defenseman's skate and went directly back to me."

By now, Lindbergh is the subject of trade rumors and the Spectrum crowd has started to turn against him. He confides his worries to Parent, who once again advises him to stop putting so much pressure on himself. "Pelle, all you can you do is keep working through this. If you get traded, well, there actually are other teams in the NHL," Parent says. Years later, Parent recalls,

> Pelle was such a positive guy, but he was allowing negative
> thoughts to get in his mind. That's when a goalie gets in trouble.
> But that's something every goaltender goes through sooner or later.
> I told Pelle it would be a beautiful thing when he worked through
> it. The only way to succeed is to learn how to deal with failure.

Pelle never lets out his private worries in the locker room or in public. During Lindbergh's struggles, his sense of humor remains intact. He does a tongue-in-cheek television interview with Gene Hart. "OK, here we have Pelle Lindbergh," Hart begins. "Pelle, you've won 248 consecutive games for the Flyers." "Yaaah, that's true," Lindbergh replies with a grin. "But now you really stink, with eight goals against in every game." "Yaaah, forgive me,"

Pelle pleads. "Well, now the Flyers have traded you to the Colorado Rockies," responds Hart. Lindbergh chimes in, "Yaaah, thanks a lot." The Colorado Rockies no longer exist by this point, as they have relocated to NJ and become the Devils.

Pelle's struggles on the ice hit rock bottom on Sunday, February 12. With the Flyers leading the Vancouver Canucks 5-4 midway through the third period, Darcy Rota flips the puck in from the neutral zone, and it caroms on net off the board. On the seemingly harmless play, Lindbergh gets crossed up and loses his balance as the puck goes into the net off his skate. The Spectrum crowd howls. Sitting on the ice, Lindbergh covers his head with his glove as the grinning Canucks celebrate the game-tying goal at center ice. "That goal was an absolute nightmare," Thomas Eriksson remembers years later, still shaking his head at the memory. It gets worse. With 1:54 left in regulation, Brad Marsh ties up Vancouver tough guy Dave "Tiger" Williams up in front of the net. A shot by Gary Lupul deflects off Williams and trickles in on Pelle. It's an easy save, but the goalie once again stumbles and falls down. The puck knocks off the goalie and inches over the goal line.

Now the crowd really lets Lindbergh have it. Even as he skates to the bench for an extra attacker, the booing continues. The Flyers fail to score the equalizer and the game ends in a 6-5 loss. From his place in the press box, all Bernie Parent can do is agonize at the depths to which his protégé has sunk. Lindbergh has become his own worst enemy. "It was hard to watch," he says today. "Afterwards, we had a long talk." Lindbergh feels so low after the game that he fights back tears. McCammon attempts to make a joke of the situation but makes his goaltender feel worse in the process. "We booked you a plane ticket to Sweden," he says. "It leaves at midnight."

The coach then repeats the quip to the local media. Afterwards, Pelle is asked about the booing he received from the fans. "I heard them, but I guess they heard enough from me, too. Do you know what it feels like to play like a zero, to feel like an absolute fool, in front of more than17,000 people? It feels horrible," he says. Speaking to Al Morganti of the *Philadelphia Inquirer*, Lindbergh asks, "Al, what the hell has happened to my game? I can't figure it out."

Two days later, on Valentine's Day, the Flyers send Pelle down to the AHL Springfield Indians. McCammon tells him that it will be a short-term assignment, but the length of his minor league stay will depend on Pelle himself. "We were forced to do something," McCammon recounts. "Pelle needed games in an environment where he could get his confidence back again." Adds Parent, "It was easier to make the adjustments Pelle had to make if he was playing in front of 3,000 people instead of 20,000."

At the same time, Lindbergh decides to view the situation as a challenge rather than a demotion. He's advised to do something different. He starts by ordering a new mask for his AHL games. "I want one like the one (New York Islanders' goalie Billy) Smith has," Pelle tells Kevin Cady. Lindbergh's Parent-style mask remains in his equipment bag for the time being. He wears a wire-cage mask, decorated with a Swedish flag on the forehead and a small angry wasp (the logo of Sweden's national *Expressen* newspaper) on the sides. Pelle gives Cady the thumbs up after testing the mask out. "Kev, when you see me on TV from Springfield, you'll think of me as a new, tough Billy Smith, not the old useless Pelle Lindbergh you know today. Now I'm just going to have fun and get back into the groove," Lindbergh says.

Pelle and Kerstin pack a suitcase and move into a hotel in Springfield, a city they experience as gray and depressing. "It was tough living at the hotel, but above all it felt like a big letdown for Pelle," Kerstin recounts. "Before the hand injury the previous year, he was on the way to a big breakthrough. What I can say about the weeks in Springfield is that Pelle felt low and really didn't enjoy being there."

To cheer himself up, Pelle calls his friends at home in Stockholm on nearly a daily basis. "Normally, we mostly wrote letters, instead of talking on the phone. But during this period, he called and wanted to talk often. I don't remember the exact words, but he wasn't feeling very good," says Ankan Lånström.

The Flyers are worried about Pelle's mental well-being. McCammon and Parent both realize that the goalie could just as easily continue spiraling downward as get his career back on track. Parent is concerned enough to travel to Springfield to spend two days with Lindbergh. "I went up from Philly and worked a lot to help him get back to the Flyers. We talked a lot, and it was a tough time," Parent recalls.

Pelle spends two weeks with the Indians and plays four games, giving up just 12 goals. More importantly, he gets better with each game and by the end rediscovers his joy for playing. The negative thoughts are replaced by anticipation of the next save. Bob McCammon attends Lindbergh's final game, and watches with great relief from the stands. "The other team outshot them by double, and the Springfield players were nowhere to be seen. But Pelle looked like himself again, and they won game, 1-0. So I met him in the room after the game and say, 'Gump, pack up your gear, you're coming back.'"

The next day, February 26, 1983, Pelle starts for the Flyers in Hartford, and he rides with McCammon to the team's hotel. "We were in the car for an hour and we talked a lot about what was happening in his life and how he felt. I got to explain to him that we didn't send him down because we didn't have faith in him, we did so he could find himself again," McCammon says.

The Hartford game is another fiasco, at least on the scoreboard. Lindbergh gets strafed for six goals on 24 shots in the first period, and the Whalers go on to win by a 9-6 score. The lone highlights for the Flyers are two goals by Mark Howe and a three-point game for Tim Kerr, which includes the big winger's fortieth goal of the season. "The score looked real ugly but it wasn't Pelle's fault in that game and I told him that. He actually played well in Hartford when he had a chance to make the saves," McCammon says.

Kerstin checks them out of the hotel and moves their things back to South Jersey. With each successive start, Lindbergh regains his form a little bit at a time. McCammon rotates the goaltending chores between Froese and Lindbergh.

The next year, in an interview with *The Hockey News*, Pelle looks back at his trials and tribulations. From the safe vantage point of his breakthrough 1984-85 season, Lindbergh says that the biggest lesson of his struggles was that he needed to have more faith in himself as an NHL player and be more patient. "The problem was that I began to listen to everyone else. I listened too much to a bunch of different advice and I tried to make everything right all at once. But if you forget to play your own game, you've got problems," Lindbergh says. "In some of the games, I could hardly believe what was going on. It felt like every time the puck came in the zone it would go off a skate and come right in on goal. I lost my self-confidence."

Three days before the start of the 1984 playoffs, Pelle has his first appointment with psychologist Dr. Steven Rosenberg. The sessions go a long way toward helping Lindbergh revamp his mental approach, and continue for the rest of his life. Even as Pelle starts to piece his professional life back together again, the spring of 1984 is a tough time for the entire Lindbergh family. Pelle's older sister, Ann-Christine is diagnosed with cancer, and undergoes a hellish course of treatment. When he's not discussing his hockey career with Dr. Rosenberg, Pelle often tries to work through his feeling of helplessness about Ann-Christine's condition. "I'm a little down," he tells Rosenberg the first time. " It's so unfair! Mentally, my mind is back in Sweden. It's hard to focus on hockey right now." Kerstin recalls,

> Pelle's family meant the world to him. In a certain way, he wanted to give back to them for all they'd done for him, and now he could try to help. Ann-Christine's sickness hit him very hard, but there was really nothing he could do. Pelle was frustrated that he couldn't live near her and be a support when she was fighting for her life. He had several long phone conversations with Ann-Christine and begged her to come over with her family after the operation so he could help. But that was impossibile because of her condition and the planned treatment of the cytoxin.

> According to Anna-Lisa, Pelle's talks with his older sister were therapeutic for both of her children. "Ann-Christine's conversations with Pelle cheered her up. Pelle came to understand that, too."

The regular season ends with Pelle posting a 16-13-3 record, 4.05 goals against average and .860 save percentage in 36 games played. Froese had some ups-and-downs of his own, but was the better of the two goalies in all but October. He ends up with a 28-13-7 record, 3.15 goals against average and .887 save percentage in 48 games. The Flyers finish with 98 points, good enough for third place in the Patrick Division (the Rangers win the division with 105 points). As usual, the Flyers are dominant at home (25-10-5), but they are barely more than a .500 team on the road this year. Philadelphia draws second-place Washington (101 points) in the first-round mini-series. McCammon names Froese as his starting goaltender for the series opener. Lindbergh is disappointed, but also realizes that Frosty has outplayed him over the bulk of the season and deserved the first start.

The Caps take the first game, 4-2. Pelle gets mop-up duty late in the game with Washington well ahead. In the second game, Froese is not sharp and the Capitals breeze, 6-2. Lindbergh gets the start in Game 3. In one of the ugliest playoff games in team history, the dispirited Flyers get thrashed while the Spectrum crowd boos throughout the game and calls for McCammon's head with chants of "Bob must go!" Pelle hears some boos, too. He's pulled for Froese just 1:23 into the second period after Gary Sampson makes it a 3-0 game on Washington's thirteenth shot of the game. The Capitals go on to win, 5-1. Shortly thereafter, McCammon is fired as head coach and general manager, and Bobby Clarke retires as an active player and becomes the new GM. After considering various coaching candidates, he narrows the choices down to Flyers' assistant Ted Sator and University of Toronto bench boss Mike Keenan.

With the help of real estate agent Ed Parvin, Pelle and Kerstin find a new home they love in the Kings Grant neighborhood of Marlton, NJ. The house at 28 Landings Drive is located in a development that is 15 minutes away from the Cherry Hill area where they'd been living. They settle into their house before heading back to Stockholm two days after the Flyers are knocked out of the playoffs.

On May 24, 1984, Pelle has his 25th birthday. The couple celebrates with a one-week vacation in Mallorca, and Kerstin gives Pelle a special birthday gift: She has had his Olympic ring redone into something bigger and more valuable. "I had worked in a jewelry boutique, and I went back there and took the ring that Pelle got from the King at the Olympics in Lake Placid. All the players on the team had gotten the same ring; it had the interlocked Olympic rings on it. It was very beautiful, but it wasn't set in real gold. So I had it set in gold for Pelle," Kerstin recalls. Pelle wears the ring every day for the rest of his life.

CHAPTER 21

WEDNESDAY, NOVEMBER 13, 1985

Kerstin sleeps in her bed at home, for the time since the accident. It's a very hard night, as she knows that she'll never wake up next to her fiancée again. In the morning, she receives a phone call from Pelle's agent, Frank Milne, who will be flying to Philadelphia to attend the memorial service at Gloria Dei Church. He wishes to meet with Kerstin.

The Canada-based attorney has the unpleasant duty of telling Kerstin that together they need to make an estate inventory for Pelle, and there will be a need to coordinate the dispersal of Pelle's assets in accordance with Swedish as well as American law. Under Swedish law, an inventory must be drawn up of Pelle's assets within three months of the date of his death. The inventory must then be registered with the district court, and an inheritance tax calculated which is based on all property and cash assets left to Pelle's family. As a further complication, there is the issue of Pelle's unsigned contract with the Flyers. Although Bob Clarke has pledged to honor the agreement in full, nothing is in writing.

Another legal challenge is the fact that Kerstin and Pelle are not yet married, and there's a chance Pelle's life insurance company will balk about Kerstin being a beneficiary. In any kind of a settlement, Pelle's parents would have to be represented separately, because they are the next-of-kin and reside in Sweden. "Frank, it's very hard for me to even think about anything like this right now," Kerstin says. "I know it is," he says softly. "And I'm very sorry."

The Flyers hold their last practice session at the Coliseum prior to the game against the Oilers, and Keenan puts the team through the paces. Privately, he's proud of the extraordinary focus and determination which his players are showing. He knows that their hearts ache, yet they go about their business on the ice in a crisp, high-tempo practice. "It's one thing to talk about mental toughness and character, and quite another thing to display it. I've been blessed with many teams that have had tremendous character…It took extraordinary fortitude for the players on the Flyers to come back and prepare to play after Pelle Lindbergh died," Keenan said in a 1994 television interview.

In front of his players, however, Keenan is back in full "Iron Mike" mode: yelling at everyone, demanding everyone dig a little deeper, and seemingly incapable of being pleased. The Flyers suffer a major setback at practice. Bob Froese gets drilled full-force between the legs. Despite wearing a protective cup, he's in an agony that worsens throughout the day. Despite this setback, Froese attends the memorial service for Pelle in the afternoon, but Dr. Ed Viner declares that he is in no shape to play hockey.

The Flyers are left without a proven NHL goalie for the Edmonton game, as Clarke and Keenan huddle quickly. There's no way the team can risk starting fringe minor leaguer Mike Bloski against the power-packed Oilers. They also cannot obtain a serviceable veteran from another NHL team at anything less than an astronomical price. The team does not wish to put undue pressure on Hershey prospects Ron Hextall or Darren Jensen, even in a backup capacity. Now, however, they have no choice but to recall one of them to start until Froese recover. The Flyers opt for Jensen, the second year pro, and inform him that he's going to start against the Stanley Cup champion Oilers.

As a schoolboy, Pelle Lindbergh was never very interested in learning about history. But the man whom Flyers' announcer Gene Hart deemed "Sweden's gift to Philadelphia hockey" was a latter-day arrival to a region that traces its earliest European settlements to Lindbergh's Swedish homeland. The first European settlers of the modern-day Delaware Valley were not William Penn and the British Quakers. The Swedes came first. In 1638, Swedish settlers arrived on two ships (the *Kalmar Nyckel* and the *Fogel Grip*) in what is now Wilmington, Delaware. They established a colony called New Sweden. In 1700, some 19 years after establishment of William Penn's Pennsylvania colony, the Swedish community dedicated a new brick church building at what is now Columbus Boulevard and Christian Street in Philadelphia. Three hundred years later, the Gloria Dei Church (also known as Old Swedes Church) is a US national landmark as the oldest church building in Pennsylvania and the second-oldest in the Unites States.

During his lifetime, Pelle Lindbergh never set foot in the Gloria Dei Church, for he was not a religious man. Nevertheless, in putting together the arrangements for Pelle's memorial, the Gloria Dei Church seemed to be especially appropriate to remember Lindbergh.

The mourners file into the church and pass the two lit candles in front of the entrance. The Flyers players and club personnel arrive by bus and most are too distraught to speak. In addition to the Flyers players, several of Pelle's hockey friends and former teammates from other clubs attend the service, including Mel Bridgman, Anders Hedberg and Ulf Nilsson. There are also representatives from the Philadelphia Phillies, Eagles, and 76ers.

The *Expressen* reporter and photographer, Gunnar Nordström and Hasse Persson, realize that they do not have any funeral-appropriate clothing at their residences in Manhattan. Hurriedly, they purchase black suits off the rack and drive to Philadelphia for the private memorial service. Kerstin has cleared with Bob Clarke that they be allowed to attend the service, while all other media members must remain outside. Photographer Hasse Persson stations himself up on the balcony and takes the only pictures permitted at the memorial. Reporter Gunnar Nordström sits in one of the back pews.

Sigge, Anna-Lisa, and Kerstin arrive in the white limousine, which the Flyers arranged, and they walk into the church last. Kerstin walks in the middle and holds Pelle's parents' hands. Pelle's family sits in the front pew and Reverend Evert Olsson begins the service. Apart from Reverend Olsson, the only person who speaks is Dave Poulin. Speaking softly but resolutely, the Flyers' captain delivers his handwritten eulogy:

> Pelle experienced more in his short time than many of us will in an entire lifetime. He traveled across the world, he forged many friendships, and wherever Pelle went, he left an impression.…We will remember Pelle for his broad smile. We all teased him for his slightly unusual ways, but I believe we were all a little envious. …I said to Pelle that I was friends with the winningest goaltender in the National Hockey League, and I was always proud of that.

Poulin continues by dropping several Swedish phrases which he learned during his season playing in Ängelholm,

> The first thing my wife and I learned to say when we moved to Sweden was *'Jag älskar dig'* ('I love you'). And now I'll say in English or any other language, that I believe I speak for all of my teammates when I say, *'Pelle, jag älskar dig, vi älskar dig alla'* (Pelle, I love you, we all love you').

The service concludes with the Lord's Prayer (called *"Father Vår"* in its Swedish version). The prayer is recited, both in English and Swedish.

In the evening, *Aftonbladet* reporter Bert Willborg meets with Kerstin at the house in Kings Grant. He asks Kerstin about the reports of Pelle's blood alcohol level. She sighs,

> Right from the beginning, I found out that alcohol was involved. Everyone who knew Pelle knew that he liked to go out almost every evening when he was at home. It's not true that he drank all the time, but if he did drink, he didn't take the car.... The first year I was here, Pelle and I would go out on Friday nights, and maybe I'd want a glass of wine with dinner, but he would drink milk. That was his usual (behavior). Otherwise, he wouldn't have become the best goaltender in the NHL....It's strange that he would drink before taking his Porsche. He was (usually) so careful about that. But when he did drink, he could tolerate a lot. I'm sure he certainly didn't think he was drunk.

The Edmonton Oilers arrive at their Center City hotel. This has been a tough week for them, too. At first, they're not sure if the game against the Flyers will even take place. Now they have to try to stay focused on the game while at the same time being respectful of Lindbergh's death. "We would have understood if they wanted to postpone the game," said Wayne Gretzky. "Now that we're here, we have to do our best to win. But right now, it's hard to think about how we can go out and have a good game."

245

Elsewhere in the NHL, moments of silence are held in Buffalo, Hartford, Chicago, Calgary, and Los Angeles. In Sweden, Hammarby players wear black armbands on their green uniforms during their game against Vallentuna. The following day, Lindbergh's memory is honored before the four games taking place in Elitserien.

CHAPTER 22

PHILADELPHIA, PA.
OCTOBER 10, 1984

It's the evening before the Flyers' regular season opener, and the club has been dubbed "The Broad Street Babies." With an average age of 24 years and four months the Flyers are by far the youngest team in the NHL. What's more they have a 34-year-old rookie coach behind the bench and a novice general manager in Bob (no longer Bobby) Clarke. The team gets even younger with the surprise trade of veteran Darryl Sittler to the Detroit Red Wings for 21-year-old forward Murray Craven and 25-year-old winger Joe Paterson.

Around the NHL, expectations for Philadelphia are modest. Some have predicted that the Flyers could finish as low as fourth in their own division, and few think Philadelphia is destined to break its string of first-round playoff exits while in the midst of a transitional season. But the Philadelphia Flyers and goaltender Pelle Lindbergh have a surprise in store for the pundits. Over the course of the next eight months, the club will reestablish itself as an elite team, while its Swedish goaltender will blossom into the league's best goaltender. "There's a symbiotic relationship between confidence and winning," recalled team captain Dave Poulin,

> In our case, we had a strong belief in ourselves and in one another, and I think it's fair to say that the whole was greater than the sum of the parts. Pelle was an indispensable part of our team success. When you have a goalie playing the way he did all year, it makes you skate with more confidence as a hockey team. We had a team where you knew everyone had your back, and we played in

a building where the fans were almost like the seventh man on the ice…. It was always just a matter of time for Pelle and, fortunately for all of us, his time coincided with when we had the right pieces in place around him.

At the end of April 1984, former coach and general manager Bob McCammon worked his last day as a Philadelphia Flyers' employee. New general manager Clarke quickly narrowed the field of coaching candidates down to current assistant coach Ted Sator and an outside candidate, 35-year-old Mike Keenan. Ten days later, the Flyers name Keenan their new coach. Hyper-organized, extremely intelligent, and often arrogant, Keenan had won at every level at which he'd coached. He was a complex man who could almost seem to be several different people wrapped up into one. Keenan reveled in his own contradictions, and called himself "predictably unpredictable."

After his graduation from college in 1974, Keenan worked as a teacher in a school near Toronto, and by night, he was a player-coach in a local hockey league. By the end of five years, he was a professional coach who was considered a protégé of the legendary Scotty Bowman. In 1979, Buffalo Sabres GM Bowman hired Keenan to coach the Sabres' AHL farm team, the Rochester Americans. As coach of Rochester, Keenan saw enough of Maine Mariners goalie Pelle Lindbergh to know that the MVP-winning keeper had an extremely bright future ahead of him. In 1982-83, when Lindbergh was an NHL rookie and Bob Froese joined him midseason, Rochester swept Maine (with Sam St. Laurent in goal) in the Calder Cup Finals.

Feeling like he'd hit a glass ceiling in the Sabres' organization, Keenan stepped out of pro coaching for one year to return to the University of Toronto as its head coach, and the team won the Canadian collegiate championship. After the season, the Flyers, NJ Devils, and Vancouver Canucks contacted him about coaching opportunities. When Keenan interviewed for the job, he presented himself well by dressing impeccably and speaking in a calm, self-assured, and polite tone of voice. He spoke frequently of the need for a coach and a team to have mutual understanding and strong communication. The Flyers' brass soon discovered that Keenan was the polar opposite of Bob McCammon. There were, however, rumors that Keenan's players in Rochester and University of Toronto were contemplating mutiny had he not left on his own accord. Flyers' management decided that the contrast between his meticulous style and McCammon's fly-by-the-seat-of-the-pants ways as a head coach would do the young team some good. The one constant in Keenan's philosophy of coaching: Never let there be an excuse or a tolerance for losing. Everything is geared toward making sure his players are single-mindedly focused on winning hockey games. Keenan could challenge his players to think about hockey in situations where it wouldn't ordinarily occur to them.

Keenan retains Ted Sator and adds E.J. McGuire, his assistant from Rochester, in addition to Bernie Parent as the goaltending coach. Lindbergh respects both assistants immensely, although he feels closer to Sator because he's been with him longer. Having coached in Sweden, the coach can communicate with him in Swedish when necessary. "Pelle could always get me to laugh, whether he was speaking English or Swedish," Sator recalls.

He could say something funny after allowing a bad goal at practice, and I'd have to laugh….but no one is always happy during a hockey season. Sometimes there are hard days on the job, even for the league's best players. There were certain days where Pelle had something on his mind, and he'd tell me how he felt or what he was worried about. There were a few times he couldn't say exactly what he wanted in English, so it was good that we could speak Swedish at those times. But most of the time, there were a whole lot of days where the Flyers needed Pelle Lindbergh more than Pelle needed the Flyers.

In August, Keenan conducts one-on-one meetings with his new players. One of the first players he talks to is Poulin. The first question he asks is, "Do you think we have the goaltending to win the Cup?" Poulin's answer is immediate, "Yes, both Gump and Frosty can do it." When Keenan meets with Pelle, he has a pleasant surprise in store for the Swede. Coming off his rough 1983-84 campaign, Lindbergh expects to have to compete with Froese for the starting spot. Keenan says, "I've enjoyed watching you play, and I was impressed by what you did for Maine. I was thinking about rotating you and Froese, but I've decided that you're going to start. The only thing I demand is that you do your best all the time and believe in what I tell you to do." They shake hands.

Pelle turns down an invitation to play for Sweden at the 1984 Canada Cup. The situation causes tension between Lindbergh and Tre Kronor coach Leif Boork. "Pelle had a tough year the previous season, and Ann-Christine was very sick, so he turned it down and tried not to focus on hockey until it was time to get ready for the Flyers camp. Leif Boork called him selfish, questioned his patriotism, you name it," Reino Sundberg says. The situation ended up hitting the national Swedish newspapers, with Lindbergh defending his refusal to play in the tournament.

In the mid-1980s, players and teams begin to place much greater emphasis on off-season conditioning. It's no longer good enough for players to "work their way into shape" at camp after spending the summer fishing and drinking beer. Soon, the acceptability of coming to camp in less than peak condition will go the way of players without helmets.

The Flyers, under the auspices of Pat Croce, are one of the NHL clubs at the forefront of the movement toward greater physical fitness. Training camps become shorter, but more intense. Pelle is not a big fan of the change. "Pelle never enjoyed that. He couldn't turn on to the idea that he could be an even better goalie with harder physical conditioning," says Dave Poulin. When Keenan took over, he connected fast with Pat Croce. Together, they really elevated the expectations of what the players needed to do. "They had the players gather and they took the players' pulses before and after practice, measured their body fat and did other tests to measure conditioning. They also paid attention to things like how much water players drank." Croce then creates personalized fitness plans for different players. Pelle gets nabbed for having a little too much fun during the summer. "Because Pelle was seldom in really good shape when he came to camp, it gave me a reason to make sure he puked. I gave him hell," Croce recalls with a grin. Eventhough he privately grumbles about the regimen at first, Lindbergh does everything he's asked, and gets into the best shape of his career. As he notices his stamina increase, Pelle credits Croce for helping him remake his training habits. Another part of the reason why Pelle buys into the routine is that it comes with Bernie Parent's seal of approval. "Bernie told him it was good to hold the position as long as possible, because he wanted Pelle to be strong in his abdomen, back, and diaphragm," says Sator.

Pelle and Bob Froese are as different as two goaltenders can be, both on and off the ice. They've never been close friends, but they've gained a mutual respect for each other over their three seasons as teammates. Away from the game, Pelle likes fast cars, hanging out with friends and going to rock concerts. He's not religious. Froese on the other hand is a devout Christian (he becomes a minister after his playing days are over) and his non-hockey life revolves around the Bible, his wife Ruth, and sons Robbie and David. In Pelle's third full NHL season, he begins to interact more comfortably with Froese, especially when the team is traveling.

During the 1983-84 season, Pelle got off to a tremendous start only to crash in November and steadily see his season disintegrate. The 1984-85 season, like the previous one, starts with Lindbergh playing a strong game against the Washington Capitals (he's named first star of the game with a 30-save performance in a 2-2 tie, with Ilkka Sinisalo and Tim Kerr providing the offense). But this time around, there's no drop-off for Lindbergh or the Flyers. Philadelphia goes 6-2-2 in October, highlighted by a 13-2 win over the Vancouver Canucks on October 18. Froese sees only 19 shots to 58 generated by the Flyers.

In November, the Flyers post an 8-2-2 record. On November 19, Pelle is named NHL Player of the Week for the second time in his career. After blanking St. Louis by a 6-0 score on 29 shots, he beats the Edmonton Oilers and downs Hartford 6-1 on Bobby Clarke Night at the Spectrum. Philadelphia television station KYW-TV 3 interviews Lindbergh after Clarke Night. He is named third star of the game. "There was always Bernie Parent and Bobby Clarke when you think of the Flyers," Lindbergh says. "Bernie was my hero, because I'm a goaltender, but you also can't think about the Flyers without Bobby Clarke. He's always been a big help to me and so this was a special game for me." Over the course of the next several days, Pelle outduels former teammate Pete Peeters in a 5-3 Flyers' win at the Boston Garden, and earns first-star honors after turning back 37 of 40 shots in a 3-3 home tie against the Islanders.

December sees the Flyers hit their first mini-slump of the season, by losing five of six before righting their ship. Philly closes out the calendar year with wins in Vancouver (7-4) and Los Angeles (3-2). The New Year begins with a rousing 5-2 win in Edmonton. After the Flyers drop a hard-fought 4-3 game in Calgary the next night, Philly reels off a 6-1-1 record over the next eight games. The stretch sees Lindbergh get revenge on the Flames by stopping 24 of 25 shots in a game. Next the Flyers hit their second rough patch of the season, as they deal with injuries to stalwart defensemen Mark Howe and Brad McCrimmon. Lindbergh gets a one-game rest after starting 24 straight games. Rookie Darren Jensen starts and loses 7-5 against the Islanders.

Philadelphia begins to fly again on February 9. In a rousing game in Landover, MD against the Capitals, Pelle has a pedestrian game but the team picks up for him. Lindbergh yields four goals on 24 shots and takes a costly slashing penalty, but the Flyers keep coming back to erase deficits. Twenty-four hours later, Pelle is chosen as first star in a game that sees the Flyers prevail by a 3-2 score and Lindbergh stops 32 of 34 shots.

As the Flyers hit the NHL All-Star break, Lindbergh is selected to represent the Wales Conference for the second time in his three-season career. His first All-Star game was one of the most humiliating performances of his career, with Wayne Gretzky picking him apart. The second time around goes much better. Lindbergh and Buffalo's Tom Barrasso (the starter) split the game. Pelle pitches the *equivalent* of a shut out period despite the wide-open play in front of him. Finally, his old All-Star nemesis, Gretzky, solves him. In all, Lindbergh stops 11of 13 shots – very respectable by All-Star game standards. The Wales Conference wins, 6-4. "I was nervous before I came in," Pelle says afterwards. "My self-confidence was OK, but I'm going up against the best attackers in the world in this type of game."

Lindbergh has a love-hate relationship with Keenan. On the one hand, he's grateful for the coach's confidence in him, but on the other, Keenan's tantrums and public humiliations of players grate on him. In spite of all of this, he makes a point of shaking Keenan's hand after every victory before he changes out of his uniform. In interviews, Lindbergh invariably points to the playing time Keenan gives him as a key to his newfound ability to keep bad goals or bad games from snowballing. "Pelle and Mike had a unique relationship," recalls Dave Poulin. "Sometimes Mike would openly get on Pelle. He'd lay into him and complain that the team needed a better goalie. But I think Mike knew Pelle was strong enough mentally to handle it… In the season-plus Pelle and Mike were together, the results were almost magical."

There's nothing wrong with Lindbergh's focus late in the regular season. After the All-Star break, he wins 15 of 19 decisions, is named NHL Player of the Week for the second time (April 8) and grabs his first NHL Player of the Month award. Among the highlights are a 34-save shutout over the Islanders, another win over Edmonton, a 31-save performance against the Rangers in the midst of an eight-goal Flyers offensive explosion, and a 38-save night as Philly closes the regular season with a 6-1 win over NJ. Lindbergh wins the inaugural Bobby Clarke Trophy as Flyers' team MVP. He accepts the award as thunderous "Pell-lee! Pell-lee!" chants reverberate around the Spectrum. He receives the award at the final home game of season.

In what was initially predicted to be a transitional year, the Flyers win the President's Trophy for the best regular-season record in the NHL. The club posts a 53-20-7 record (113 points) and goes 32-4-4 at the Spectrum for an extraordinary .850 winning percentage on home ice. Lindbergh boasts a 40-17-7 record in 65 games. In the midst of the NHL's highest scoring era, he posts a 3.02 goals against average and .899 save percentage. The Swede later learns that his extraordinary regular season has earned him NHL First-Team All-Star honors and the Vezina Trophy, but his more immediate concern is the playoffs. As the press frequently reminds them, the Flyers have been ousted in the first round of the playoffs in each of the last three years, and neither Pelle nor Froese have fared well in the postseason.

Bernie Parent, as usual, knows just what to say to Lindbergh. Pelle isn't outwardly nervous about the playoffs, but the Flyers goaltending coach knows the constant talk of postseason failures could weigh on any young goalie. At the team's final practice before the start of the playoffs, Parent says,

"All this 'Can't win in the playoffs' talk is bullshit. You wanna know something, Pelle? I never won a playoff series before we won the Stanley Cup for the first time. Just go out and keep on doing what you've done all season, and you'll never hear a thing again about not winning in the playoffs."

Despite the Flyers' youth, the club is stacked for a lengthy playoff run. The only element of a Stanley Cup championship squad missing from the team is a prolific playmaking forward. The team has offensive depth, a stellar top defensive pairing, a collection of gutsy two-way forwards, toughness, leadership, and outstanding goaltending. In the offensive end, Tim Kerr has blossomed into an unstoppable force, racking up 54 goals and 98 points. Brian Propp is right behind him with 43 goals, 54 assists and 97 points. Ilkka Sinisalo scores 36 goals and 76 points despite missing 10 games with injury. Dave Poulin hits the 30-goal plateau, while rookie callup Todd Bergen surprises everyone with 11 goals and 16 points in 14 games and Murray Craven chips in 26 goals and 61 points in his first year with the club.

The team also gets significant offensive contributions from the blueline. Mark Howe shrugs off his injuries to contribute 18 goals and 57 points, while Brad McCrimmon takes advantage of the attention paid to Howe by chipping in eight goals and 43 points in just 66 games. Two of Keenan's less-favored defensemen, Thomas Eriksson and Doug Crossman also help spark the offense. Eriksson hits double-digit goals, while Doug Crossman adds 33 assists. Defensively, Howe (plus-51) and McCrimmon (plus-52) anchor the team, with Brad Marsh (plus-42) serving as the third defenseman.

Over all the locker room is exceptionally close-knit, and is bonded both by their experiences dealing with Keenan and by the joy of winning on nearly a nightly basis. "We loved coming to the rink every day. That season was a lot of fun," recalls forward Dave Brown. "We had a hard-working team, but when you're winning and everyone is committed the way this group of guys was, it never feels like you're working hard. It's just fun."

Even though Poulin barely had a full year's worth of NHL experience under his belt coming into the season, the 25-year-old center quickly gains the reputation of being one of the game's premier leaders. "A lot of attention gets focused on the player with the "C" on his uniform, but one person can't possibly lead alone. Winning teams have a strong leadership group. That's something we definitely had in Philadelphia," Poulin recounts. One of Poulin's key roles as captain is to serve as a buffer between the players and the intensely critical Keenan. When necessary, Poulin is not afraid to support his teammates and stand up to Keenan in a respectful way. "Perfection is impossible to attain in this sport. But there are variables that are under your control, and that's what Mike Keenan constantly harped on. Never get beaten because the other team was more prepared than you, physically or mentally. There was no hiding from Mike. He figured each one of us out very quickly, and he harped on the areas we needed to improve," Poulin says. Under the new captain's leadership, the other Flyers fall in line. The team's mental toughness and focus are nothing short of remarkable.

Two days before the Flyers open the playoffs, the players are shown films of the Flyers' 1974 and 1975 Stanley Cup Final victories. "We don't want to compare teams, but maybe you can get a feeling of how it can happen for you," Bob Clarke explains. For many of the players, it's their first time of watching the historic clinching wins against Boston and Buffalo, but Pelle Lindbergh, having seen the games countless times on the film projector at his family's home in Stockholm, knows every play by heart "I bet I know what's gonna happen next!" Pelle shouts, laughing. "Fifty bucks says Rick MacLeish is going to score on a deflection."

The Flyers take on the Rangers in the best-of-five opening round. Although the Flyers finished the regular season a staggering 51 points ahead of the Blueshirts, the Flyers have learned the hard way that the Rangers are a dangerous first-round opponent. Philadelphia was ousted by New York in the 1978-79 quarterfinals as well as the 1981-82 and 1982-83 divisional mini-series.

Game one takes place at the Spectrum on April 10. The crowd grows nervous as an early 3-0 lead steadily evaporates by early in the third period. Kerr restores the lead at 6:04 of the third period and the Flyers cling to the lead. In the final minute of play, the Rangers pull Glen Hanlon for an extra attacker. Anders Hedberg ties the game at 4-4 with just 26 seconds left on the clock.

Keenan rages at the team during the intermission, and questions the guts and determination of his club. The Flyers dominate the overtime, by firing nine of the 10 shots sent on goal during the extra frame. Finally, Mark Howe sneaks past Hedberg and sends the crowd home happy, by sealing a 5-4 overtime decision. Despite recording his first playoff victory on 27 saves, Lindbergh isn't satisfied. "I wasn't too happy with myself," Lindbergh says to Prism television afterwards. "I need to play better than this, but the guys picked me up. Hey, I'll take the win and we'll go back at it tomorrow."

The second game is a rough-and-tumble affair with the Rangers out-playing the Flyers in the first period, but Lindbergh is flawless in turning away 15 shots. The Rangers finally break through in the opening minute of the second period, but Lindbergh holds the score right there until his team finally gets its skating legs going. Todd Bergen ties the score midway through regulation and the Flyers' keeper holds the fort through a late-period penalty that erupts into near brawl at the end of the period. In the final period, Bergen gives the Flyers the lead early in the period and Sinisalo provides some much-needed insurance with 2:40 remaining in the game. Lindbergh, who stops 38 of 39 shots, earns a standing ovation at the end when he's named the game's first star. The win turns out to be costly, as Poulin suffers a ligament tear in his left knee in the second game against the Rangers. He misses a total of six out of the next eight games, including the entire second round against the New York Islanders before returning for the Wales Conference Finals.

Game three is the Tim Kerr show. The Flyers power forward takes over the game in the second period, turning a 3-2 deficit into a 6-3 lead by scoring four straight goals over the span of eight minutes, 18 seconds. The Rangers fight back for two third-period goals, but it's too little too late. The final goal is scored by Hedberg – his last goal in the NHL before he retires. "I've always kept that puck, not because it was my last NHL goal. I see it as my goal against Pelle," Hedberg recalls. "Pelle was excellent in that series and the Flyers were too tough for us." The Flyers survive the Rangers final, desperate push. At the final buzzer, Brad Marsh is the first teammate to embrace Lindbergh.

The New York Islanders are the Flyers' opponent in the Stanley Cup quarterfinals, and the aging nucleus of the four-time champions has finally begun to show its age. At least one prominent pundit predicts the Islanders will win the series: Don Cherry. Not surprisingly, the notoriously anti-European *Hockey Night in Canada* commentator points to Lindbergh as the reason why he thinks the Flyers will fall short. "You can't win with a Swedish goalie in the playoffs," he says. Lindbergh responds by shutting out the Islanders in the opener, once again taking first-star honors. After a scoreless opening period, Rick Tocchet and Ron Sutter solve Kelly Hrudey, and Ron Sutter adds some extra insurance with 3:36 left in the game.

Three nights later, Lindbergh keeps the Islanders at bay until the final minute of the second period, when Clark Gillies finally breaks Pelle's shutout stretch on the Islanders' forty-fifth shot of the series. By this point, however, the Flyers already have a 4-0 lead built up on a rare Ed Hospodar goal and a natural hat trick by Brian Propp. Tim Kerr scores to make it 5-1 in the third period, and then Bobby Nyström scores a meaningless goal late in regulation to close the final deficit to 5-2. Lindbergh is named second star for stopping 26 of 28 shots.

The scene shifts to Long Island for the third game. Lindbergh spots the Islanders an early goal after an attempted centering pass by Anders Kallur banks into the net off his skate. He then settles in as Doug Crossman and Rick Tocchet give the Flyers a 2-1 lead by the end of the first period. In a fight-filled middle frame, Ron Sutter extends the lead and Brian Propp adds to the cushion with a shorthanded goal. The Islanders then answer back with goals by Brent Sutter and John Tonelli. Philadelphia clamps down defensively in the final period, by allowing just four shots. Ilkka Sinisalo seals the game in the final minute with an empty-netter, which puts Philadelphia just one win away from the Wales Conference Finals.

The Islanders don't go down without a fight. In Game 4, sharpshooters Pat LaFontaine, Brian Trottier, Denis Potvin and Mike Bossy pick corners to give New York a 4-0 lead by the middle of regulation. Keenan pulls Lindbergh from the net and sends in Bob Froese to finish out the game. New York wins, 6-2.

Back at the Spectrum for Game 5, Lindbergh plays like a man possessed. He makes a second period Ilkka Sinisalo goal stand up, turning aside all 25 shots he sees for a 1-0 series-clinching win as the "Pell-lee! Pell-lee!" chants grow deafening. He no longer even needs to make saves to get his name called, for as soon as Lindbergh steps on the ice for the start of the third period, the fans begin the chant anew. The keeper slams the door on the Islanders in the third period and grabs first-star honors yet again. "I was nervous the whole way," Pelle admits afterwards. "But now it just feels so damn good. At this time of year, I'm usually going home to Sweden and trying to answer the old question about why everything always goes good in the regular season but never in the playoffs." Asked what it's like to beat the Islanders in five games, a beaming Lindbergh has a one-word reply: "Unbeeel-ievable!" Before he heads to the showers, he has one last thing to say to a certain Canadian hockey commentator. "Where's Don Cherry now?" he asks.

The Flyers play the speedy Quebec Nordiques in the Wales Conference Finals. Led by the Stastny brothers, Michel Goulet, and the pugnacious Dale Hunter, Michel Bergeron's club was one of the highest-scoring teams in the league and had just stunned Montreal in a seven-game quarterfinal round.

The Flyers settle for a split the first two games in Quebec, losing 2-1 in overtime in Game One before bouncing back to take Game Two by a 4-2 count. In the second game, Poulin suffers cracked ribs when he takes a stick to the ribcage from Quebec's Mario Marois. Before going to the locker room, Poulin cradles a lead pass from linemate Craven and beats goaltender Mario Gosselin to give the team a 1-0 lead while shorthanded.

Back at the Spectrum, Lindbergh is sensational in goal the third game, and enables the injury-riddled team to win 4-2 despite the absences of Poulin, Kerr, and McCrimmon. Murray Craven, Ilkka Sinisalo, Brian Propp, and fill-in forward Joe Paterson provide the offensive support.

Quebec takes the next tilt 5-3 to knot the series at two games apiece. It's not one of Lindbergh's better performances and the loss breaks a streak of 22 consecutive home wins by the Flyers. The media, accustomed to Pelle's A-game, grills him afterwards. He's relaxed. "You can't be great every night," he says. "You guys make it sound like I gave up 20 goals tonight. They've got a good team, too."

In Game 5, Poulin, donning a flak jacket to protect his injured ribs, returns to the game. The Flyers are outplayed in much of the game, but Lindbergh (who suffers a knee injury after getting struck in the back of his leg by a shot from Mario Marois, but remains in net) preserves a 2-1 win. Pelle's 30-save performance earns him first-star honors for the fourth time in the playoffs.

With a chance to clinch the series and avoid a seventh game, the Flyers head back to Philadelphia for Game Six on May 16, 1985. After practice, Poulin calls a players' only meeting. "If we're going to do this, let's do it with class," the captain says. "We've played well the whole season, but it feels like we've sometimes relied too much on individual players. Now let's push ourselves to see if we can all play well at the same time."

The Spectrum is hopping several hours before opening faceoff, and the "Pell-lee" chants start in the parking lot even before the doors open. Every seat is filled well in advance of the pregame warmup, and fans on the top level hang a huge banner reading "Pelle for President."

Rick Tocchet gets the Flyers on the board late in the first period. The Flyers cling to their slim lead, but find themselves in dire straights early in the second period. Minor penalties to Paterson and Propp leaves Philadelphia at a five-on-three disadvantage. In one of the most dramatic moments in team history, Lindbergh and Dave Poulin come to the rescue. Poulin picks off a cross-ice pass by Marois in the defensive zone and races off on a clean break-away. The sold-out Spectrum crowd collectively rises to its feet, holding its breath as Poulin skates in on butterfly stylist Gosselin. "I knew I had a clean breakaway even before I got to the red line, which is way too much time to think about what you're going to do. All series long, we kept preaching to shoot high on Gosselin, so I was looking to shoot high all the way," Poulin recalls. He beats Gosselin cleanly over the glove and the Spectrum crowd goes bonkers. The Flyers go on to dominate the rest of the game. Lindbergh, who faces just 15 shots for the entire game and five over the latter half, gobbles up the few pucks that get through to him. The Flyers win the game, 3-0, and earn their first trip to the Stanley Cup Finals since 1980. "It's like a big dream," Lindbergh tells Philadelphia's WPVI-6 television.

The series is a glorious, but costly one for Philadelphia. A six-game victory comes at the expense of broken ribs suffered by Poulin, a season-ending separated shoulder suffered by McCrimmon, and knee injuries to Kerr and Lindbergh.

Afterwards, a throng of jubilant Flyers' fans crowd around the smiling goalie as he leaves the Spectrum. It takes him nearly 30 minutes to get back to his car, but he waves off the security guards from clearing a path for him. As others mug for the camera, a middle-aged woman tells the Swedish news crew documenting the raucous celebration, "Tell everyone in Sweden that we love Pelle and we will take care of him! Amen!" Meanwhile, a camera crew later shows up at the Lindbergh at home in Kings Grant. He's in agony every time he tries to bend or straighten his legs. "Oh! It's brutal," he says in English to unidentified person on the other end of a telephone conversation. "I did the same thing in Maine [in 1981], you know. ...Well, I don't remember if it was the same knee, but I hurt myself the same way in the finals. I couldn't stop a thing in the final game because of that, and it cost us the championship." Despite the pain, there's no way Lindbergh would miss playing in the Finals against Edmonton. He takes anti-inflammatory injections, while Kerr also returns, fitted with a special knee brace, and Poulin needs the flak jacket to protect his ribs. McCrimmon is done for the playoffs with his severe shoulder injury.

As the Flyers hold their final practice for Game 1 of the Finals, Pelle continues to feel considerable pain. His almost freakish mobility has been hindered, and he tries to adjust his positioning to play a little more conservatively. After his heroics in the last two series, no one is about to second-guess anything he does. "Pelle had been so good against the Islanders, you almost had to laugh, but his play against Quebec was the best I've ever seen from a goalie. In all the years I played and coached, I've seen a lot of good goalies. But Pelle's semifinals were beyond comprehension. I can hardly describe it," Poulin recalls. Ted Sator adds, "Pelle was the backbone of our team. Without him, there's no way we beat Quebec."

The Flyers have beaten Edmonton eight straight times at the Spectrum and have swept the season series during the regular season. No team in the NHL can game up to the Oilers when it comes to superstar talent, for the club featured a quintet of Hockey Hall of Famers at the height of their powers – Wayne Gretzky, Mark Messier, Jari Kurri, Paul Coffey, and Grant Fuhr. The defending Stanley Cup champions enter the 1985 Finals as the favorites. By now, the Oilers have plenty of Stanley Cup Finals experience, by having reached the championship round in three straight seasons. The Flyers, conversely, have only one player with Stanley Cup Finals experience. Brian Propp was a rookie during the Flyers run to the 1980 Finals.

The Flyers need to win the first two games at the Spectrum to ensure a return trip to Philadelphia. The series is played in a 2-3-2 format, with the middle three games in Edmonton. The Flyers go out and surprise everyone but themselves with their two-way play. Philadelphia throws a defensive blanket over the champs, and Ilkka Sinisalo scores on the powerplay to give the Flyers the lead at 15:05 of the opening period. The slim lead holds through the middle period as Philly continues to outwork Edmonton on the boards and prevent them from getting any skating room. Lindbergh flawlessly handles the routine shots he sees in the first two periods.In the third period, goals by Ron Sutter and Tim Kerr give the Flyers some breathing room. With 3:08 left in regulation, Edmonton's Willy Lindström finally gets a puck past Lindbergh, but it's the only goal he allows on 26 shots (14 of which came in the final period). Dave Poulin adds an empty netter to punctuate the 4-1 win. "We're not dreamers any more. We're believers," said Ron Sutter.

Afterwards, the press asks Keenan what he said to his team before the game. "I just said, 'Go out and have fun!" Before he leaves the locker room, Lindbergh shakes hands with Keenan and gets congratulated by Parent.

The psychological gamesmanship begins in earnest the day after Game One. Edmonton coach Glen Sather complains about the water bottle Lindbergh keeps on the top of his net, despite the fact that it's been there all season. "You can't have surprises in the Stanley Cup Finals," he says. "Maybe we'd like to have a bucket of fried chicken on top of our net. Maybe a hamburger. I mean, what's the difference? If we're going to take water out there, let's take out lunch." Sather also complains about the condition of the Spectrum ice. "It was like we were stuck in quicksand the whole night," he says. Two decades later, Willy Lindström recalls, "It was warm outside, but we were convinced that the Flyers deliberately melted the ice. It was slushy the whole game and it affected us. We lived by playing a high tempo and controlling the puck."

Meanwhile, the press learns that Wayne Gretzky was playing through a fever. "I'm not going to use that as an excuse," he says. "I just played a bad game." In the *Philadelphia Inquirer,* Al Morganti writes that the Oilers will come up with a much better effort in the second game "unless they're complete frauds." Gretzky and the Oilers use the "frauds" quote as a rallying cry, although the article's context makes clear that the first game was simply a case of the Flyers playing their best hockey while the more talented Oilers team got outworked.

On Wednesday night, the Flyers players have the evening to themselves.

Pelle chooses to spend a rare quiet night at home with Kerstin, in order to rest for the next game. The Oilers head to Veterans Stadium to watch the Phillies take on the San Francisco Giants. The Phillies have been a National League powerhouse for much of the last decade but have begun to slide from contention after winning the 1980 World Series and losing in the 1983 Series. Early in the game, the Phillies show Wayne Gretzky in the stands on the stadium video screen in the outfield. On cue, the Philly crowd boos. The Oilers strike back in the second game. This time, Edmonton controls much of the play, and Lindbergh is tested much more severely than he was in the first game. Edmonton can muster only a mid-first-period Wayne Gretzky goal. "The Great One" follows up his own rebound at 10:29 of the first period. Lindbergh keeps his team close. Despite outshooting the Flyers by an 18-6 margin over the first half of the game (30-18 for the entire game), Edmonton's lead remains a single goal. At the 10:22 mark of the second period, Tim Kerr ties the score. Bedlam ensues in the Spectrum but the joy lasts for only six minutes. Willy Lindström cuts into the slot and wrists a shot into the net to give Edmonton a 2-1 lead at 16:08. Late in the period, with the Flyers' pressing the attack, Oilers defenseman Paul Coffey appears to deliberately push the net off its moorings. The referee Fraser refuses to call a penalty and Mike Keenan screams from the Philadelphia bench. With nine seconds left in the period, Kerr gets sent off for cross-checking. The crowd screams obscenities at Fraser, an Ontario native who makes his home in the Philadelphia area.

Edmonton limits the Flyers to four shots during the third period. Lindbergh makes seven stops to keep his team close, but Philly never gets an equalizer. With the goaltender pulled for extra attacker in the final minute, Tim Hunter scores into the empty net to make it a 3-1 final. "We didn't play like the last game, we weren't as aggressive," Pelle says afterwards. "Now it's going to be a tough series. But we've won up there [in Edmonton] before." Looking back two decades later, Thomas Eriksson believes that the Stanley

Cup slipped away from the Flyers on this night. "We should have won that second game. We played well, and Pelle kept us right there. That was our chance," he says.

The ice is considerably better and the crowd quieter at Edmonton's Northlands Coliseum, but the Oilers make plenty of noise early in Game 3. Before the game is a minute and a half old, Wayne Gretzky has already scored two goals with the teams skating four-on-four. Flyers checking liner Derrick Smith temporarily stops the bleeding by scoring just 16 seconds after the second Gretzky tally. But "The Great One" completes the hat trick midway through the period to send his team off with a 3-1 lead and a 20-12 shot advantage.

"You know that he's going to make the same move every time he comes in, and which corner he wants to put the puck into, but you still can't stop him," Lindbergh marvels after the game. Mike Keenan switches goalies at the start of the second period but sends Lindbergh back in for Bob Froese after the first stoppage of play. He remains in the game until Mike Krushelnyski pots a powerplay goal at the 6:58 mark to give Edmonton a 4-1 advantage. Froese goes back into the net, and stops all seven shots he faces. In the third period, the Flyers get a mid-period goal from Mark Howe and a late-period one from Brian Propp, but go down to a 4-3 defeat that was not as close as the final score implies.

After the game the Philadelphia journalists are concerned about the news that Tim Kerr, who has scored a combined 64 goals between the regular season and playoffs, has reinjured his knee and will be lost for the remainder of the series. Meanwhile, Ilkka Sinisalo (combined 42 goals) has a shoulder injury. Nothing is said of Lindbergh's physical problems, but he's still feeling pain just above his knee.

The next game takes place on Tuesday, May 28. The Flyers come out like a different team. Rich Sutter forges a 1-0 lead just 46 seconds after the opening faceoff and the Flyers get off to a 3-1 lead at 11:32 when Murray Craven scores shorthanded. Despite a missed penalty shot by Ron Sutter, Philadelphia seems well positioned to knot the series at two games apiece.

It is then that the walls cave in on Philadelphia. Charlie Huddy scores a late first period powerplay goal, and Glenn Anderson ties the game, 3-3, just 21 seconds after the start of the second period. At the 12:53 mark, Wayne Gretzky puts the Oilers ahead. At this point, Lindbergh, sweating profusely, suffers from mild dehydration symptoms despite gulping down fluids every chance he gets. "Marshy, I need a water bottle," he tells defenseman Brad Marsh. Instead, Keenan pulls Lindbergh from the game so he can get hydrated on the bench. Froese goes into the net with a faceoff deep in the Edmonton zone. Five seconds later, there's another stoppage of play. Lindbergh returns to the net. Several minutes later, Lindbergh goes down to make a save and gets hit just above the knee by a Mike Krushelnyski slapshot. Pelle feels shooting pain in the same spot he injured in the Quebec series. Lindbergh finishes the period, but he's in bad shape. Sudsy Settlemyre tends to him in between periods, but quickly realizes that Lindbergh won't be able to finish the game. Froese goes into the net for the third period. Early in the period, Gretzky scores an insurance marker on the powerplay. The Oilers win, 5-3, to move within a victory of their second Stanley Cup championship.

Lindbergh receives an anti-inflammatory shot in the locker room but feels no relief. He meets after the game and the following morning with team orthopedist, Dr. John Gregg. "Doc, it feels pretty good now," Lindbergh lies. Dr. Gregg has a reputation for giving players the green light to play if there's even the slightest possibility of suiting up for a big game. Lindbergh hopes he can con the doctor into getting clearance for Game 5, but Gregg sees right through him. "Forget it," Gregg says, "You've got a slightly torn quadricep. It doesn't seem too bad, but you can't play with it. If you play, you can make it worse, and you'll need surgery over the summer. The kind of injury you have usually needs about six weeks of rest."

Just like that, Lindbergh's season is over after a combined 83 games played between the regular season and playoffs. He finishes the postseason with a 2.50 goals against average and .914 save percentage. All he feels right now, though, is disappointment as he speaks with Al Morganti of the *Philadelphia Inquirer* and tells him about the injury. "Pelle could hardly walk up a single step, let alone play hockey," Morganti recalls. Adds Ted Sator, "Pelle had tears in his eyes. He was almost crying, and he couldn't even bend his leg anymore."

Nevertheless, rumors circulate that the Flyers' Swedish goaltender has pulled himself out of the series when his team needs him the most. "There's no way Pelle could have played," Morganti says. "Gregg didn't baby the players. If there was the slightest chance Pelle could have played, Gregg would have shoved him out on the ice. I remember that Gregg clarified Pelle's injury for us reporters and said it was torn. Anyone who said that Lindbergh was afraid to play either didn't have the facts or else they were making it up."

Lindbergh's re-aggravated injury forces Keenan to start Froese in the fifth game. The Flyers also recall Darren Jensen to back up Froese for the remainder of the series. Frosty has played only parts of three games during the playoffs and has started only one game since early March. Froese often seems impervious to rustiness, but starting against the Oilers with the Stanley Cup at stake is an exceptionally tough order. No team since the 1941-42 Toronto Maple Leafs had come back from a three games to one deficit in the Finals.

Froese had posted an extraordinary 58-19-9 career record and a goals against average of 2.80. Statistically he'd always been superior to Lindbergh, although few (apart from Froese himself) believe that he's of Lindbergh's quality as a starting goaltender. In order to get the series back to Philadelphia, the Flyers need Froese to play the game of his life, and for the rest of the squad to game its effort from the opening game of the series. It doesn't happen.

On May 30, the Oilers crush the Flyers, 8-3, and win the Stanley Cup. In the final five minutes of play, fights break out and coaches Sather and Keenan scream at each other from their benches. After shaking hands with the Oilers at the final buzzer and quickly vacating the ice so as not to see their opponent celebrating with the Cup, the Flyers convene in the dressing room. Several players cry openly. Keenan waits until he's alone to let the anguish register.

Pelle Lindbergh

CHAPTER 23

THURSDAY, NOVEMBER 14, 1985

Even before the 1985-86 season started, many Philadelphia Flyers players had circled November 14 on their calendars. This game marks the first meeting between the Flyers and the Edmonton Oilers since the Stanley Cup Finals. Anticipation for the game grew even more intense as Philadelphia built its current 10-game winning streak.

Now no one is quite sure how to feel about the game. Pelle's death makes it seem trivial on the one hand, but on the other it feels almost cathartic to be able to play hockey again. The Flyers players feel it's nearly imperative to win on the night their fallen teammate will be memorialized to the public. Lindbergh's death has begun to make the players realize how bonded they are to one another. "We knew the character of this team. We knew how we all felt about one another. But a lot of those feelings had never been expressed, not just because we're athletes, but because we're males. As much as Pelle's death pulled us together, I think it showed us how close we already were," said Dave Poulin to *Sports Illustrated* just 11 days after the accident.

Pelle's family spends the day at the house and tries to keep themselves as busy as possible. With a little help from Sigge, Göran finishes rebuilding the deck outside the house. Anna-Lisa prepares food in the kitchen, and she irons clothes for the family to wear to the memorial at the Spectrum. Kerstin's day is spent going over funeral arrangements, meeting with Pelle's agent, Frank Milne and talking to the Flyers. Bob Clarke informs her that the team's entire management group hopes to be able to attend Pelle's funeral in Sweden. The gesture means a lot to the family.

The choice of locations for the funeral is obvious. To the extent that Pelle identified himself with any church congregation, it was with the Sofia Church in south Stockholm. Located near his family's home, the church was the setting of some of Pelle's key life events. He was baptized there and he and Kerstin had planned to have their wedding ceremony there as well.

The funeral is set for the following Wednesday, November 20. Sigge wants a female minister to lead the service, so Kerstin goes about contacting her. The Flyers take care of first-class plane tickets via SAS for the family and the transporting of Pelle's body back to Stockholm.

Darren Jensen checks into his hotel room in Philadelphia. He had been on a road trip with the Hershey Bears in Canada when he learned of his recall to the Flyers. Since the Flyers are not practicing today before the game, Jensen has the day to collect his thoughts. The rookie tries not to think of the pressure on him to crank up a strong game against the Oilers on such an emotionally-charged night. He's nervous even though he knows the team will give him as much support as possible, but the game will still come down to whether he makes the saves he needs to make. Such is the life of a goaltender.

The flags at the Spectrum hang at half mast. In Pelle's memory, a Swedish flag has been placed next to the American flag. The electronic message board outside the arena, which usually promotes upcoming events, simply says "Pelle 31." Inside the building, workers carry and unpack boxes containing postcards to be given to everyone in attendance that night. On the front side, there's a black-and-white photograph of Lindbergh. On the reverse, it says, "In Loving Memory of Pelle Lindbergh: Our Goalie, Our Friend." By happenstance, the tickets for the game feature a color photo of Lindbergh in goal. Each game has a different player pictured on the ticket, and every player on the opening night roster is featured at least once during the season. Lindbergh so happens to be the photo subject for this game. Arena management asks the ticket-takers not to tear people's tickets as they walk through the turnstiles. Instead, the ticket-takers are given markers to write an X on the reverse of the ticket.

As fans enter the building prior to the pre-game warmups, many hang banners or bring hand-held signs dedicated to the fallen player. Among other messages are sentiments such as "He's on your team now, God, take good care of him." "Win the Cup for Pelle," and a misspelled sign in Swedish reading "Pelle jag alskar dij" and "We miss you Pelle." Down at ice level, work crews have whitewashed the boards of all advertising. The message from management is clear: Tonight is about honoring Lindbergh's memory and not about making money.

The Flyers players gather at the Spectrum two hours before the game. They're quieter than usual and simply go about their business of preparing for the game. Several players glance over at Pelle's stall in the locker room. Others try not to look at it at all.

Flyers' management has arranged for a limousine to pick up Pelle's family at the house and bring them to the game. Sigge, wearing a dark double-breasted suit, steps from the car first. Anna-Lisa is clad in a plaid dress while Kerstin wears a knee-length skirt and matching jacket. Göran, unprepared for this formal occasion, has borrowed a suit that belonged to Pelle. As they arrive, a photographer from *Aftonbladet* snaps a picture.

Elsewhere in the building, Swedish reporter Gunnar Nordström sits in an office, as he works on a special assignment. The Flyers Gene Hart will lead the memorial ceremonies and Bernie Parent will deliver the eulogy. Both men have graciously agreed to share copies of their speeches with Nordstrom, who remains in one of the Flyers' offices, as he painstakingly translates the speeches in their entirety. The cramped pressbox would not be conducive to focusing on such tasks. *Expressen* photographer Hasse Persson sits beside him.

In the sparse visitors' locker room at ice level, the Oilers attempt to go through their normal pre-game preparations but it's exceptionally difficult. The prematch memorial ceremony will be followed by a 15-minute delay before the start of the game.

Mike Keenan is usually unapproachable before games because he doesn't want anything to interrupt the preparations. On this night, however, he understands the need to speak on behalf of himself and the team to people watching the game on television. Keenan does a formal interview with *Prism* commentator Bobby Taylor and speaks fondly of Lindbergh's talent and charisma. He recalls some of the goalie's idiosyncrasies and game-day superstitions; it's a side of Keenan's personality that Pelle himself rarely got to see. The coach tells Taylor (who was Bernie Parent's backup when the Flyers won their two Stanley Cups) that it's impossible to replace a goaltender of Lindbergh's caliber, but the team as a whole is strong enough to persevere. The pre-game broadcast features several other tributes, clips of old interviews with Pelle, and highlights and still photographs from his five years in the Flyers organization.

At 7:30 pm, the lights are dimmed. Only the center ice area is illuminated and prominently features an orange floral tribute to Lindbergh arranged in the shape of the number 31. Kerstin, Sigge, Anna-Lisa, and Göran sit in the Snider family's private box. At ice level, Gene Hart stands front and center with Bernie Parent, Ed and Jay Snider, Bob Clarke, Keith Allen, team chaplain John Casey, and NHL president John Ziegler. A hush falls over the building as Hart begins his speech,

My good friends, what was to have been a shimmering evening of spectacular hockey, with the two greatest teams in the professional game, has become instead a deeply more personal occasion as we, the Flyers family, the team, the organization, and especially you fans, gather to grieve the loss of one of our own. But, really, since Pelle Lindbergh's entire existence exuded nothing but the positive things in life, what I'd like to do this evening is to make the theme of our ceremony not the mourning of his death but the celebration of a life that we, in Philadelphia, were privileged to share.

Hart goes on to assure the fans that their sorrows will ease over time and be replaced by happier memories. He then briefly recounts Lindbergh's life story and career. "And so," Hart continues,

That far-fetched, hundred-thousand-to-one dream that began so long ago and so many thousands of miles away came true....Add to that the personality that endeared him to everyone with whom he came in touch. And he was able to do all of this with a fiancée who was able to make his every day a joy, a young lady whose courage and strength this past week have been magnificent.

After Father Casey gives an invocation, Hart concludes by informing the crowd that Pelle's family is at the game and thanking all of the fans on behalf of the team and the family for the outpouring of support and condolences.

It is now Parent's turn to speak. Clad in a dark blue suit, white shirt and dark red tie, he approaches the podium. Several times, he has to pause to compose himself as he addresses the crowd. Midway through the eulogy he says, "The papers have said that I was his hero. But I wish I could have only told him this – told him how much I admired him and how much I cared about him." Parent's lip quivers and he brushes away a tear. The crowd cheers and Parent takes a deep breath and continues the eulogy. "A goalie stands on a very lonely island, and I'm grateful that I was able to share some of that island with him, but for too brief a period. Pelle Lindbergh had become, without question, one of hockey's greatest goalies. When death defeats greatness, we mourn. And when death defeats youth, we mourn even more." At the end of his speech, Parent can only manage to say a few words at a time as the emotions well up inside him. He says in a low, staccato voice, "Pelle, you will always live in our hearts. Pelle, we miss you."

Parent hands the microphone back to Hart. The announcer ends the ceremony by reciting the final period of Robert Frost's "Stopping by the Woods on a Snowy Evening." Many in the stands cry openly throughout the ceremony, as do several Flyers players watching from the ice. At the conclusion, a loud and cathartic "Pell-lee! Pell-lee! Pell-lee!" chant fills the building one final time.

Hart introduces Hildegard Lindström, a singer the Swedish consulate recommended to the Flyers. She performs a stirring rendition of "Du Gamla, Du Fria," the national anthem of Sweden.

Up in the pressbox, former Maine Mariners and Flyers head coach Bob McCammon watches the ceremony with an aching feeling. Now an assistant coach with the Oilers, he can't help but think of the times he spent with Lindbergh in Maine and Philadelphia. "I don't get it. It's tough to take in what happened," he says aloud, and stares at the memorial postcard of Lindbergh which he, too, has been given. The players retreat to the locker room as the organist plays "The Moment of Triumph."

In the Flyers' locker room, the Flyers players quickly compose themselves and are anxious to get the game underway. Mike Keenan chooses his words carefully and speaks calmly. "Gentlemen, you are professionals, and now you have a job to do," he says. Poulin rises and loudly echoes the same sentiment. "We're professionals, boys! We're going to go out and do our job!"

Darren Jensen is the first player to step out as the Flyers take the ice. Backup Mike Bloski takes a seat on the bench. Twenty minutes after the memorial ceremony, referee Don Koharski raises his arm and the opening faceoff is dropped at center ice.

The Oilers get the game's first scoring chance but Jensen stops the shot from Mike Krushelnyski. At the 2:52 mark, a cheer erupts in the building as Ed Hospodar tussles with Kevin McClelland, but the cheers turn to groans as the Flyers' defenseman gets the only penalty. Philadelphia kills off the disadvantage. Over the course of the first period, the two clubs trade off several penalties and Philadelphia outshoots Edmonton, 14-9. Finally, at the 17:25 mark of the period, the Flyers get on the board. With the Flyers on their third powerplay of the period, Poulin wins a faceoff cleanly back to Mark Howe at the point. Poulin and Murray Craven move toward the net to screen Oilers goaltender Andy Moog as Howe unleashes one of his deadly wrist shots. The puck goes in the net. Howe's mind momentarily drifts as his teammates congratulate him and he skates back to the bench. "I felt tears welling up and I had the urge to cry," Howe recalls two decades later.

Up in the Snider family's box, Sigge and Anna Lisa stand up and applaud wildly after Howe gives the Flyers the lead. Throughout the game, they continue to cheer loudly for the Flyers and yell in Swedish at Koharski when he makes calls that go against Philadelphia.

Gene Hart wrote in his book, *Score!* "I can recall thinking, 'How with all the grief of a son dying the day before, can they cheer and applaud like that?' Then I realized that they were cheering and applauding Pelle's team for what they considered to be a tribute to Pelle, and rightfully so!"

In the second period, the Flyers are still clinging to a 1-0 lead, but the lead seems precarious. Howe has gotten injured and has to leave the game with a groin injury. Later, Wayne Gretzky gets a shorthanded breakaway against Jensen. The emergency call-up stones the reigning Hart Trophy winner. The fans and the Lindbergh clan roar for the most dramatic of the seven saves Jensen makes on Gretzky in the game.

At the 17:53 mark of the middle period, Edmonton ties the game on its twenty-third shot of the game. On the next shift, Rick Tocchet drops the gloves with Edmonton center Craig MacTavish. With 13 seconds left in the frame, Dave Hunter gets whistled off for slashing Brad Marsh. The Flyers press the attack and gain an offensive zone faceoff with two seconds left on the clock. Mark Messier skates into the circle to take the draw against Tim Kerr. As linesman Gerard Gauthier holds the puck, Messier drops to his knees hoping to occupy the puck long enough for the clock to run out on the period. The lineman refuses to drop the puck and warns Messier, who barks at the official. Koharski intercedes and calls an unsportsmanlike conduct penalty on Messier, and gives Philadelphia a carryover five-on-three advantage for the first 1:44 of the third period.

Edmonton coach Glen Sather is thrown out of the game by Koharski, which necessitates McCammon coming down from the pressbox to finish the game behind the bench. The Oilers refuse to send their players out on the ice to start the period and tack on an additional delay of game penalty. The Flyers now have a lengthy powerplay to start the third period, and Philadelphia takes full advantage. At the 24-second mark of the third period, Pelle Eklund threads a perfect feed to Ilkka Sinisalo, who snaps a shot past Moog to give the Flyers a lead they'll never relinquish. As Edmonton continues to self-destruct with penalties, a frustrated Moog gets tagged with a slashing penalty, and Brian Propp turns the latest 5-on-3 advantage into a goal at 3:56. The sniper fires a tracer from the circle that beats the keeper to give Philly a 3-1 lead.

When one team enjoys a series of powerplays, it's almost inevitable that there will be even-up calls at some point. Sure enough, Brad Marsh (holding) and Brad McCrimmon (high sticking) get sent off in quick succession. Minus their top three defensemen and facing a two-man disadvantage, Philadelphia tries to minimize the damage. Paul Coffey scores on the 5-on-3 to cut the deficit to 3-2, but Edmonton is unable to retie the game. At the 11:04 mark, Rich Sutter goes wide on Melnyk and scores past Moog to temporarily restore breathing room for the Flyers.

Seconds later, two rounds of fisticuffs break out, as Hospodar fights McClelland and Dave Brown takes on Dave Semenko. Brown and Semenko are assessed game misconducts and escorted to the locker rooms. One minute and 21 seconds after all the penalties are sorted out, Messier gets Jensen to commit early and brings the Oilers back to within a single goal. Finally, with 3:10 left, Rich Sutter connects with McCrimmon. The defenseman gives the Flyers a 5-3 margin. Few of the 17,380 fans leave the building before the final buzzer.

The Flyers' players receive a standing ovation at the conclusion of the game. The applause is in recognition of the team's 11-game winning streak, the tremendous effort involved in beating Edmonton and, most of all, in respect for all the team had been through over the past five days. Jensen, who stopped 29 of 32 shots from the NHL's most explosive team, is named third star; Rich Sutter is second star for his clutch goal and assist in the final period; and, Brian Propp gets top honors. After the game, Mike Keenan is effusive in his praise for his players and delivers the same message both to the team and to the media. "Winning or losing wasn't a factor tonight," he says. "I'm just so proud of the way they played."

The Flyers' locker room gets silent as Sigge Lindbergh appears in the doorway. Unable to speak a word of English, he is nevertheless able to communicate his feelings. One-by-one, he approaches each player in the locker room, looks him in the eye and shakes his hand. Thereafter, Pelle's father meets with Bob Clarke and Kerstin translates. Sigge tells Clarke that the family would be honored if it at all possible that Bernie Parent could attend the funeral in Sweden. "You're all welcome to come together," Sigge says. "When Pelle was in the States, he saw Bernie as his second father. That felt good for us at home." Without hesitation, Parent agrees to come along to Stockholm. The team also gives Thomas Eriksson permission to take a bereavement leave and be with the Lindbergh family during the funeral.

CHAPTER 24

TORONTO, ONTARIO, WEDNESDAY, JUNE 12, 1985

Clad in a newly purchased tuxedo, Pelle Lindbergh has come to Toronto's Metro Convention Center for the 1984-85 NHL Awards gala. He's a finalist for both the Hart Trophy as the league's most valuable player and the Vezina Trophy as the best goaltender. Pelle knows it's extremely unlikely that he's won the Hart Trophy, because the perennial honoree Wayne Gretzky has posted a mind-boggling 208 points during the regular season and should win the award.

It's the Vezina that Pelle covets. While he knows that he has strong credentials to win the award, it's no guarantee. Reigning Vezina winner Tom Barrasso should receive some first-place votes as well as Pelle. He had a lower goals against average (2.66) than Pelle's, although Lindbergh's record was superior and he played in more games. If playoff performance were considered, Pelle would be a shoo-in for the award; however, the postseason does not figure into the equation because balloting takes place at the end of the regular season. When the final votes of the 21 NHL general managers are tallied, it's likely to be either Lindbergh or Barrasso who walks away with the prize.

The 1984-85 NHL Awards ceremony is broadcasted nationwide throughout Canada. Modeled on the Oscars or Emmy Awards, the presenters announce finalists for the awards and then the winner. The finalists are the top three finishers in the balloting for each category.

Pelle sits nervously in his chair as the Vezina Trophy presenter is escorted up on stage. He knows beforehand that the presenter will be Bernie

Parent. Lindbergh can hardly articulate, in Swedish or English, just what it would mean to him to share the moment with Parent, himself a two-time winner of the trophy. "The winner of the Vezina Trophy is Pelle Lindbergh!"

Lindbergh later says that he has no recollection of rising and walking up to the stage as the assembly cheers. A beaming Parent stands off to the side as Pelle approaches the podium. He keeps his speech short, and speaks from the heart. "First of all, I want to thank all my teammates. Without them, this wouldn't be possible. But the person I really want to thank is the man standing to the left of me, Bernie Parent. He taught me everything I know…to play hockey in America. Thank you, Bernie!"

Parent warmly embraces Lindbergh. The television cameras capture the defining moment of a rare and special relationship between a young man and his idol, a pupil and his mentor, and a surrogate son and his second father. Looking back two decades later, Parent still smiles at the memory.

That night in Toronto was the finest memory I have from the time with Pelle. I was even happier and prouder than when I won the Vezina. I saw all the hard work that went into it, and I saw Pelle make his dreams come true. He was so determined. We didn't say much to each other during the night, but to see him walk up from the floor to the stage, and look him in the eye and hand him the award and give him a big hug, it really said more than any words we could say to each other. Several times during the night, we looked over to each other and caught each other's eyes. We both knew what it took to get there. He had to battle for it and get through some really tough times. When it came time to give interviews, I went off the side. It was his night, and he earned it. I was just glad to watch him a little in the hall and see how pleased he was.

Lindbergh talks with Al Morganti and several other Philadelphia reporters. He poses for pictures with the Vezina Trophy and later stands side-by-side for photos with Mike Keenan, who has won the Jack Adams award as the NHL's Coach of the Year.

"I'm very proud to be the first European to win this award," Pelle says. "There's a lot of people who said we can't handle the pressure. There will probably be a lot of people who wonder if I can do this more than one time, so that's something I've got to show them next season."

Before the night is over, Pelle learns that he's also been selected as the NHL's First-Team All Star goaltender, becoming the second Swede (Börje Salming was first) to earn the honor. In the Vezina balloting, he got 14 of the

Shortly after being announced as the 1984-85 Vezina Trophy winner, Pelle Lindbergh discusses the honor with the media. Reporter Al Morganti (right), then with the Philadelphia Inquirer, was a friend of Lindbergh's away from the rink. [Getty Images]

21 possible first-place votes (the rest went to Barrasso). Lindbergh finishes third in the Hart Trophy balloting. There are no Swedish media representatives at the NHL awards, so Pelle makes sure his family and friends at home get the news first hand. After the ceremony, Lindbergh joins many of the other elites in the NHL hockey community at an after-party at a bar in walking distance from his hotel. Standing at a pay phone in the bar, he repeatedly screams into the receiver, "I got the Vezina! I got the Vezina!" In the wee hours of the morning, Pelle returns to his hotel room. The next day, he flies to Philadelphia and meets with several friends to celebrate his success. He also does an endorsement appearance as a paid spokesman for a newly built IKEA store in the Philadelphia suburbs.

After arriving back in Sweden, Pelle finds for the most part that the summer of '85 is a mixture of personal business and carefree fun. In his public and professional life, Lindbergh participates in a televised celebrity soccer competition and agrees to several lengthy interviews (including an English interview for *Hockey Night in Canada* conducted on Pelle's speed boat). He once again serves as special guest goaltending instructor at a summer hockey camp in Leksand. In late August, he works out with the Hammarby IF senior team.

For the first time in his hockey career, Lindbergh works out in earnest during the summer of 1985. "Pelle definitely slimmed down that last summer," Kerstin recalls. He does it partially out of fear of facing Pat Croce if he reports to camp again in less than ideal physical condition. But Lindbergh also wants to make sure that once his torn quadriceps heal, he'll get a head-start on being ready to play 65 or more regular season games again in 1985-86. "Pelle drove himself pretty hard that last year. He was one of the first goalies who suddenly looked like a real man," Croce quips.

Pelle also stays in regular communication with Frank Milne. The agent has begun negotiations with the Flyers on a new long-term contract, but the early progress is slow. The goalie learns that he's also in demand for additional paid public appearances, especially in the Philadelphia area.

Meanwhile, Lindbergh's unique pace of life remains largely unchanged. His toys have gotten more and more expensive and his circle of friends grows wider all the time, but he's fundamentally the same charmingly boyish and down-to-earth person he's always been. On the one hand, hardly a day or night goes by where he's not meeting with friends, racing around the Stockholm harbor on his speedboat, or taking friends for hair-raising spins in his sports car. He's also consumed by arranging the details for the delivery of his newly customized Porsche to the US when he returns for the next hockey season.

In the midst of his busy schedule, he somehow makes time to visit his parents and his sisters' families. His private time with Kerstin is limited, but she often comes along with him on group outings. Above all, the young couple looks forward to starting a family of their own in the years to come. Despite his growing celebrity status, Pelle's relationship with Kerstin is stable and happy. They remain very much in love and devoted to each other. The couple's life together is usually filled with laughter and Pelle's laid-back demeanor makes most problems seem minor. They are, however, human beings. Like any couple, they have their spats and the occasional arguments can sometimes become heated. Kerstin recalls,

> I remember one time we had argued over something. I don't remember what but I had a towel in my hand. A glass dropped and broke. I was cleaning up with the towel. He said something that made me furious and I threw the towel in his face. I remember how strongly he reacted. It was very clear that he was angry, but also afraid. He could have gotten glass in his eyes, and that

was his livelihood. I was mortified right away. That was the first and last time I threw something at him.

Lindbergh gets a summer visit from Ed Parvin Jr., a bartender at Kaminski's, a Cherry Hill bar and grill that is one of the Flyers' players' favorite hangouts. Parvin's father is a successful real estate agent who is the realtor of choice for many in the Flyers' organization. "I knew most of the players and had season tickets at the Spectrum," the younger Parvin says. "When I got to know Pelle, we clicked immediately. We got along great." The players stop by Kaminski's after games for a bite to eat and a beer or two, but usually don't stay too long. "They would stay maybe half an hour to wind down before they went home. The schedule was tough. They didn't have almost any days where they could stay longer," Parvin recounts.

Shortly before the end of the 1984-85 season, Pelle asked Parvin if he'd like to take a trip to Sweden during the summer. "Can I bring along a friend of mine?" Parvin asks, already knowing the answer. "Yeah, absolutely, Eddie. No problem." Parvin's friend is a man named Frank Coille, whom Lindbergh has only met in passing. They stay in Stockholm for 10 days with Pelle as he is fishing and racing around the archipelago on his speed boat. "We were out on the islands and only came ashore to have fun. Certainly there was a bit of partying. We thought it was fantastic, because the sun was still up at midnight," Parvin says. At the end of their trip, Pelle drives Parvin and Coille back to Arlanda airport. As it turns out, the next time he sees Parvin is on the night of the accident.

Late in the summer, Pelle also has a much more low-key visit from a North American. He has grown to view psychologist, Dr. Stephen Rosenberg, as a friend as well as a therapist, and takes him out in Stockholm as a gesture of gratitude for the positive visualization techniques Rosenberg has taught him. In the days that follow, Pelle shows Dr. Rosenberg the sites around

Stockholm and takes him out to eat at several of Lindbergh's favorite restaurants. Lindbergh, who does all the driving, doesn't drink any alcohol while he's out with Rosenberg. As he once explained to Kevin Cady, Lindbergh tells Dr. Rosenberg, "If you get caught driving here in Sweden after you drink beer, you go to prison. It's not worth it."

In August, Pelle is the subject of an interview conducted by *Hockey Night in Canada*. He takes the crew out on his boat and talks at length about his Vezina Trophy winning season, the Flyers run to the Cup Finals, Bernie Parent, the 1980 Olympics, the 1981 Canada Cup debacle, his relationship with the fans, and a host of other topics. He says of Parent, "Bernie has been my coach and one of my best friends since I came over to America or the Flyers. During my first year in Maine, he came up to me, and we didn't just talk about hockey. He took me out to dinner and we talked about everything you can imagine, about boating and fishing and other things. I felt that he was good friend, someone I could talk to about anything." At the end of the interview, he's asked how he thinks he'll be remembered in 20 years. "If there's really anyone who remembers me in 20 years it will probably be because there's some new Swedish super goalie who wins the Vezina Trophy. …Maybe there will be some old players who remember that I was the first European goalie to win the Vezina. But I don't think anyone will remember me in 20 years," Lindbergh says.

Before he departs Stockholm for Flyers' training camp, Pelle works out the final details for his customized Porsche 930 Turbo to be delivered to the United States from the Porsche factory in Stuttgart, Germany. Several weeks later the car arrives in Baltimore and Pelle is ecstatic. "It's perfect! It's got 380 horsepower and it's beautiful. The acceleration is so smooth," he reports to friends at home. In the weeks to come, everyone close to him will get to know all the specs on the car by heart, because Pelle talks so often about the car.

Stories abound of Pelle's obsession with sports cars and his love of driving at tremendous rates of speed. Virtually everyone who spent significant time with him has at least one tale of a close call he had while behind the wheel. "I wasn't scared being in the car with him," Kerstin says. "Pelle knew how to drive. But of course he drove too fast, and I was worried about him getting in an accident for that reason. I would bring it up and he'd just laugh and say not to worry."

While driving one of his sports cars, he often exceeds 120 miles per hour on the open road. Regardless of whether he's behind the wheel of his car, his boat or even pedaling a bicycle, Pelle inevitably tries to test the vehicle's top speed, and make light of warnings to slow down. "Anna Lisa, Sigge and, later, Kerstin, all talked to Pelle about the risks," says Björn Neckman. "But Pelle felt he was in control, and he loved the feeling he got from driving fast. So he kept increasing the horsepower."

Pelle has plans to purchase an even faster boat in the near future. In March 1985, Pelle drove to Lancaster, Pennsylvania with Kerstin and Reino Sundberg. He began discussions to buy an Apache with a more powerful motor than his Century. Along the way up and back, Lindbergh's Porsche passed by local Amish inhabitants driving in horses and buggies. The contrast could hardly be starker. "Hey, do all those horses have the same horsepower?" Pelle jokes.

Several years before, during Pelle's stint with the Maine Mariners, some of the team members went to the Sugarloaf Mountains over the Christmas break. Coach Bob McCammon forbade the players from doing any skiing. Many ignored the warning, including Pelle. He joined Kerstin and Neckman on the mountain and had no interest in taking one of the beginner slopes. "Pelle had hardly ever stood on skis, but he was very confident about it, even though he was doing something dangerous," Kerstin recalls. "So he goes full speed, right down the mountain with hardly a single turn. There was never a thought about whether he could get hurt. As long as he had control of it, whether it was going skiing or driving, he never worried."

Pelle always loved fancy cars but his options were limited in his early years by what he could afford. His first car was a little Fiat 128, light green in color with Hammarby IF and the number 1 (his jersey number) painted on the front doors. He leased the car for 500 SEK per month. Lindbergh was drawn to the Fiat because many of the senior level players in Stockholm drove the same car, and Sigge owned several Fiat 1300 cars over the years. Next, he saved money and bought a white, two-door Pontiac Grand Prix. Björn Neckman was one of his few friends who dared to ride with him on a regular basis. "Pelle loved to test all sorts of limits. Not just with speed, but even with things like the gas tank. I remember when he got the Pontiac, we were always running on empty or getting the warning light. Pelle would ask, 'Do you think we'll make it?' One time, we got to intersection and the power shut down. We almost drove into a traffic light," says Neckman.

By the time he played for AIK and had begun to make a name for himself as Sweden's fastest-rising young goaltender, Pelle traded in the Pontiac and bought a Lincoln Continental. Later he thought the big, wide car was too sluggish and soon opted for a black Saab Turbo. At the time, it was considered the slickest Swedish car on the road. A female friend from Gothenburg with whom he sometimes hung out in those days, Annika Nilsson, remembers that Lindbergh already had set his sights even higher on the sports car scale. "Pelle was proud of his Saab but he'd say, 'When I get to the NHL, I can get myself a really fast car. I want to get a Porsche,'" she says. "One time we were in the car and we met up with Reino Sundberg, and Pelle was speeding as fast as he could. I was afraid." He laughed and told Reino, "Annika was really scared when I was driving, but good God, someday we've all gotta take in the oars." Annika remembers, "I didn't know what he meant by that and he laughed even harder." He said, 'You know, we've all gotta drive the spike in the lid sooner or later.'" Pelle meant that everyone will eventually die.

When Pelle and Thomas Eriksson signed their first contracts with the Flyers, they bought matching Corvette Sting Rays. The two cars, especially Pelle's, soon became infamous among the Portland police. As Pelle's local fame grew and he befriended many of the cops, he was usually able to avoid speeding tickets. By the time he blossomed into NHL stardom with the Flyers, he was virtually immune to being held accountable for his driving habits. Usually, he tried to play the ignorant foreigner when he got pulled over. But in the early days of his rookie season with Maine, Pelle quickly racked up several tickets. Sometimes Pelle would remember to pay his tickets, other times he'd forget. On one occasion, he got stopped and cited for driving more than 60 miles an hour in a 30-mile-per-hour zone. Pelle set down the ticket when he got home, and forgot about it as the Mariners headed out on a road trip.

Shortly thereafter, he received a summons. Scared, Pelle went to coach Bob McCammon and asked what to do. "Just relax," McCammon said. "I'll call up our [team] lawyer, and maybe he can pull some strings." A few hours later, the lawyer called McCammon. "Everything's OK, Pelle," said McCammon. "You just have to go downtown by 3:00 pm today and pay your tickets." Lindbergh thanked the coach and departed. The next day, he walked into McCammon's office and laid a speeding ticket down on the desk. "What the hell? You should've paid the goddamn thing!" McCammon exclaimed. "Yeah, I did," Lindbergh replied. "But I got this one yesterday afternoon when was going down to pay the other tickets." Such was McCammon's introduction to Pelle's driving habits.

Over the course of their four years together in Portland and Philadelphia, McCammon became all too familiar with the way Lindbergh drove. "There were plenty of times I'd be driving to practice, and Pelle would drive right by me," McCammon recalls a quarter century later. "He'd fly by me. One time, I hollered at him about it and he said, 'Ah, Cagey, that was nothing. I was just in second gear.'"

During Pelle's first winter in Portland, on January 4, 1981, Kevin Cady was involved in a serious car accident. The accident was not the fault of 18-year-old assistant equipment manager. During the morning rush hour, Cady sat at a red light at a busy intersection. As the light turned green, he stepped on the gas pedal. Unfortunately, a driver going the other way ran the red light and slammed into Cady's car. Cady, who was not wearing a seatbelt, got thrown forward, and his head went through the windshield. At the hospital, doctors worked on him for five hours to save his life, because he lost a massive amount of blood. Cady woke up with over 500 stitches in his face.

In this 1981 photo, Pelle poses at his home in Maine with the Corvette he bought with his first professional contract. [Courtesy Ann-Louise Hörnestam]

Pelle and Neckman came to visit and brought a traffic light for a present. "We bought a little traffic light, which actually worked and would change from green to yellow to red," Neckman says. "We put it beside Kevin's bed in the hospital room. We were relieved that Kevin was OK, but we didn't think about the risks [to ourselves] just because we visited a friend in the hospital. We were young and we didn't think about what could happen to us, and Pelle thought he was a good driver." Cady's strongest memory from the visit, apart from the blinking traffic light, is that Pelle couldn't stop asking questions about the accident. "He was totally fascinated by all the details of the accident and how the doctors had saved my life and stitched my face," Cady says.

Pelle bought his first Porsche after earning an NHL spot with the Flyers. He purchased an original Porsche 930 (manufactured in 1969) from Rolf Tellsten's Porsche garage in the Stockholm suburb of Täby. Lindbergh drove it both in Philadelphia and Stockholm, and would take it to Tellsten for service during the summer. Reino Sundberg recalls, "Pelle and I took a drive from Nacka to Värmdö in his first Porsche. We went out when there wasn't any traffic. Pelle kicked the speed up to 255 kilometers (153 miles) per hour, and then Pelle even got the car up to 260 KPH (156 MPH). I told him afterwards that he needed to calm down with it." Lindbergh decided that he'd found the maximum speed his Porsche could reach on the open road, but now he wanted a car that could go even faster.

In 1983, while competing for Team Sweden at the IIHF World Championship in West Germany, Lindbergh and Thomas Eriksson took a tour of the Porsche factory in Stuttgart. "I loved Porsches almost as much as Pelle did, and we were like kids in a candy store at the factory," Eriksson says. It's at about this time that Pelle decided he was going to get a new Porsche. Not just a new "ordinary" Porsche, either. He wanted a one-of-a-kind car, regardless of the cost. After returning to Sweden from the tournament, Lindbergh and Eriksson went together to a Porsche dealership on Lindhagsplan in

Stockholm. Pelle bought a new-generation Porsche 930 Turbo (1984 model) in red and Eriksson picked a Porsche Carrera Targa. Lindbergh offered most everyone he knew a ride in his car. Few took him up on it more than once.

Sudsy Settlemyre recalls, "When we were together, I almost always drove, because I refused to sit in a car with Pelle behind the wheel. He was crazy. One time I went out on a double date with Pelle and Kerstin, and Pelle starts showing off, spinning the car and leaving round black tracks on the asphalt and smoke around the whole car. I screamed at him from the back seat, 'We're just going out to dinner with the ladies, cut that shit out!'" Pelle stopped. But he'd give Settlemyre other occasions to yell at him for his recklessness behind the wheel. "Pelle drove my son, Derek, home when Derek was 14. He wanted to show off for my kid, so he floors it and drove 130 miles an hour. When Derek told me what happened, I flipped out on Pelle. I put my both my hands on his neck and shouted, 'You goddamn fool! That's my boy! If you ever drive like that again with him in the car, I swear to God, I'll strangle you to death!'" Lindbergh apologized profusely. Settlemyre forgave him, but he remained extremely concerned. "I remember that in the fall of 1984, I said to my girlfriend Roberta that Pelle's car is like a red rocket and this whole thing is going to end up real bad some day."

Jack Prettyman shared the same concern. He's warned Lindbergh on many occasions to slow down and the plea always falls of deaf ears as does advice from Lindbergh's other friends on the force. Prettyman decided to try to scare Pelle straight. The officer phoned trainer Sudsy Settlemyre at the Coliseum. "Pelle is going to be driving up in about 30 seconds," the police officer said. "How do you know that?" Settlemyre asked. "I was just in touch with an ambulance that was out on call. Pelle just overtook it in his car. So now I want you to scare him. If he keeps driving that way, something bad is going to happen."

When he's not tempting fate behind the wheel of the Porsche, Lindbergh takes care of his favorite toy with almost paternalistic concern. "When Pelle was home on a Sunday afternoon, he loved to go outside to wash and polish the car," Kerstin recalls. "Also, he didn't like to drive it in bad weather and almost never drove it after dark." If Kerstin's Mercedes had not broken down on the night of November 9, 1985, Pelle would have driven her car to Bennigan's and the Coliseum.

Pelle was unable to take his Porsche along on the Flyers' road trips, but that didn't mean he was off the road. "Everyone knew how Pelle loved cool cars. I remember that whenever we were in Los Angeles and had free time, he went up to Beverly Hills and rented a sports car," Dave Poulin says. Lindbergh tried out several different cars, by renting a Ferrari or a Lamborghini for the day. Sometimes he'd take along *Philadelphia Inquirer* beat writer Al Morganti, who also loved fast cars. Morganti remembers,

> Eventually, I stopped driving with Pelle. When he got the red Porsche, he really started driving like a maniac. I told him to slow down and he just smiled and sped up. If I tried to kid him and tell him I just saw a cop, he also sped up. I drove pretty fast myself at the time, but when I went with Pelle, I got scared. That Porsche went entirely too fast. It was beyond any conceivable speed limit. That car was extremely difficult to drive, especially with the turbo kick. It was hard to steer, and when the turbo kicked in, the back wheels would lift off the road. I told that to Pelle and he just said, 'Yeah, yeah, but you just have to learn your car.

The last time Morganti rode with Lindbergh was a few weeks before Anna Lisa and Göran's visit. Pelle and Morganti were in Atlantic City, and Lindbergh showed off the recent renovations on his car, by hitting speeds of over 120 miles per hour with scarcely any effort. "I said to him, 'You're going to die,' and he laughed at me," Morganti recalls.

Late one night in March 1985, about nine months before his fatal accident, Pelle had a serious scare with the Porsche. The incident occurred during Reino Sundberg's visit. The guys met up with several Flyers players at the Coliseum. Afterward, Sundberg drove the car back toward Pelle's house. "A deer ran out in front of the car," Sundberg says. "There was a leftward curve not very far from the house and we were driving too fast, and braked too late." The car careened off the road and came to a stop in a meadow. The guys tried to back up the car but the wheels were stuck and merely spun in the soft soil. Everyone got out of the car as smoke rose from the car. They started walking back to the house through the woods and shortly thereafter, the grass ignited and the car caught fire. A passerby saw the blaze and called the fire department. The front half of the car was badly burned. "We heard the sirens but we didn't think there was any danger to us or the car," Sundberg recalls. With the car ablaze and no sign of the driver at the scene of the accident, the police were notified. Jack Prettyman went to the scene of the accident as Lindbergh and Sunberg made the roughly 20 minute walk back to the house. Prettyman's patrol car beat them there. "Kerstin," Prettyman said, "Pelle's Porsche is on fire and the guys are missing." A few minutes later, Pelle and Sunberg come walking into the house unharmed, although Pelle has been scratched up by the brush and his shorts are ripped.

Pelle chose not to tell Flyers' management about the mishap. The next morning at practice, teammate Rick Tocchet noticed the deep scratches all over the goaltender's legs. "Where the hell did those come from?" he asked. "I bought a little lion cub. They scratch like you wouldn't believe." Tocchet plays along with the joke. In the days to come, everyone finds out about what happened. Prettyman, relieved that his friend is unharmed, places a handwritten sign at the scene of the accident. It says "Reino's Curve."

With the Porsche more or less totaled, Pelle decides to go ahead and send the car back to the Stuttgart factory to get the modifications he's been wanting. The car gets a new, aerodynamic front, new tires and rims, a new red paint job, and an upgraded (and illegal in the USA) motor with 80 additional horsepower. The car can now go zero to sixty in fewer than four seconds.

CHAPTER 25
FRIDAY, NOVEMBER 15, 1985.

The Philadelphia Flyers' charter flight lifts off for Hartford. Despite the emotional victory over the Edmonton Oilers the previous night and the team's 10-game winning streak, the usual banter and joking is missing during the short trip. Thomas Eriksson makes the trip with the team, but has permission to leave right after the game to attend Pelle's funeral in Stockholm.

Back in Marlton, NJ, Pelle's family sits at the breakfast table and talk about how moved they were by the memorial at the Spectrum. Across the ocean in Sweden, it's already the afternoon. The two biggest national newspapers, *Aftonbladet* and *Expressen*, have extensive coverage of the memorial and the game at the Spectrum. The conversation continues and they discuss the upcoming trip to Sweden. Kerstin talks to Kevin Cady and asks if he will come to Stockholm for the funeral. Cady, who had originally planned to head back to Portland, says, "Yes." "I'll call the Flyers and arrange it," Kerstin replies. "You'll meet us at JFK in New York tomorrow." Later, Anna-Lisa and Göran pack everything they've brought to the US and Kerstin prepares a bag for a one-week stay in Stockholm.

Kerstin asks Jack Prettyman if he'll drive her to visit Ed Parvin Jr. at Cooper Hospital and Kathy McNeal at Kennedy Memorial. She buys flowers to bring to both of Pelle's passengers. Parvin is still unconscious, his parents remain nearby and are consumed by their own sorrows. She tries her best to comfort them, but feels like she's intruding and is still grief-stricken herself. The visit is brief.

Kerstin returns to Prettyman's car. They travel southbound toward Kennedy Memorial, while discussing the arrangements for Pelle's Stockholm funeral as they go. Prettyman nears his exit, and starts to pull off the highway. Suddenly, a tow truck changes lanes and pulls right in front of the car; the collision is unavoidable. Prettyman's car slams into the back of the tow truck. The front of the car is smashed. "Are you OK?" Prettyman asks, turning to Kerstin. "Yeah, I'm OK." Neither Prettyman nor Kerstin is hurt, but Kerstin is a little freaked out that she's just been in a car accident in the same week as Pelle's fatal accident. Prettyman calls his wife and asks, "Can you come here and pick up Kerstin? I don't want the reporters to find out what just happened." "I'll be right there," she replies. Ten minutes later, Kerstin goes to Kennedy Memorial Hospital to visit Kathy McNeal. The conversation is short and stilted.

Early the next day, the casket containing Pelle's body is discreetly loaded into the cargo hold of an SAS plane bound for Stockholm. Pelle's family members board the plane, sit in the first-class section, and try to get some sleep during the flight. When the plane lands at Arlanda airport, it's just a few hours before Hammarby IF's memorial for Pelle before a game at Hovet. "I want to go to the game," Sigge says. "OK, but we don't have a lot of time," Anna-Lisa replies. There are only a few minutes to spare when Sigge (clad in his Hammarby jacket) walks through the entrance with Kerstin and Ann-Louise. They're escorted to the stands and sit with Pelle's former national team coaches Leif Boork and Anders Parmström.

A crowd of 2,000 fans, significantly higher than the usual attendance for a Hammarby IF game, has come out for the game. The arena is darkened with a single spotlight on the ice and the players stand with bowed heads during the ceremony. Former Hammarby IF executive Sivert Svärling leads the memorial by talking about Lindbergh's love for Bajen and by recalling his first meeting with an 11-year-old Pelle. "He was the smallest on the team but he was the best player. He was already so good that when the older Hammarby kids played in the playoffs of the St. Erik's Cup, they wanted Pelle in goal," says Svärling.

Pelle's former teammate Jan Lindberg (who played with Lindbergh on Hammarby's junior and senior teams) then gives a short speech on behalf of the players. "You were a one-of-a-kind local kid who put the whole world at your feet. We were proud of you, Pelle," Lindberg says. After Lindberg finishes, Pelle's final letter to Bajen management is read aloud: "Finally, here comes the money I promised. I hope it can benefit the little guys." Pelle wrote the letter earlier in the fall and donated the $2,000 prize money he'd gotten for being named first star of the game in a 2-0 shutout of the Hartford Whalers on October 24. Hammarby management announces that it will be starting a memorial fund for its junior team, with Pelle's donation as the first contribution. In addition, a 29,000 SEK portion of the ticket sales from the night's gate will also go to the fund.

The ceremony ends with a minute of silence. After the game, which Hammarby lost on a bizarre deflection goal, Sigge talks to an *Aftonbladet* reporter. "It feels good to be back. In Philadelphia, everything was so heavy and big with limousines and film cameras everywhere," he says. After traveling the world in his sailing days, Sigge would much rather stay put in Stockholm.

Monday is a chilly and lonely Swedish autumn day for winter is in the air. With the funeral still two days away, Pelle's family members spend much of the day home alone for the first time since the crash. On Barnängsgatan, Anna-Lisa walks into the kitchen, only to realize that the days of her standing there yelling at a teenaged Pelle to turn down his blaring bedroom stereo are now a bittersweet memory. She'll never get the pleasure of watching him stand in the kitchen, wolfing down her cooking, and asking for more. She cries as Sigge sits pensively on the living room sofa.

It's also a rough day for Kerstin. She's staying with her parents at their home on Gökvägen in the Stockholm suburb of Täby. It's the first time in many years that she's gone home without Pelle. So much of their life together revolved around the hockey season. "The hardest times early on were when I was alone and I wasn't able to try to make things feel as normal as possible," Kerstin recalls two decades later.

Barely more than a week ago, Kerstin thought she knew what her future held. Pelle was the spontaneous type and usually not much for long-term planning, but he and Kerstin knew they wanted to be husband and wife after their long engagement. She'd marry Pelle after the season, and the couple would continue to make their in-season home in the Philadelphia area and return to Stockholm for the summers. Now all those plans are gone, shattered as suddenly and violently as Pelle's Porsche hit the wall.

On Tuesday afternoon, a delegation from the Philadelphia Flyers, Bernie Parent, Bob Clarke, Jay Snider, and Keith Allen, arrives at Arlanda airport. Thomas Eriksson and Kevin Cady are already in Stockholm. The Flyers' leaders check into a Sheraton hotel in central Stockholm, but they spend the early part of the evening having dinner at Kerstin's family's home on Gökvägen in Täby. Sigge, Anna-Lisa, Ann-Louise, Ann-Christine, and Kevin Cady are also there.

There's a biting chill in the air on the morning of Wednesday, November 20, 1985 as a limousine pulls up in front of the apartment building on Barnängsgatan. Clarke, Snider, Allen, and Parent enter the building and walk up to the second floor where Anna-Lisa, Sigge, and Kerstin are already waiting for them. Kerstin translates as necessary. This is the first time that any of the people in the Flyers' contingent have seen Pelle's childhood home. It's emotional for all of them, but especially for Parent. He goes into Pelle's bedroom and sees the various mementos, photos, and old equipment Pelle kept in his room. He also sees a poster of himself, a copy of his autobiography and other tangible testaments to the way a young Pelle idolized him. More than 20 years later, Parent vividly recalls standing in Pelle's childhood room. It was one of the most emotional parts of the trip for him. He recalls,

> I had the chance to be alone in Pelle's room for a few minutes, and it was a very, very special moment. The room was full of Pelle's private memories, but it didn't feel strange to be there. I felt at home, and, well, this is hard to explain, but I got a warm feeling in there. Pelle was talking to me. He was saying that everything would be good, everything was OK, and I could go on.

The magnificent Sofia Church overlooks south Stockholm from the peak of the White Mountains (*Vita Bergen*) in Södermalm's Vitaberg Park (*Vitabergsparken*). Standing on the grass plain at the top, a visitor is treated to a spectacular unobstructed view of all of south Stockholm. On this day, the skies are overcast and few pay much notice to the vista, with the temperatures below the freezing point. Hundreds gather in front of the church an hour before the funeral. There have been so many floral tributes donated for the funeral that there are enough bouquets to place flowers at every pew.

Ann-Louise and Ann-Christine are near the front with their families. As the clock strikes 1:00 pm, Sigge, Anna-Lisa, and Kerstin walk into the church last with Kerstin holding Sigge's arm. Sigge wears a Swedish flag lapel pin on his dark suit. Anna-Lisa enters directly behind them, next to vicar Inga-Britt Lindell. The mourners stand as the procession moves past them. The inside of the church is filled beyond capacity with over 700 people of all ages filling the pews or standing in the back. Outside there's at least another hundred people who could not get into church.

In the middle of the church's meticulously maintained wooden floor stands an upraised closed casket, white as a new sheet of ice. Lindell, who hails from Täby and is a friend of the Pietzsch family, begins the ceremony with a psalm chosen by Anna-Lisa. The only speech made during the ceremony is by Lindell, who talks about "all the energetic, gentle, and trusting traits of Pelle's personality." She concludes by speaking directly to Pelle:

> You who were so eager to achieve, who trained extra and
> reach the status you dreamed of and strived for from the time you
> were little… you, Göran Per-Eric Lindbergh from Söder in
> Stockholm, Sweden, are here in the earth at just 26 years.

The funeral ends with several of Pelle's favorite songs by Elton John. With Anders Eljas on piano, Vicki Benckert sings "Your Song," a tune that reminded Pelle of Kerstin. The next song is "Sorry Seems to be the Hardest Word." Finally, Eljas plays the instrumental "Song for Guy," which Elton John had written for a young friend who died in a traffic accident. The only lyric in the song, repeated at the end, is "life isn't everything." When the music ends, everything is still for a moment as Kerstin and Anna-Lisa lay a rose on the casket. One-by-one the most important people in Pelle's life then head out of the church as dusk falls over Stockholm.

After the funeral, the family hosts a buffet reception for 200 invited guests. At each place setting, there's the same black-and-white memorial card that the Flyers distributed at the game against the Oilers the previous Thursday. Kerstin walks around to each table and thanks the guests for coming. Afterward, the guests are shown a video with parts of the tribute show that aired on television before the Flyers-Oilers game. There's also a sequence of video clips and still photos of Pelle on and off the ice.

The guests start to file out by saying their goodbyes to Pelle's family. After the reception, Al Morganti stands with Kerstin as the reception hall staff cleans off the tables. "What were those blue bottles on the tables?" he asks. "It's called Ramlösa," she replies. "It's for guests who are driving. We don't drink alcohol and drive here in Sweden." She shares personal thoughts, "This is all so upsetting. We were going to get married next summer and we were going to have our reception here. What a shame that you had to come here for such a sad reason instead."

Pelle Lindbergh

CHAPTER 26

JANUARY 16, 1986 TO OCTOBER 9, 1987

Time goes by but the scars are still fresh for Pelle Lindbergh's loved ones and teammates. On January 16, 1986, Pelle is buried in The Woodland Cemetery (*Skogskyrkogården*), a cemetery in south Stockholm considered by many to be a marvel of architectural design. His tombstone has a Flyers' logo and his number 31 on it, and Pelle's parents visit the grave every Friday.

Pelle's parents soon stop granting interview requests. They focus much of their attention on Ann-Christine and their grandchildren. Although Ann-Christine had a brief reprieve from her illness, the long-term prognosis remains ominous. For all of her sadness, Anna-Lisa is determined to take things as they come but Sigge struggles to reconcile what's been going on around him. His world has collapsed.

As a team, the Flyers are fortified to survive. They try to deal with Pelle's death the same way they would if a teammate were traded or suffered a season-ending injury. They prepare for the games the same way and try to get back to their normal routine. As individuals, many have days where they're hit by waves of grief or anger. On those days, the players lean on each other for support.

In public, Mike Keenan is complimentary and supportive of the way his players have handled Pelle's loss. The team leaders respond in kind. In a *Sports Illustrated* article written weeks after Pelle's death, Dave Poulin deemed Keenan "a players' coach" and insisted "despite the tragedy, we're a happy

team". Behind closed doors, though, Keenan has become even more tyrannical and sometimes downright cruel to his players. In early December, the
Flyers drop four of five games. Keenan explodes and questions his players'
manhood and accuses them of using Pelle's death as an excuse for slacking off.
"Human nature wants comfort," Poulin said a decade later in *Full Spectrum*.
"Obviously he thought anger at him would help us play better. You wanted to
win just to shut him up."

On December 10, the Flyers end their mini-slide with a 7-4 win over
the Bruins at the Spectrum. Philadelphia goes on to win eight of nine games,
which brings the team's record to 28-9-0. But Pelle is still very much on
everyone's minds. "The mourning we all felt after Pelle's death touched the
team the whole season," recalls Kevin Cady. "We had a tremendous team, but
I remember there was a major worry in management that the players wouldn't
sufficiently recover, off the ice as well as on."

On a much happier note, the Flyers' family has a happy occasion to
celebrate during the holiday season. Brad and Patti Marsh welcome the arrival
of their first child whom they name Erik in honor of Pelle.

Kerstin continues to attend all of the games at the Spectrum. The team,
especially the players' wives and girlfriends, try to make sure she's included in
the team's family-related activities. She attends the team Christmas party and
her input is sought for the club's annual Flyers' Wives Fight for Lives charity
carnival in February.

Flyers supporters and fans around the NHL have not forgotten Pelle
Lindbergh. He is posthumously elected as the Wales Conference starting
goaltender for the 1985-86 All-Star Game, and is the first player in any major
sport to be honored this way. In the awarding of the Vezina Trophy at the
season's conclusion, winning goaltender John Vanbiesbrouck dedicates the

award to Pelle Lindbergh's memory during his acceptance speech. "There was an automobile accident in November," he says. "I would like to honor Pelle Lindbergh tonight in accepting this."

There's no telling how the Flyers would have fared in the 1986 playoffs if not for Pelle Lindbergh's accident. Perhaps Vanbiesbrouck would have outdueled Pelle in similar fashion, or perhaps the presence of Lindbergh in goal would have swung the final game at the Spectrum. What is for certain is that Pelle's death took an enormous toll on everyone associated with the Philadelphia Flyers. By the time the playoffs rolled around, there was precious little energy left to deal with the physical and mental rigors of the postseason. "It was a very long and tough winter, even though Pelle's passing happened early in the season," recalls Pelle Eklund. "After the Rangers series, many of us thought, 'finally, it's over.' Mentally and emotionally, we were drained." Former club president Jay Snider echoes the same sentiment. "There's no doubt that our team never recovered that year after Pelle's death," he says. "From the start, it felt like it was going to be our season. But then we lose Pelle so suddenly. He was enormously missed, both on and off the ice. Even before the playoffs, we were mentally finished."

On the day that the players clean out their lockers and say goodbye for the summer, Mike Keenan conducts his usual one-on-one meetings with each of the players. Thomas Eriksson informs him that he's going back to Sweden for good, even though he has one year remaining on his contract. He's already informed Bob Clarke.

Reino Sundberg finishes the season in Switzerland. As soon as the season ends in March 1986, he heads to the US to visit Kerstin and the accident scene. "In peace and quiet, I wanted to see what happened," he recalls.

Pelle's car is still at the same shop. After an investigation by police, it has been determined that the car did not malfunction. Human error caused the crash. Parts of the car, especially the motor, are salvageable and the usable parts are later sold to one of the Philadelphia Eagles' football players.

In the wake of Pelle's accident, the Flyers and many other NHL teams stop providing beer to players in the postgame locker room. Instead, the players have a choice of mineral water, sports drinks, or soft drinks. "That was a bigger change back then than it might sound like today. If a player wanted to be part of the team, he drank with the guys. Otherwise, he was an outsider. Beer was a huge part of the NHL in those days. It was a part of the hockey culture," says Al Morganti. Adds former Boston Bruin Micke Thelvén, "After a win, we'd all sit in the locker room, celebrating with a few beers. That disappeared right away after Pelle's accident."

The 1986-87 season proves to be the both the zenith and the beginning of the end of the Mike Keenan era. As they did the previous two years, the Flyers capture the Patrick Division championship with a 100-point season. "The adversity we went through with Pelle helped to fortify us the next season," recalls Poulin. "For the most part, we had the same team intact, but we'd grown up a lot. Everyone faces challenges and trying times, and facing them in the context of a hockey season just makes it a tougher test. But in many ways you learn more from those times than when things go the way you want them to," said Poulin, who also played through cracked ribs in the 1985 playoffs.

One year and eleven months after Pelle's death, the Lindbergh family is in mourning again. On October 11, 1987, 37-year-old Ann-Christine loses her long battle with cancer and is buried next to Pelle at *Skogskyrkogården.*

CHAPTER 27
STOCKHOLM, SWEDEN MAY 1990

Kerstin Pietzsch has come back to life. Over the past four-and-a-half years, she has picked up the pieces and rediscovered love and laughter. Pelle's "Kärran" always had remarkable inner strength, but coping with his loss took every ounce of courage she could muster. Now Kerstin is getting married and Pelle's family couldn't be any happier for her.

After Pelle's burial in November 1985, she returned to the house in Marlton and her mother, Gudrun, stayed with her. "The first half year, I tried to continue like nothing happened. Everything was so hard to fathom. It was like Pelle was on a road trip and he'd come home again soon," Kerstin recalls. "It was easier to go to the games and the team Christmas party than to sit home."

Kerstin visited Ed Parvin Jr. in the hospital in the months following the accident. She was one of his first visitors when he finally awakened after undergoing emergency brain surgery. By December 1985, he was able to jot down short notes, although he was still unable to speak. "Where's Pelle?" he asked. "He's dead, Eddie," Kerstin struggles to say. She also meets with Kathy McNeal to see if she can offer any insights into the accident. "Neither of them could really tell me very much," Kerstin says.

In early 1986, Kerstin agreed to be interviewed on national television in the United States on the ABC news show, *American Almanac*. Reporter Connie Chung presented a story tying Pelle's death to the question of whether bar owners could be held liable if patrons subsequently get involved in car accidents that cause injuries or death. "I can't hold anybody responsible for Pelle's death. No one except himself," Kerstin said to Chung.

After the 1985-86 hockey season, Kerstin wasn't ready to return to Sweden. As each day passes she became lonelier and lonelier in the house which they had shared despite people's efforts to keep her company and offer support. She spoke with the Snider family, who suggested she move to Los Angeles, where they had many good contacts. As a faithful friend, Jack Prettyman helped her empty the house. In appreciation, Kerstin gave him much of the equipment Pelle used in his final season.

Kerstin lived in Los Angeles for two years. It was the road city Pelle enjoyed the most during his NHL career, but her early days in Los Angeles were tough. Eventually, she forged a new social circle. "I got to be good friends with Wayne Gretzky's girlfriend at the time, Vicky Moss, who was a singer. We hung out a lot," she recalls. "Wayne was still playing in Edmonton then but we were all together a couple of times. He was sympathetic and wondered how he could help me in coming to grips with what happened. It took me a couple years to feel like myself again."

After two years in LA, Kerstin longed to move back home to Sweden. When she returns, she meets Kurt Somnell, an aircraft engineer. The two fall in love and marry in May 1990. They settle in the Stockholm suburb of Täby. Nineteen years later, the Somnells have two daughters, Mikaela and Petra, and a son Jens. Kerstin teaches youths as a member of the athletic faculty of the Åva gymnasium in Täby. All along, Kerstin has remained close with the Lindbergh family, especially Anna-Lisa, but she has never been back to Philadelphia. "It's unfortunate, but I haven't been back since I moved. I've thought about it many times," she says, "I've lost contact with people there…. after Pelle passed away…we're not in contact anymore."

The economic aftermath of Pelle Lindbergh's death was complicated. If not for the close relationship between Kerstin and Pelle's family (and their fundamental caring for Pelle above a desire for money), the situation could have torn them apart. At a press conference after Pelle's accident, Flyers GM Bob Clarke pledged to make sure the player's family received every cent of his still-unsigned six-year, $2.1 million contract. "As far as we're concerned, there's an agreement," he said. But Clarke's words were spoken out of emotion and compassion for the family in the hours following the accident. It did not reflect a business decision made by the organization or a legal recommendation from its attorneys. Pelle's contract was never paid in full to Kerstin or Sigge and Anna-Lisa, either directly by the Flyers or through Lloyds of London, which insured Lindbergh's assets. The insurer refused to pay the claim, and eventually settled out-of-court with the Flyers.

Attorneys had contacted Kerstin and offered her a settlement of $200,000, less than 10% of the value of the contract Pelle had agreed to. Lindbergh's agent Frank Milne hit the roof. He encouraged Kerstin to file a lawsuit to battle for the entire amount, and to make sure she got an equal share to Pelle's family in any settlement. But Kerstin didn't want to fight it out with the Flyers' organization that meant so much to Pelle, and she certainly didn't want to battle over money with people she loved. With the full support of Sigge and Anna-Lisa, she declined to file a lawsuit and accepted the $200,000 settlement. "We didn't have the desire to do it, and it wasn't going to bring Pelle back," Kerstin recalls. "We're not the type of people who sue over an accident. With the money, I was able to get a fresh start in Los Angeles and later had enough left to buy an apartment when I went back to Stockholm."

According to the Lindbergh family, the club offered to help Kerstin out with her living expenses as long as she lived in the Philadelphia area. She forwarded household bills to the club which the Flyers paid.

Pelle's parents later accept a life insurance settlement (Kerstin was ineligible to receive anything because she and Pelle were not yet legally married) and a $300,000 settlement from the Flyers. The organization tried to arrange the settlement for the family to avoid as much of the 70 percent Swedish inheritance tax as possible, but it was still worth far less than a "paid-in-full" $2.1 million contract.

The family says that Milne also suggested that even if they didn't want to pursue a case against the Flyers, they should explore a lawsuit against Porsche for manufacturing a car that may have been too dangerous to be used in everyday traffic. The ultra high-powered car was technically illegal for use in the United States. "We said no to that, too," Kerstin says. "It didn't matter to me or to Pelle's mother and father. We weren't out to get money for Pelle's death." Had they sued the car manufacturer, the family may not have had much of a case. Considering Pelle's history of reckless driving and the presence of alcohol in his body at the time of the accident, it may have been tough to prove the car's manufacturer caused his death. In addition, the car was custom-built to Lindbergh's specifications.

Pelle's family members also declined to take part in the legal processes surrounding the settlement of his estate. "We didn't check into any of the details," Kerstin says. "Again, to us, Pelle was suddenly gone and we didn't worry about money. So I don't know what his estate was worth, but when the house was sold, there was nothing left."

Frank Milne did not oversee the settlement of the estate, according to the family. He was replaced by an attorney recommended by the Flyers, and the Lindbergh clan simply stayed out of it.

After the accident, the two injured passengers in Pelle's car on the night of the accident filed lawsuits against the owners of the Coliseum and Bennigan's. They later reach settlements. Attorneys also filed for shares of Pelle's estate settlement.

In one of her few public statements after the accident, Kathy McNeal, seated next to her attorney, appears on *American Almanac*. She tearfully described the lingering physical and emotional effects of the accident. McNeal subsequently declined all interview requests, by citing the need to put her life back together and move on. She later relocated to another part of the country. Two decades later, she still refuses interview requests.

Ed Parvin eventually recovered his faculties after the accident, but the brain damage suffered in the accident left him with permanent slurring of his speech. He remembers,

> I was bed-ridden for a long time and it took a long time to recover. It was extremely hard, because I didn't know how I could move on. For a long time, it felt like we'd never leave the accident behind us. And the money really had no value. We did it [the lawsuit] in good faith. But I said to my lawyer that I didn't want the case to end up in the newspapers. Pelle was my friend. I miss him so much. Money doesn't replace that, and it doesn't give me back the time in my life that I lost.

For Ed Parvin Jr., the passage of time heals his wounds in ways that money can't. He gets his life back again and moves on without bitterness while learning to appreciate each day he has.

Pelle Lindbergh

CHAPTER 28

STOCKHOLM, SWEDEN. DECEMBER 28, 2006, 4:45 PM.

The sky is already pitch black by the time the American couple arrives at Stockholm Central Station after a three-and-a-half hour bus ride from Leksand. They're greeted by a Swedish friend, who leads them out to another friend's waiting car. The driver, Roffe Alex, is an old friend of Pelle Lindbergh's who has remained in contact with Pelle's surviving family members in the 21 years since his death. The passengers are the authors of this book, as well as Bill Meltzer's wife, Laura.

Roffe and Thomas Tynander have arranged a special evening: a trip to Pelle's gravesite at Skogkyrkogården, a stop at the Sofia Church where Pelle was baptized and eulogized, and a visit to Pelle's childhood home on Barnängsgatan to meet Anna-Lisa, Ann-Louise, and Göran. The Lindbergh family was away for the Christmas holiday, but has come back to Stockholm just to meet the American visitors.

Roffe drives everyone to the cemetery. Pelle is buried with his sister Ann-Christine and father, Sigge. Ann-Christine lost her battle with cancer shortly after Pelle's death, and Sigge passed away at age 85 on February 12, 2002. There are already lit candles placed along either side the grave site. Roffe and the others realize that someone else has been there that day, perhaps Anna-Lisa and Ann-Louise. The cemetery is huge, and if one doesn't know exactly where Pelle's grave is located, it would be virtually impossible to find without a map. Roffe knows the way, and the car rolls slowly to a stop on the paved road adjacent to the quadrant where the Lindbergh family's burial plot is located. Roffe and the others stand by the grave and contemplate how the life journeys of the three people laid to rest at this site were each remarkable in his or her own way – at once tragic and inspiring.

Life was never easy for Sigge Lindbergh, but he did everything in his power to make sure his children had what they needed and were raised with the correct values. His three children made him as proud as a father can be. The loss of two of them did something that backbreaking and dangerous work, economic hardship, and his own medical issues could never do – it broke his spirit. The final 17 years of Sigge Lindbergh's life were filled with sadness and regret for he had become increasingly bitter and withdrawn after Pelle and Ann-Christine died.

Ann-Christine was every bit the battler in life that Pelle was on the ice. She was determined to win her fight and her will remained strong even as her body got weak. For Ann-Christine, death meant a release from the ravages of cancer, but it also meant leaving behind her children and her husband at age 38. For her parents it meant losing their middle child after the sudden death of their youngest.

Pelle loved life and had everything to live for, yet threw his away and left others to pick up the pieces of their own shattered hearts. Pelle made the mistake of believing he was indestructible. Others believed, too, only to find out he was as mortal as the rest of us. The beauty and complexity of human life is that we're all fallible and imperfect. Honoring Pelle for how he lived does not mean one cannot be angry at the way he died. Any time the world loses such a person, whether it's a world-class athlete or someone who toils in the everyday work world, we're all a little poorer.

Before heading back to the car, Roffe and Thomas lay flowers at the grave. Bill and Laura pay respects by placing blades of grass at the foot of the grave.

The Sofia Church stands majestically as ever at the peak of the White Mountains in Södermalm's Vitaberg Park, but it is empty on this night. The visitors' footsteps echo as they walk into the magnificent chapel of the century-old church. The contrast to Pelle's funeral 21 years earlier could hardly be more striking. On that day, the church was filled to overflowing, and hundreds more people had to stand outside.

The last stop is Barnängsgatan. The grass field beneath the balcony looks very much like it did when Pelle used to play hockey outside for hours on end. The vestibule, Pelle's first 'rink,' carries a lot of tinny sound, so it's easy to see why neighbors objected to Pelle and best friend Mikael Nordh bouncing off the walls and banging sticks. Anna-Lisa has lived here since she and Sigge moved from their one-room apartment in 1964. Now an 86-year-old widow, she has been in poor health in recent years. Her expression is pleasant and she remains a gracious host, but her eyes and weathered face betray the many tears she's shed in the past 21 years of her life. Enduring the pain of losing people whom she'd have given her own life to save. Despite her losses, she still enjoys people: talking proudly about her grandchildren, seeing old family friends like Roffe, and meeting new people.

Ann-Louise and Göran, who live in a suburb southeast of central Stockholm, greet the guests warmly. Anna-Lisa and Ann-Louise lead the guests to the living room, where they've set out coffee and Christmas refreshments. The apartment furniture and decorations have not changed much in the years since Pelle's death. "I think about Pelle and Ann-Christine every day," Anna-Lisa says. "I see something that reminds me."

A photo of Pelle with Bernie Parent sits on a table near a deep sofa, next to a Dala horse that Pelle got during one of his summer hockey camps in Leksand. They have been in the same place for many years. She also keeps photos of Kerstin's three children among those of Ann-Louise and Ann-

Christine's children. Kerstin's youngest plays youth hockey and is a goaltender. For all intents and purposes, Anna-Lisa still considers Kerstin her third daughter, and they remain in regular contact.

When Thomas was in the process of researching the original Swedish version of this book, Kerstin (who lives outside Stockholm) came to the Lindbergh family home and sat beside Anna-Lisa on the sofa and held her hand as the author interviewed them. "Despite the dark time after Pelle's death, my memories of him are light, happy ones. Pelle's life was a Cinderella story," Kerstin says:

> But what I remember most is how Pelle was so unassuming and good to everyone. He had a single ambition, and he made his dreams come true but never forgot all his old friends. He was extremely social and modest and it was pretty easy to see the person behind all the goalie gear. It's very sad that there is still a lot of talk about him being drunk that last evening. He loved the speed of fast cars, but was very careful in taking care of himself. He hardly ever drank alcohol during the season, because he wanted to be fit and ready for every time he got out on the ice for the Flyers. Pelle loved being loved, so I was happy to see so many people turning up for his funeral. That felt good during all the sorrow and grief. But I look back on those dark days and still feel it was a horrific thing that happened. I've learned today to really appreciate the things I have in life.

The conversation is in Swedish. Bill understands roughly 25% of what's being said (there's a significant difference between skills with the written and spoken language). He tries to respond to questions in Swedish and to interpret the discussion for his wife, but it's a struggle. Anna-Lisa knows this situation all too well, from having experienced the same barriers whenever she traveled to the United States to visit Pelle. Even the simplest interactions in the US required an interpreter. She wants to make sure her American guests feel comfortable in her home. "Translate! Translate!" Anna-Lisa repeatedly insists to Roffe and Thomas. Just before the trip to Sweden, Bill's 93-year-old grandmother baked cookies to bring along to the Lindbergh home. He explains in Swedish to Ann-Louise, who repeats the information in a louder, clearer tone to her mother who smiles. "Take some more coffee now," Anna-Lisa says. "We have more cheese in the kitchen, too."

"I heard from Thomas that Pelle usually jumped over the balcony instead of leaving through the door," Bill says in halting Swedish. Thomas clarifies for Anna-Lisa who laughs. "Oh, yes. He'd jump down to go play with his friends outside," she says. Ann-Louise brings out a family photo album for she and Göran got married the same year Pelle was born. There's a striking picture of the two of them as a young couple with Ann-Louise holding her baby brother.

After everyone finishes eating and takes his or her last sip of coffee, Ann-Louise leads the guest to Pelle's old bedroom. The small room tells the story of an energetic, wide-eyed child from a working class neighborhood in Sweden who dreamed of playing for the Philadelphia Flyers and becoming the next Bernie Parent.

The small bedroom, with Pelle's old bed, tells the story of that dream coming true. The room is filled with photos, trophies, medals, and mementos spanning his youth hockey days, international tournaments, and his AHL and NHL careers, arranged exactly as Pelle left them. Among the dozens of items, there's Pelle's first goaltending mask, made by his father. There's a photo of him as a member of Hammarby's '59 team, with a dated note from Curt Lindström extolling the 11-year-old's boundless potential as a goaltender. There's his NHL All-Star Game jersey, his much tinkered-with pads, his memorabilia from Lake Placid, and more. On the other side of the room, there's Pelle's copy of Bernie Parent's autobiography, his music collection, and memoribilia accumulated during his hockey travels. Above Pelle's bed, there's a picture of his beloved Porsche, taken shortly before his fatal crash.

There's one more object in the room, easy to miss among the priceless hockey objects: a small stuffed animal. It's the same blue-and-yellow octopus that Pelle used to keep in the guest room of his house in NJ. He gave it to Anna-Lisa just before heading out on the night of the crash. The stuffed animal now sits on the pillow atop Pelle's childhood bed, and forever waits for Anna-Lisa's son to come home.

CHAPTER 29

STOCKHOLM, SWEDEN AND PHILADELPHIA, PA, MAY 24, 2009

Pelle Lindbergh would have celebrated his fiftieth birthday today. It's a reminder of just how young he was when he died 24 years ago. In Stockholm, Ann-Louise, Göran, Rolf Alex, Thomas Tynander, and members of the Hammarby IF fan club attend a small graveside memorial, just as they did for Pelle's birthday the previous year. Elsewhere in Philadelphia and in Stockholm, people go about their usual business.

Over the last two years, 2008 and 2009, many of the tangible parts of Pelle's hockey career have started to disappear. In 2008, Hammarby IF announced that its hockey section was bankrupt after operating at a deficit in recent years. The Bajen senior team had not played in Elitserien since 1985, and the cost of operating the hockey program with declining sponsorship and membership revenues had become prohibitive. Despite efforts to save the team, the hockey club was disbanded on April 22, 2008, after 88 years of existence. At about the same time, Comcast-Spectacor, the owner of the Flyers, announced that the Philadelphia Spectrum would close its door for good after the 2008-09 season. The Flyers' original home, the rink where Pelle spent many of the happiest times in his adult life, was to be demolished and replaced by a hotel and shopping center.

The collection of mementos in Pelle's childhood bedroom is no longer intact, either. At the age of 88, Anne-Lisa is physically unable to care for Pelle's materials. An unscrupulous profiteer convinced the family that Pelle's old trophies, medals, equipment and papers may have had plenty of sentimental value to the family but very little monetary value to the general public. He acquired the collection from the family for a small sum, and then promptly turned around and made a hefty profit by auctioning the entire collection online. Most items netted between $200 and $2,300, with seven items selling for over $1,000. Two very-prized collectibles (Pelle's Cooper leg pads and his jersey from the 1978 World Junior Championships) sold for over $2,000 apiece.

The collection is now scattered to the winds and is doomed to be resold piecemeal. Like the Spectrum and the Hammarby IF hockey team, it's all transient. Fortunately, the real measure of Pelle Lindbergh's legacy is not found in the objects he owned or within the walls of a brick and concrete building where he used to play hockey. Pelle's immortality is found in the hearts of the people whose lives he touched, and in the stories they've passed along for posterity. It's manifested in the influence he has had on a new generation of goalies, just as Pelle found inspiration in Bernie Parent and Parent in Jacques Plante. Last but not least, it's found in the permanence of his role as a pioneer in the NHL – the first European goaltender to win the Vezina Trophy. He carved a role in hockey history that can never be taken away by death or the passage of time.

Brad Marsh was one of Pelle's best friends on the Flyers, and a very well liked player within the entire hockey world. Brad and Patti Marsh celebrated the birth of their first child one month after Pelle's death, and named the baby Erik in memory of Per-Eric Lindbergh. The Lindbergh family was deeply touched, and sent a special gift to the Marshes. "Through Kerstin, Pelle's parents gave us a medallion that belonged to Pelle," Marsh says,

It was an extremely thoughtful gift. On one side, Pelle's family had it engraved 'Erik David,' and under Erik's name is the Swedish word, 'Lycka.' On the other side, there's a four-leaf clover and engraved around it is, 'In memory of Pelle Lindbergh, Phila-

delphia Flyers # 31. We gave the medallion to Erik on his six-
teenth birthday. To this day, he still wears it with pride.

Lycka is a special word in the Swedish language. Depending on the
context, it can mean luck, happiness, or success.

Brian Propp has given away many of his hockey mementos and lost
track of others, but there are two objects that aren't going anywhere. One is a
photo of a smiling Pelle Lindbergh and the other is a Flyers' jersey with a #31
memorial patch on the shoulder, worn the remainder of the 1985-86 season
after Pelle's death. " I keep a framed photo of Pelle in my office," Propp says,

The jersey is the only game-used one from my career that I still have.
Pelle will always be with me – and all of us who were his teammates. The
memories I hold closest are the ones of a guy who was more than just a good
goaltender and teammate.... He was also very competitive on the rink. He
and I used to have breakaway competitions after practice, and we'd have a
great time. Neither one of us wanted to let the other guy get bragging rights
on the last shot....Pelle was only just beginning to tap into his potential, and
he was already a Vezina Trophy winner. One of my few regrets in my career is
that we couldn't have enjoyed Pelle longer, because he was a joy to have as a
teammate and as a friend.

During his career, Captain Dave Poulin was always known for his
leadership ability. Never did he face a more trying time than when he had to
be strong for his teammates while his own heart ached after Pelle's death.

Pelle's death shook every one of us to our core. It shattered the illusion of invincibility that athletes – especially young ones – often feel. Playing hockey was cathartic for us, but it was very hard to carry on in the beginning. We were already a close-knit group, but losing Pelle made us realize just how much we meant to each other. We helped support one another," he says. When I think of Pelle, there are two images that resonate. First of all, he was a very dedicated hockey player. He was always striving to get better. Secondly, he was a truly genuine, caring, and compassionate human being.... You have to learn from your own mistakes, and you have the potential of learning from others' mistakes as well. Back in those days, we all drank a few beers or partied and then we drove our cars home. I did the same thing, but after the night Pelle died, I never did it again....You experience an array of emotions when you suddenly lose someone close to you, the way we lost Pelle – denial, anger, despair. Ultimately, you come to understand that it's all part of the grieving. Everyone faces challenges and trying times. Sometimes, the most valuable lessons you learn are the ones that come from adversity.

Thomas Eriksson never looked back to the NHL after leaving the Flyers in the summer of 1986. Eriksson had put his hockey days behind him for the most part, but Pelle Lindbergh remains very much in this thoughts. "I've spoken with Pelle many times after what happened," Eriksson says. "I dream that we get together and every time it feels like things are back to normal, and we talk about everyday sorts of things. It can be about a practice or a game or about going out to do something. At the same time that I've had every dream, I've had a feeling like, 'This shouldn't be working like this,' but at the same time I think, 'Nah, this is nothing strange.' There were many dreams like that, especially in the first few years. Afterwards, it's tailed off a little, year by year."

Ed Parvin Jr. sustained permanent injuries in the crash, but the 51-year-old carries no ill-will toward his friend who was driving the car. "I think about Pelle just about every day. Every day! He was a great guy and a great goaltender. Pelle was a hero in Philadelphia and, naturally, people still remember him. When I went to the Spectrum for my first Flyers game after the accident, I felt 17,000 people staring at me. But accidents like that happen. I'm not bitter."

Policeman Jack Prettyman retired from the force at the end of 2008 and moved to Arizona. His memories of a close friend have come west with him. "I still think about Pelle, and we talk about him in my family," he says. "I still have trouble accepting the accident.... He was one of my best friends. I miss him."

Former Flyers equipment manager Kevin Cady left the team after five years to become a police officer in Portland, Maine. Later, he served on the FBI's Joint Terrorist Task Force and on the US Customs maritime contraband enforcement team. His days of lugging and fixing hockey equipment are long gone, but the very mention of Pelle's name brings back those times and his friendship with Lindbergh. "Gump lived life like he'd only be 26 years old. He had fun and lived for the moment, and always with a smile.... I looked up to him and the things we experienced together have influenced and shaped me into what I am today. Pelle used to say to me that anything is possible if you just try." In the summer of 2009 Cady took a side job as an assistant equipment manager with the AHL's Portland Pirates.

Pelle's childhood friend Björn Neckman, who lived in Pelle's home in the United States during Lindbergh's first two years in North America, has remained close to the surviving members of the Lindbergh family. When he has a chance, he'll still drop by Barnängsgatan to visit Anna-Lisa and reminisce about Pelle. "Things were extremely tough for the family after his death, but today we all feel like Pelle is still right nearby. We can laugh about the things Pelle and I did together," Neckman says.

Likewise, the memories of Pelle that Reino Sundberg and Rolf Alex think of are inevitably the happy ones. "I often smile to myself when I think back at stuff we did when Pelle was along," Sundberg says. "He's sitting up there in his heaven and laughing at us down below.... I remember the positive, because there was never a dull moment when Pelle was around." Adds Alex, "When I think of Pelle today, I think of a pleasant guy who was extremely goal-driven, and it was something I learned a hell of a lot from. When that passion burns inside you, you're truly alive. He had a tremendous enjoyment for life."

After leaving Hammarby IF, Curt Lindström went on to coach both Sweden (1987) and Finland (1995) to IIHF World Championships. He still remembers Lindbergh among his favorites. "I got to know Pelle and his family when he was only six years old. It didn't take many years before he said that he wanted to play in the NHL...."The fact that he passed away so early is a real tragedy. I don't believe anyone back here in Sweden truly understands [today] that he was becoming very big in the NHL."

Bernie Parent did not know Pelle nearly as long as Lindström but bonded with the young goaltender in a profound way, on and off of the ice. Parent recalls,

I only knew Pelle for a few years, but our relationship was as beautiful and meaningful as a father's relationship with a son. Everyone talks about how I was his hero and helped him as a goalie. I did my part as a coach but I'll tell you what – Pelle was the one who put in the work and he was a pleasure to be with. When we had good times, we laughed together. When there were tough times, we cried together. When Pelle needed me, I was always there.... I'm just grateful that he was there at that time, even if it was way too short....If you're lucky, you meet the right people at the right time in life, and that's how it was with me and one from the top of the mountain to the deepest valley after I had to retire with the eye injury. But then God brings this wonderful kid into my life, and we share part of it together Pelle really was the right person at the right time for me. The only thing you can't take away is the beautiful memories that we have of Pelle. He was a wonderful person who lives in our hearts.

When Pelle grew frustrated at his inability to crack the Flyers' roster in the second season of his North American career, and when he struggled badly in his second NHL season, Parent was there to preach patience. Kerstin recalls one piece of advice that struck home with Pelle. "Bernie told Pelle that he had tough times in his career," she says. "He was French-Canadian and sometimes felt like an outsider. And on the ice, he had to mature as a player. It took time. To Pelle, that meant a lot coming from Bernie."

The Flyers organization as a whole has also taken steps to make sure their fallen goaltender is always remembered with an honored place in team history. Lindbergh's number 31 jersey has never been officially retired, but no Flyers player has worn it since – and it's unlikely that anyone will in the future. Also, in 1993-94, the club named an annual team award for the most improved player in Pelle's memory, recalling his 1984-85 Vezina Trophy season after his difficult second NHL campaign the prior year. Fittingly, the first winner of the award was Mikael Renberg – an earnest, well-liked young Swede who took the team by storm in his rookie year.

Indeed, one of the most inspirational pieces of Pelle Lindbergh's legacy is his ongoing influence over the new generation of Swedish goaltenders who are emerging on the hockey scene. The late keeper is still an inspiration to Buffalo Sabres prospect Jhonas Enroth, former Montreal Canadiens draftee Christopher Heino-Lindberg, and New York Islanders hopeful Stefan Ridder-wall, among others.

"Pelle showed all Swedish goalies that there is a chance of making it in the big league, the same way Henrik Lundqvist does today," Ridderwall says. "I never had a chance to see him play," says Enroth, who was born in 1988. "But he means a lot for us young goalies from Sweden. He won the Vezina and it shows that Swedish goalies can do it." Today, the Swedish goaltender who most publicly idolizes Lindbergh is 23-year-old Christopher Heino-Lindberg. Although Heino-Lindberg was less than a year old when Pelle died, he feels a personal connection to the late goalie, both in on-ice demeanor and an off-the-ice love of music. "I've read a lot about Pelle and even met his mom, Anna-Lisa, who sought me out. She thinks that I'm a lot like Pelle," he told the Färjestads BK website.

Anna-Lisa Lindbergh knows how she'd like for her son to be immortalized when she's gone: having a street near the family's home on Barnängsgatan named in his honor. "Pelle would have liked that," she says with a smile.

CHAPTER 30

PELLE LINDBERGH BY THE NUMBERS

Born	May 24, 1959 Stockholm, Sweden
Died	November 11, 1985
Height	5-foot-9
Weight	195 pounds
Position	Goalie
Catches	Left
NHL Draft	Philadelphia, 1979 (2nd, 35th)

			Regular Season								Playoffs							
Team	League	Season	GP	GD	G	A	P	PIM	GAA	PCT	GP	GD	G	A	P	PIM	GAA	PCT
Team Sweden	EC	76	3	5	0	0	0	0	1.33	.960								
Hammarby IF	U20 (Swe)	76/77																
Team Sweden	EJC	77	3	6	0	0	0	0	1.00									
Team Sweden	WJC	77	7	7	0	0	0	0	4.05									
Hammarby IF	Division 1 (SWE)	77/78	36w		0	0	0	4										
Team Sweden	WJC	78	4	7	0	0	0	0	2.50									
Hammarby IF	Division 1 (SWE)	78/79	35		0	0	0	2										
Team Sweden	WJC	79	6	6	0	0	0	0	2.00									
Team Sweden	World Champ.	79	6	8	0	0	0	0	6.33									
AIK	Elitserien	79/80	32		0	0	0	6	3.44	.869								
Team Sweden	Olympics	80	5	7	0	0	0	0	3.60	.873								
Maine Mariners	AHL	80/81	51		0	5	5	2	3.26	.893	20		0	0	5	4		
Team Sweden	Canada Cup	81	2	5	0	0	0	0	5.87									
Maine Mariners	AHL	81/82	25		0	0	0	2										
Philadelphia Flyers	NHL	81/82	8		0	0	0	0										
Philadelphia Flyers	NHL	82/83	40		0	4	4	0	2.98	.890	3		0	0	4	4		
Team Sweden	World Champ.	83	9	10	0	0	0	0	3.00	.905								
Springfield Indians	AHL	83/84	4		0	0	0	0										
Philadelphia Flyers	NHL	83/84	36		0	1	1	6			2		0	0	1	0		
Philadelphia Flyers	NHL	84/85	65		0	0	0	4	3.02	.899	18		0	1	1	0		
Philadelphia Flyers	NHL	85/86	8		0	0	0	0										

CHAPTER 31

WHERE ARE THEY NOW?

PHILADELPHIA FLYERS TEAMMATES (1984-85 AND 1985-86 SEASONS)

BOB FROESE: Senior pastor, Faith Fellowship Church, Clarence, NY

BRIAN PROPP: Health benefit consultant, Crawford Advisors, Radnor, PA

TIM KERR: Owner, Tim Kerr Powerplay Realty, Avalon, NJ

ILKKA SINALO: European scout, Philadelphia Flyers

DAVE POULIN: Vice president of hockey operations, Toronto Maple Leafs.

PELLE EKLUND: European scout, San Jose Sharks

RON SUTTER: Pro scout, Calgary Flames

RICH SUTTER: Working for a skate company in Alberta

MURRAY CRAVEN: Youth hockey association director, Whitefish, MT

PETER ZEZEL: Deceased-May 25, 2009-rare blood disorder

RICK TOCCHET: Head coach, Tampa Bay Lightning

DAVE BROWN: Director of Player Personnel, Philadelphia Flyers

MARK HOWE: Director of Pro Scouting, Detroit Red Wings

BRAD MCCRIMMON: Assistant coach, Detroit Red Wings

BRAD MARSH: Owner of Marshy's bar and grill, Ottawa, Ontario

DOUG CROSSMAN: Real estate agent, Ocean City, NJ

DERRICK SMITH: Employed by Fury Hockey, Toronto

THOMAS ERIKSSON: Police detective, Stockholm, Sweden

OTHER PHILADELPHIA FLYERS TEAMMATES (PRE 1984-85)

PETE PEETERS: Goaltending coach, Edmonton Oilers

RICK ST. CROIX: Owner and head instructor, Rick St. Croix Goaltending School, Winnipeg

MEL BRIDGMAN: Financial consultant, Smith Barney, Manhattan Beach, CA

GLEN COCHRANE: Scout, Anaheim Ducks

MIROSLAV DVORAK: Deceased (June 11, 2008 at age 56)

PAUL HOLMGREN: General Manager, Philadelphia Flyers

BOB CLARKE: Senior Vice President, Philadelphia Flyers

COACHES

MIKE KEENAN: Fired as head coach, Calgary Flames after 2008-09 season

BOB MCCAMMON: Retired from hockey in 2008. Resides in Vancouver, BC.

PAT QUINN: Head coach, Edmonton Oilers

FAMILY

ANNA-LISA LINDBERGH: Lives in Stockholm, Sweden in the apartment where she raised Pelle

SIGGE LINDBERGH: Deceased

ANN-LOUISE AND GORAN HORNESTAM: Live in suburban Stockholm

ANN-CHRISTINE: Deceased

KERSTIN SOMNELL (NEE PIETZSCH): Married to Kurt Somnell, mother of three children, resides in Taby, Sweden